Critical Perspectives on Child Abuse

Critical Perspectives on Child Abuse

Edited by

Richard Bourne
Children's Hospital Medical Center
Northeastern University

Eli H. Newberger
Children's Hospital Medical Center
Harvard Medical School

Lexington Books
D.C. Heath and Company
Lexington, Massachusetts
Toronto

Library of Congress Cataloging in Publication Data

Main entry under title:
   Critical perspectives on child abuse.

   1. Child abuse—Addresses, essays, lectures. 2. Child abuse—Prevention—
Addresses, essays, lectures. 3. Child abuse—Services—Addresses, essays,
lectures. I. Bourne, Richard. II. Newberger, Eli.
HV713.C74   362.7'1   77-18565
ISBN 0-669-02109-1

Second printing, September 1979.

Published simultaneously in Canada.

Printed in the United States of America.

International Standard Book Number: 0-669-02109-1

Library of Congress Catalog Card Number: 77-18565

Contents

Concerning the Infanticide, Marie Farrar

Bertolt Brecht

Marie Farrar, born in April,
No marks, a minor, rachitic, both parents dead,
Allegedly, up to now without police record,
Committed infanticide, it is said,
As follows: in her second month, she says,
With the aid of a barmaid she did her best
To get rid of her child with two douches,
Allegedly painful but without success.
But you, I beg you, check your wrath and scorn
For man needs help from every creature born.

She then paid out, she says, what was agreed
And continued to lace herself up tight.
She also drank liquor with pepper mixed in it
Which purged her but did not cure her plight.
Her body distressed her as she washed the dishes,
It was swollen now quite visibly.
She herself says, for she was still a child,
She prayed to Mary most earnestly.
But you, I beg you, check your wrath and scorn.
For man needs help from every creature born.

Her prayers, it seemed, helped her not at all.
She longed for help. Her trouble made her falter
And faint at early mass. Often drops of sweat
Broke out in anguish as she knelt at the altar.
Yet until her time had come upon her
She still kept secret her condition.
For no one believed such a thing had happened,
That she, so unenticing, had yielded to temptation.
But you, I beg you, check your wrath and scorn,
For man needs help from every creature born.

From *Selected Poems,* copyright 1947 by Bertolt Brecht and H.R. Hays; renewed 1975 by Stefan S. Brecht and H.R. Hays. Reprinted by permission of Harcourt Brace Jovanovich, Inc.

And on that day, she says, when it was dawn,
As she washed the stairs it seemed a nail
Was driven into her belly. She was wrung with pain.
But still she secretly endured her travail.
All day long while hanging out the laundry
She racked her brains till she got it through her head
She had to bear the child and her heart was heavy.
It was very late when she went up to bed.
But you, I beg you, check your wrath and scorn,
For man needs help from every creature born.

She was sent for again as soon as she lay down:
Snow had fallen and she had to go downstairs.
It went on till eleven. It was a long day.
Only at night did she have time to bear.
And so, she says, she gave birth to a son.
The son she bore was just like all the others.
She was unlike the others but for this
There is no reason to despise this mother.
You too, I beg you, check your wrath and scorn.
For man needs help from every creature born.

Accordingly I will go on with the story
Of what happened to the son that came to be
(She says she will hide nothing that befell)
So let be a judgement upon both you and me.
She says she had scarcely gone to bed when she
Was overcome with sickness and she was alone,
Not knowing what would happen, yet she still
Contrived to stifle all her moans.
And you, I beg you, check your wrath and scorn,
For man needs help from every creature born.

With her last strength, she says, because
Her room had now grown icy cold, she then
Dragged herself to the latrine and there
Gave birth as best she could (not knowing when)
But toward morning. She says she was already
Quite distracted and could barely hold
The child for snow came into the latrine
And her fingers were half numb with cold.
You too, I beg you, check your wrath and scorn
For man needs help from every creature born.

Between the latrine and her room, she says,
Not earlier, the child began to cry until
It drove her mad so that she says
She did not cease to beat it with her fists
Blindly for some time till it was still.
And then she took the body to her bed
And kept it there with her all through the night:
When morning came she hid it in the shed.
But you, I beg you, check your wrath and scorn
For man has need of every creature born.

Marie Farrar, born in April,
An unmarried mother, convicted, died in
The Meissen Penitentiary,
She brings home to you all men's sins.
You who bear pleasantly between clean sheets
And give the name "blessed" to your womb's weight
Must not damn the weakness of the outcast,
For her sin was black but her pain was great.
Therefore, I beg you, check your wrath and scorn.
For man needs help from every creature born.

Preface

This book of essays on child abuse is intended to promote intelligent analysis of a topic that usually stimulates outrage, despair, and confusion. Child abuse is an old problem, but it has been newly discovered. The many claims for its effective "treatment," and the equally numerous, if less frequently voiced, proposals for its prevention, reflect the professional and technical inability to come to terms with issues involving intense feelings, divergent values about children and families, and social and economic inequality.

The uncertainty about how to solve so visible a phenomenon as child abuse is also demonstrative of the limits to which clinical experience and science can inform practice and social policy. Kempe and Gil[a] have asserted that based on present knowledge we can effectively treat and prevent child abuse. What remains to happen, they comment, is for society to make the commitment and to apply its resources.

But what commitment and which resources? These respected scholars disagree on issues of *focus* (Kempe, the home; Gil, the society); of *definition* (Kempe, the violent injury of children; Gil, the compromise of a child's potential); and of *method* (Kempe, the public health visitor's opening "life lines" between abusers and helping institutions; Gil, the changing of such social-structural causes of child abuse as poverty, racism, regressive employment policy, acceptance of violence as a means of conflict resolution, and the emphasis on competition rather than cooperation).

To whom does the secretary of health, education and welfare turn when instructed by Congress to develop a child abuse policy? If $20 million of a $3 billion American child welfare commitment are appropriated, how may such funds initiate effective action to protect children?

In this book we intend to present analytic approaches to knowledge, practice and policy. There are no simple solutions to child abuse, and our hope is that, short of providing answers, this collection will help formulate good questions.

We mean no slight to C. Henry Kempe and his coworkers, for whose contributions to the study and treatment of child abuse we are deeply grateful, in not including them in the book. Their four edited volumes[b] are already widely read and appreciated.

[a]C.H. Kempe, Statement on the Child Abuse Prevention Act of 1973 (Public Law 93-247), Subcommittee on Children and Youth, United States Senate) Washington, D.C.: U.S. Government Printing Office, 1973, pp. 167-208; D.G. Gil, *Violence Against Children: Physical Child Abuse in the United States* (Cambridge, Mass.: Harvard University Press, 1970).

[b]R.E. Helfer and C.H. Kempe, eds., *The Battered Child*, 2nd ed. (Chicago: University of Chicago Press, 1973); C.H. Kempe and R.E. Helfer, eds., *Helping the Battered Child and His Family* (Philadelphia: J.B. Lippincott, 1972); R.E. Helfer and C.H. Kempe, eds., *Child Abuse and Neglect: The Family and the Community* (Cambridge, Mass.: Ballinger, 1976); H.P. Martin, ed., *The Abused Child* (Cambridge, Mass.: Ballinger, 1976).

We thank Mary Lee Cox and Judy Risch for patient and consistent technical support in the preparation of this collection. We are indebted to the following professional colleagues for their contributions to our thinking and understanding: Roberta Goodfader, Sally Mack, Joanne Michalek, Marva Serotkin, Betty Singer, and Maren Stavig. Our wives, Carole Rice Bourne and Carolyn Moore Newberger, are ever supportive of our work, and we wish to publicly express to them our admiration and gratitude.

Boston, Massachusetts   *Richard Bourne*
April 1978   *Eli H. Newberger*

1

Child Abuse and Neglect: An Overview

Richard Bourne

This chapter will present some of the difficulties in defining child abuse and neglect; in explaining their extent; in detailing the various conditions which are associated with, or are seen as "causes" of, these problems; and in intervening in an effective, humane way for purposes of treatment and prevention.

Definition

Abuse and neglect are not easily defined. To begin with, they are often not clearly diagnosable in a clinical setting. If parents bring a child to a hospital with a medical problem, the physicians may have difficulty deciding whether it results from an "accident," disease, or "inflicted injury." They may be unable to judge whether the causal explanation offered by the family is a reasonable one or whether it is inconsistent with the presenting trauma. Some case examples may illustrate this diagnostic problem. In the first, parents bring their child into a hospital emergency room with a complaint of fever. During the medical examination the doctors notice round red sores on the youngster's legs which they diagnose as "possible cigarette burns." They later discover that the family has recently returned from a summer retreat and that the burns are actually infected mosquito bites.

In a second case, a mother brings her daughter to the hospital with small black and blue marks on various parts of the child's body. Doctors perform multiple tests and can find no organic basis for the bruising. Social workers who meet the mother find her appropriately concerned and do not think her capable of abuse.

In a third case a child is under the third percentile for both height and weight and falls into the category of "failure to thrive." Physicians cannot exclude a biological explanation for his small size. The family is poor, and it is unclear whether the youngster's condition is a result of poverty and malnutrition beyond the family's control or of neglect wherein the family could provide better care, but fails to do so.

In a final case, a four-year-old has a second-degree burn on his hand. The mother explains that her son had been tossing his plastic car into the air and that it fell into a sink of boiling water which she had prepared for the family wash. A plastic surgeon believes that the youngster would not have been able to hold his hand under the water long enough to receive such a burn. A psychological evaluation of the child shows that he is "persistent" and "strong-willed when pursuing activities in which he is emotionally involved." These examples show the frequent problem of identification.

Not only are abuse and neglect difficult to detect, however, but also they are conceptually unclear. Abuse, for example, was initially synonymous with "battering." Over time, the meaning of the term has expanded so that it may refer to "maltreatment" or even to a failure to provide, in an optimal way, for a child's needs. Under the latter definition most parents would be seen as abusive.

Abuse generally covers physical and emotional injury. Physical injury includes both beatings and sexual misuse; it denotes the *commission* of an act or acts damaging to a child's well-being.

Neglect is generally an *omission:* a failure to provide for a child's physical or emotional needs or both. Neglect occurs if parents fail to adequately feed or clothe their child, and such failure is not a result of conditions beyond their control; or if parents fail to adequately monitor their child's behavior—for example, by permitting him to play on a street full of traffic or by leaving him unsupervised for long periods of time. Leaving an infant in a crib, without changing his diapers and without giving him any contact or stimulation, represents both physical and emotional deprivation: the infant will probably have rashes and sores and might well be developmentally delayed.

Abuse: Definitional Issues

In most definitions of abuse the idea of intent is implied. That is, the injury is nonaccidental or deliberately inflicted on the child. It is questionable whether this criterion validly distinguishes abuse from nonabuse.

If, for example, a husband throws the kitchen toaster at his wife during a quarrel and it accidentally injures his child, it is arguable that abuse did not occur because the father had no desire to harm the youngster. On the other hand, if such quarrels occur frequently, and the child is prone to "get in the way," then the label might be appropriate.

If a child swallows some cherry-colored furniture polish that his mother has carelessly left in the living room, it is arguable that—given the lack of parental intent—no abuse has occurred. On the other hand, if the child is taken to a hospital because of the ingestion, and physicians warn the mother about the need to "childproof" her home, and two weeks later the youngster swallows valium pills that had been left loose on a table, then the label abuse might be appropriate. Intent, of course, implies a conscious desire to harm, while this mother and other abusers might have unconscious desires to injure their children which are unrecognized by themselves and others.

Intent, moreover, is sometimes a conclusion resulting from observer bias rather than a characteristic of the alleged abuser's behavior. When a poor minority parent brings a child into a hospital emergency ward, and the youngster has an injury whose causation is unclear, the diagnosis of "intentionally inflicted trauma" is more likely to be made than when a parent who is affluent and well-educated brings his child into the ward with an identical injury. That is, racial and social class stereotypes on the part of the professional influence the diagnosis that is made and the greater the social distance between the professional and the patient, the more readily the label of inflicted injury is applied.

Seriousness of injury is also mentioned as a criterion of abuse, though it is unclear how serious an injury has to be before it is so classifiable. For example, if a parent spanks a child, some might define the red mark that results as abuse. Others might argue that the word "abuse" is appropriately applied only if the spanking causes a black and blue mark or if it leads to a fracture. The word "serious" becomes even more problematic given the fact that, without appropriate intervention, minor injuries are likely to increase in severity over time. A minor injury, thus, forewarns of more dangerous trauma and should cause professional concern.

Obviously, the more frequently a child is injured, even if the injury is minor, the greater the concern and likelihood of intervention.

Abuse by parents is generally viewed as more serious than abuse by others. For example, children require greater protection in incest cases than they do when sexually attacked by a stranger. In incest, the sexual misuse is usually chronic and the parents, instead of easing the psychological trauma, are responsible for its occurrence.

Being attacked by a stranger, of course, is psychologically harmful to the youngster and requires response from medical, social work, and law enforcement resources. Should the parents not view it seriously, that is, if they do not feel a need to care for or protect their child after such assault, then it is considered as serious as incest—in the sense that parental obligations are not being met. The parents have neglected their child's needs, though they have not actually engaged in abuse. Such neglect might also occur in cases of physical abuse by a boyfriend or sibling should the parent(s) not take adequate measures to protect their youngster.

Neglect: Definitional Issues

Some definitions of neglect focus on family conditions. If parents are alcoholic or have psychological problems, then it is assumed that they cannot adequately care for their children, and that such children are neglected. Other definitions emphasize the child and the need for overt signs of psychological or physical harm before neglect exists. The fact that there has to be evidence of a child's condition means that children "at risk" are usually not included within the definition. Parents might be "unfit," but only children who manifest present harm are "neglected."

In order to have neglect, parents must be failing to meet their child-rearing responsibility. They are not caring for their child in ways that are clearly within their control. The issue of control is complex, however, for there might be "neglect" even if the family were doing everything possible to fulfill a child's needs. If a family is poor and is unable to afford adequate clothing and food, is it neglecting an infant if he is cold and malnourished? Perhaps not, if parents are attempting to obtain resources and are unable to do so. If the parents are spending clothing and food money on alcohol, however, and the child is suffering because of this behavior, then neglect is clearer. Defining neglect as an omission within the parents' control means that poverty alone is not sufficient criterion of neglect unless parents choose to be impoverished.

"Parental responsibility" and the issue of control may have relevance in contexts other than the economic. To illustrate, a three-month-old infant is brought by its parents to a hospital emergency ward and, shortly thereafter, dies of pneumonia. The parents explain that about two weeks before, the child had developed "a bad cold." The parents, who do not believe in modern medicine and who eat only macrobiotic foods, took the child to an acupuncture clinic and fed him herbal tea. Despite such treatment, the infant's condition worsened; regular medical care was not sought until he was comatose. Were these parents neglectful? One might argue that they did everything in their power to keep their child alive. They should not be considered neglectful because of a nonconformist life style. On the other hand, the infant is dead, and death arose because of parental beliefs and a refusal to seek appropriate attention. Had the child been treated a few hours earlier he would have lived. From this perspective, the parent's behavior is indicative of neglect, however unintentional the outcome.

Neglect vs. Abuse

The relationship between neglect and abuse is unclear. Neglect is certainly not less serious than abuse, for both neglect and abuse are potentially damaging to a child's growth and development. Leaving a youngster in dirty diapers, without adequate nourishment or stimulation, is at least as detrimental to a child as is the administration of bruises and broken bones. Physical abuse, however, frequently triggers intervention more rapidly than does neglect, commission being perceived as more life-threatening and "evil" than is omission.

Neglect, moreover, occasionally leads to abuse. If a child is ignored by its parents it might well be "developmentally delayed." Parents then might beat the child because he is slow. Or, to give a second example, an infant who is neglected by its parents and receives inadequate nourishment may begin to ruminate.

Rumination means that the child regurgitates its food, rechewing because of hunger and oral satisfaction. This rechewing causes the infant to smell and the parent further neglects, or abuses, him because of his bad odor.

Neglect is often more difficult to treat successfully than is abuse. If a mother ignores her child, refusing to satisfy any of its needs, it is difficult to "make this mother care." On the other hand, if a mother beats her child badly because the child is stealing from neighbors, this mother may be taught to use less harmful disciplinary techniques, and the abuse is less likely to be repeated.

It is frequently difficult to differentiate abuse from neglect, both clinically and conceptually. A child ignored by parents might also be scapegoated by parents. Neglect of a child's emotional needs blurs into emotional abuse. But abuse may occur without neglect. A parent who takes a child for regular medical examination and who dresses and clothes the child well might still be inflicting physical abuse upon the youngster.

Neglect and abuse are difficult to define, especially in a society that frequently mistreats its young. Many of us believe, for example, in corporal punishment: in sparing the rod and spoiling the child. If such punishment is normal child-rearing practice, and if data exist that it is damaging, then abuse might be the rule and not the exception.

If it appears that more children are injured by participation in contact sports such as hockey and football than are injured by beatings, then parents who permit such participation might well be abusive, or neglectful of their children's welfare. If parents label their children "hyperactive," and do so for their own convenience, because they do not wish active youngsters intruding on their freedom, they are not giving their children the care they deserve. In most cases none of the parents in these examples would be defined as abusive or neglectful, nor would they see themselves as such. The question as to whether their behavior should be so defined, and by whom, remains unclear.

Extent

Because the definition of child abuse is unclear, the amount of child abuse in American society is equally vague. Obviously, the broader the definition, the greater the amount of abuse.

The statistics on amount of abuse also vary depending on whether their source is official reports or self-reports. As with delinquency and crime, the frequency of abuse increases with self-reports. If a random sample of the population is questioned as to its child-rearing techniques, then more abuse appears than when the incidence of abuse is culled from cases officially processed by Departments of Public Welfare or by the police.

Self-reports also reveal that abuse is committed by a wider and more heterogeneous grouping than is indicated by official data. Official processing falls more heavily on the poor and powerless than it does on the affluent and influential.

Estimates of the amount of child abuse and neglect vary from thousands of cases per year to millions of cases per year. Professor Richard Gelles and other sociologists who recently studied a nationally representative sample of 1,142 married couples found that violence toward children was an extensive and regular pattern in many families. (See article included in this volume.) Twenty percent of the parents surveyed had hit their child with some object during the previous year, while 4.2 percent indicated they had "beaten up" the child, 2.8 percent of the parents reported having threatened the child with a knife or gun, and 2.9 percent actually had used a knife or gun on the child in question. Applying this rate to the population of (American) children aged three to seventeen, this comes to a total of about 1,200,000 children in this age group whose parents had at some time in their life attacked them with a lethal weapon.

Though the number of official cases is clearly increasing, it is doubtful that more child abuse and neglect exist now than in the past. What has changed is not the amount of abuse but the fact that abuse is now a salient social problem. Because we recognize it as an issue; because the law requires that, if recognized, it be reported to a state agency; because of intense media interest, there seems to be an increase in occurrence. In fact, the increase is more perceptual than real.

Child abuse and neglect have existed for centuries. It was in 1962, however, that Kempe and Helfer devised the phrase, "battered child syndrome." After this "syndrome" was discovered, more and more cases of abuse were recognized, the label allowing professionals to see a phenomenon which before they had overlooked. When male physicians became involved with child abuse, instead of predominantly female social workers, the problem took on an importance previously lacking, especially given the medical interest in developing an approach to diagnosis and treatment.

Causation

As the definition and extent of child abuse is unclear, so are its causes. Generally, the principal focus has been psychological: "What type of individuals would harm their children?" Recently, however, more sociological and economic explanations have been proposed: "What situations would lead individuals to injure?" Let us review some of the more common causative theories, keeping in mind that no single explanation is sufficient.

Cultural. The values of American society contribute to child abuse. An analysis of life in American society today might lead one to ask *not* "why is there so much child abuse?" but "why is there so little?" given the pressures and alienation under which we have to live.

In the economic realm many of us work at tedious jobs which give us little sense of meaning or satisfaction; we labor for fifty weeks so that we might take two weeks vacation. In the political area we have suffered through Watergate and various congressional scandals; politicians are mistrusted and government lacks the legitimacy it once commanded. Socially we feel isolated and have few friends with whom we can share intimacies; we attend large, impersonal universities and live in high-rise apartments unaware of our neighbors. Given such stress and the fact that many of our needs remain unfulfilled, it is not surprising that we scapegoat and abuse our children.

Economic. Poverty, moreover, leads to frustration which triggers aggression. In a society where material success is the principal goal, and too few resources and opportunities exist for everyone to satisfy his expectations, violence is the natural consequence. Some argue that the poor are more frequently labeled abusers because of the visibility of their behavior and because of their powerlessness. Despite the validity of this assertion, the problem of being poor in an affluent society might well cause stress which is displaced onto children.

Familial. Even if affluence were more widely shared, however, child abuse might not decline because of the nature of the family. In the family we spend much time together, the intensity and duration of the relationship causing tensions. We are taught that it is acceptable to "be ourselves" in the family—which means that there is little need to hide our nastiness. If, for example, an individual works for a corporation and his boss makes unreasonable demands upon him, he usually will not express his anger; he is afraid of losing his job. On the other hand, if he should come home and find that his wife has burned supper, there is little hesitation in showing his feelings. The marriage license has given him the "right" to be angry and to behave openly. It is clear that the police are reluctant to intervene in a "family dispute," so that the husband has little fear of arrest. In most states, even if the police wanted to intervene, they could not do so unless the assault and battery (which are misdemeanors) were committed in their presence or led to a breach of the peace.

Psychological. Less than 10 percent of abusers are clinically psychotic, though many appear anxious and depressed. Among the psychological characteristics observed by professionals are:

Low Self-esteem. Most abusers have had a bad self-image, seeing themselves as worthless.

Role Reversal. Abusers want their children to nurture and satisfy them rather than the reverse. They often describe their children as "everything that I have," and express a strong need for their presence; they hope their children will make them feel good, will give them a sense of completeness.

Unrealistic Expectations. Since abusers have low self-esteem, they frequently view children as a potential source of status and admiration. If they produce intelligent and creative children, then they as parents must be more intelligent and creative than they appear. These attitudes lead to the holding of unrealistic expectations for the children which, when not fulfilled, create disappointment and anger. To a certain degree, of course, most parents hope children will reflect well on them. Consider the anxiety over toilet training (Is my child behind the other toddlers?), and the purchase of sweatshirts with "Harvard, 19--" written on the front. Frequently the difference between abusers and nonabusers, then, is the intensity of concern, not its existence.

Fatalism, or "Inappropriate Affect." A child has a third-degree burn or a fractured leg, and parents do not appear anxious or upset. If the child is admitted to a hospital, the parents might not visit regularly despite the availability of transportation. This lack of appropriate reaction might be a result of depression or, frequently, of a fatalistic attitude towards life: "Why become upset at a burn? Children get burned all the time . . . Life is tough and these types of injuries are expected." Such a view, of course, means that parents do not take sufficient precautions to care for or protect their young.

Lack of Knowledge about Child Care. Abusing parents often are not tuned in to their child's needs and are unaware as to how these needs might be satisfied. In a hospital setting, for example, a mother is observed giving her child a bottle with the infant's head dangling between her legs, or regularly overloads the feeding spoon causing the infant to spit up and choke. Professional concern is greater if, after being shown the correct technique, the mother is still unable to nourish properly. It is clear, however, that mothering and fathering are not innate behaviors. If we do not learn them from role models, our parents or others, then they are not easily mastered.

It has been observed that abuse is intergenerational, that is, that abusing parents were frequently abused as children. This observation might be explained by the fact that abused children become "needy" adults who want infants for gratification; or by a feeling that beatings are a necessary and proper part of childrearing ("My parents beat me, and it didn't do me any harm"); or by a self-protective identification with the aggressive and more powerful adult. It is clear that psychological problems of parents are frequently passed on to their children.

Some further points should be made before ending our discussion of psychological causes: first, in most instances the abusers are as much victims as are the abused. Coming from homes without adequate nurturance and love, seeing themselves as worthless, living under conditions of stress, they are sad individuals who should not be easily dismissed as "criminals" or "wrongdoers."

Second, as implied by the discussion on "definition," a clearcut psychological distinction between abusers and nonabusers does not exist. Most parents have probably struck their children inappropriately and those who have not done so might have felt the desire to do so. By viewing abuse as what *others* do, and by picturing it in extreme terms (death, broken bones), we create rationalizations for our own difficulties in rearing children.

Third, not all abusers have the psychological characteristics generally attributed to them. If we take a narrow and specific view of what abusers are like, then many individuals who are not abusers will be stigmatized (for example, it will be assumed that if you were abused as a child, then you will inevitably abuse) and many who abuse, but do not possess the typical characteristics, will not be identified.

Fourth, abuse is a relational activity, between abuser and abused, and to understand it one must focus not only on the psyche of the abuser but also on the child-victim and his characteristics. This relationship must then be placed within a larger setting: of the family, community, society, and culture.

Fifth, other psychological characteristics are also associated with abusers: sexual repression, unmastered oral aggression, a tendency to project blame onto others, phobic thought and behavior, and poor parental relationships.

The characteristics of the child and the context in which abuse or neglect occurs are important etiological factors. Premature infants and those born with congenital defects are more likely to be abused by their parents. Both children who are normal, but who are perceived as deficient because of unrealistic parental expectations, and children who are "abnormal," and are so perceived, are youngsters potentially at risk.

Sometimes, indeed, parents view a child as "special" and are more likely to scapegoat him than they are the other children in the family. The definition of a child as "special" may exist for many reasons—from the fact that a baby resembles its father or mother to the fact that it is sickly or cranky. Whether removal of a "special child" from the family setting would trigger the selection of another child as "special" is, as yet, unclear. What is clear is that, in a family of many children, only one might be the object of parental aggression.

Children who are abused, moreover, often develop certain characteristics. They are self-destructive or have little sense of self-worth; they are negative and provocative in their interpersonal relationships; or, they appear precocious and adult-like. These characteristics are understandable given the dynamics of abuse.

If, for example, parents who are supposed to love and protect their child injure him, the child comes to view himself as "bad." He thinks that he deserves the abuse he is receiving. Such an image may cause the youngster to seek punishment—by hurting himself or by causing others to hurt him. "Being bad" might be the only way he knows to attract attention from adults. Abused youngsters are frequently afraid to be children, and seem especially mature or precocious. They think that, by controlling their behavior and by "walking on eggshells," parental anger will subside and abuse decrease. Indeed, as part of a rehabilitative program for such children, they are taught to play—taught that it is acceptable to act like a child.

Finally, family crisis may precipitate abuse: marital problems, unemployment or other threats to self-esteem, a perceived sense of social isolation. Sometimes less traumatic events such as an argument between parents or a child's temper tantrum may also produce increased stress which, in turn, triggers violence.

Prevention. Child abuse workers often lament the absence of preventive measures, the fact that intervention resembles the parking of an ambulance at the bottom of a steep mountain rather than the construction of a fence along the borders of the road.

Preventive suggestions usually take one of two forms: the introduction of family and parent effectiveness courses into public schools or the testing of parents to determine whether abuse or neglect is likely, and the consequent offering of services to those whose scores show risk.

The presentation of child-rearing courses triggers criticism because teachers might be imposing their (or the state's) values on the students. Parent testing is similarly criticized in that the tests might represent particular social class or cultural biases.

The tests are subject to what sociologists call type I and type II errors. A type I error occurs when a parent is labeled a potential abuser, because of his or her attitudes or circumstances, and the label is falsely applied. Fears are groundlessly aroused; individuals are needlessly stigmatized; and services are misspent. There is also the danger of the "self-fulfilling prophecy," in that the parent, anxious because of the concerns expressed, might become less able to provide adequate care for the child.

A type II error occurs when the potential for child abuse is present, but is overlooked. This mistake is likely when the alleged abuser is of the same racial and socioeconomic group as the individual responsible for evaluation. As we have seen, professionals are more reluctant to apply the label of abuse to those with whom they share similar characteristics. Indeed, many of the suggested concomitants of abuse: unemployment, family disorganization, and social isolation are also associated with poverty. The poor, that is, are more likely to suffer a type I error, to be overincluded in the abuse category, than are the more affluent and powerful who can better control the labels imposed on them.

Advertising and public relations campaigns (for example, "Have You Hugged Your Kid Today?") also attempt to lessen abuse, though their impact appears slight. Abuse or neglect-prone parents are unlikely to be deterred by such programs, though parents who do *not* abuse might have their positive care-taking reinforced by these techniques.

Some hospitals are attempting to prevent reinjury to children by sponsoring child abuse or trauma teams. These groups, made up of professionals from different disciplines (law, medicine, psychology, and social work), try to assist families by providing services and by referring parents to appropriate community agencies. Through having a nonaccusatory orientation toward abusers, and hoping to keep children within their families, these teams urge removal of the abused from their homes when it is the only protective measure securing a child's safety.

Treatment. The medical model is the primary way of perceiving child abuse and neglect. Abusers and abused are "sick" and require individual treatment of a supportive nature—from physicians, psychologists, and social workers. These professionals offer "life lines" to their patient-clients: psychotherapy, instruction in parenting skills, day care and homemaker services, public health nursing and medical care. Unfortunately, this treatment orientation is not always sufficient.

Human services and child protection resources are frequently in short supply or of poor quality. If support such as day care is unavailable because of a lack of state funding, then obviously such alternatives cannot be viewed as viable methods of intervention.

Even if certain treatment strategies are available, some abusing or neglectful parents are unable or unwilling to benefit from them. For example, traditional psychotherapy is often not a successful tool: it takes time for any attitudinal or behavioral change to occur; it is costly; it requires an ability to become introspective or, at the least to develop a trust relationship with the therapist; it demands a commitment from the patient and a willingness to actively cooperate. These limitations undercut the potential usefulness of therapeutic approaches.

The medical model implies that the problem is an individual one and that treatment of the person is the most reasonable intervention. As we have seen, however, child abuse is as much a social as a psychological problem. Focus on individual illness detracts from social causes such as unemployment, alienation, and values and attitudes toward children. Until such structural causes of abuse and neglect are engaged, the treating of individual abusers, though helpful to them, is relatively ineffective as a social control.

Parents Anonymous (PA), founded in 1970, represents a self-help effort by abusing parents to prevent or treat damaging relationships between them and their children. Resembling Alcoholics Anonymous and Synanon, this group has had much success in assisting its members to provide more adequate child care and protection.

Legal Issues. Traditionally children have not received much protection under the law. Parents are assumed to have the right of custody and control over the young, such right being limited only by a demonstration of gross unfitness or neglect. The state has been reluctant to intervene in family life.

Two important legal issues in child abuse are *when* to intervene and *how* to intervene. One view is that intervention should be narrowly restricted because of its defects. Criticism has focused on the fact that courts have precipitously removed children from their homes and that foster placement often has detrimental effects on the child. Great deference is given to family autonomy and the right to be free from state interference. Only the protection of a child from serious and specific harm may justify the legal use of "coercive" alternatives.

A contrary view is that decision makers should have discretion in determining the appropriateness of legal intervention. Since not all cases of abuse and neglect are predictable or easily defined, and since the purpose of intervention is to help families and protect children, it should not be narrowly restricted. The law is seen as a positive force fulfilling important needs, not a danger to be limited. Debate also surrounds the manner of intervention—whether criminal or civil law is most appropriate; whether to report a case of abuse to the Department of Public Welfare or to initiate a neglect (care and protection) petition in juvenile court.

Criminal vs. Civil Law. Some believe that abuse should be handled as a criminal matter; the beating of a child is assault and battery and the young victim should receive the same legal protection, and the perpetrator, the same punishment, as in the cases of offenses committed against adults. Others argue that use of criminal sanctions would hurt the child more than help him, and that the criminal process is unable to respond effectively in abuse or neglect matters.

Those opposed to criminal action argue that it harms the child psychologically by making him feel responsible for the punishment of a parent for whom, despite abuse or neglect, he still has positive feelings. The abuser does not usually receive rehabilitation in prison and, after release, is generally more angry at the youngster than he was prior to incarceration. The state must prove criminal cases "beyond a reasonable doubt," a difficult task in child abuse where frequently the child is too young to testify, the spouse has immunity from testimony, and the evidence of abuse (as opposed to "accident") is unclear or lacking. Finally, it is felt that the child can be better protected, and the parent more effectively sanctioned, by use of child protection statutes.

Reporting Statutes. All fifty states now have reporting statutes which require certain professionals (medical personnel, social workers, educators, and counselors) to report cases of suspected abuse and neglect to the police or to a Department of Public Welfare. The agency accepting the report investigates the allegation and, if abuse or neglect is found, offers the family whatever services are necessary to care for, or protect, the child. If the child is endangered by remaining within the home, the recipient group has the ability to file a petition in family court urging temporary foster placement.

In most state statutes there is an immunity provision that protects reporters from civil and criminal liability if their report should not be corroborated. A. long as the report is filed "in good faith," it is better to file even if the suspicion of abuse is later proved erroneous than to fail to report when abuse exists and should have been recognized.

Legal decisions seem to indicate that if a mandated reporter confronts abuse and fails to report, and the child is later reinjured, the failure to report is deemed an "intervening cause" of the reinjury and the professional, as well as his institutional affiliation, risk liability and a possible assessment of compensatory or punitive damages or both. Even if a parent is the perpetrator directly inflicting the injury, the law assumes that the parent would not have had an opportunity to reinjure had the professional fulfilled his responsibility.

The reporting statutes have not been as successful in preventing abuse as their advocates had once predicted. First, despite the compulsory phrasing of the obligation, many professionals are reluctant to report. They feel that their clients or patients will no longer trust them; that the intervention by a police or welfare bureaucracy might harm rather than help the family; that the manifestations of abuse or neglect are frequently too vague to justify official involvement. Second, some state Departments of Public Welfare receive so many reports that they are unable to adequately process them. Many reports are not investigated or are only superficially examined, the "more serious" appearing cases receiving priority. Third, poor people are more likely to be subjects of reports than are the affluent. Because of its lessened visibility, and the greater reluctance of professionals to stigmatize those with money and status, abuse by the middle class rarely triggers state involvement.

It is clear that if state legislatures refuse to appropriate adequate funds to allow investigation and the provision of services, the reporting law becomes meaningless and ritualistic, with little supportive or preventive impact for families in crisis.

Neglect Petitions. If a child cannot be protected by any other means, it might become necessary to petition the family or juvenile court. Usually such action is initiated only if services and support have not satisfactorily assured the child's safety; or if the family has refused cooperation with an investigatory agency.

The petition usually alleges that the child "is in need of care and protection" and involves a hearing in which an agency (hospital, Department of Public Welfare, etc.) presents whatever medical and social data justify its concern. The judge frequently appoints counsel for both parents and child, orders an independent investigation of the family situation, and enters temporary decrees concerning the child's legal and physical custody.

Legal custody involves the ability to make decisions about the child while physical custody relates to place of residence. In some jurisdictions, both legal and physical custody of the child are temporarily placed with the state, pending the outcome of the investigation.

Although the petitioner must prove parental unfitness and, most frequently, that such unfitness has caused harm to the child, the court's emphasis is not on adjudication, but on disposition. That is, the judge perceives the court process as a way of helping parents and protecting children, and, therefore, concentrates less on "who is responsible" and more on satisfaction of family needs. The judge, for example, might order day care services or involvement in a parent-child center, therapy or diagnostic evaluation for parents and child, placement in residential treatment, or homemaker visits.

Such legal cases often continue for long periods of time, the parents receiving services and, if the child is in the home, the family being evaluated and monitored to assess its protective capacity. If the abusing or neglecting parents make little progress and are clearly unable to care for their child, then the court might order permenant commitment of the youngster to the state, with the possibility that he will be released for adoption. On the other hand, if the parents demonstrate their ability to care and protect, legal or physical custody or both of the child will return to them and the court will order dismissal.

Court, like other methods of intervention, has negative aspects: it is more often used as an alternative when poor families are abusing or neglectful; the judge may enter orders that harm the child—for example, by ordering removal too quickly or by refusing to order removal when a life-endangering situation exists; frequently services are unavailable or of low quality; the parents are stigmatized and labeled. It is a necessary alternative, however, if a child cannot remain at home without an imminent threat to his health or safety. The removal of a child from his parents requires judicial participation to protect the rights of all parties.

The present laws on child abuse and neglect are confusing and inconsistent. The U.S. Supreme Court in the Ingraham case (45 LW 4364) has held that beatings of children by Florida school teachers, permitted by state statute, do not violate the consititutional rights of the students. If, however, the injured children—some with blood clots—had appeared at a hospital for treatment, the physicians would risk liability if they did not report such abuse to the proper authorities. Until the legal status of children is specified, and the place of law in family life clarified, those who work in the area of child abuse will remain uneasy and the law itself will play a less important protective role than its potential would allow.

2 The Myth of the Battered Child Syndrome

Eli H. Newberger

Recent work on childhood accidental injuries leads us to a more enlightened conception of child abuse from the one implied in the diagnosis of "the battered child syndrome," to a more humane view which focuses on the parent's capacity to protect a particular child rather than any "intent" he may have had to injure him. Studies by J.D. Holter and S.B. Friedman (*Pediatrics, 42*: 128, 1969), G.S. Gregg and E. Elmer (*Pediatrics, 44:* 434, 1969), and R. Sobel (*Pediatric Clinics of North America, 17:* 653, 1970) demonstrate that there is a common causal background behind childhood accidents—so called "intentional" accidents and otherwise—which has to do with a variety of real life as well as psychologic factors, including poor, crowded housing, accessible hazards, low social class, large family size, alcoholism and drugs, illness, prematurity, and unemployment.

We are coming to see that the essential element in child abuse is not the intention to destroy a child but rather the inability of a parent to nurture his offspring—a failing which can stem directly from ascertainable environmental conditions which may not necessarily be accessible to the intervention of social workers, physicians, nurses, psychiatrists, and others who offer the traditional modalities of care to distressed families.

When we at the Children's Hospital in Boston reformulated our definition for *trauma X,* our house euphemism for child abuse, we decided to define this diagnostic entity not as inflicted injuries brought on defenseless children by willfully destructive parents, the concept implicit in the "battered child syndrome" diagnosis, but as an illness, with or without inflicted injury, stemming from situations in his home setting which threatened a child's survival.

Francis Sargent, the Governor of Massachusetts, convened an advisory committee on child abuse which proposed a similar definition, also intended to be compassionate and nonpunitive. The definition read as follows: "a family crisis which threatens the physical or emotional survival of a child." The object was to define in a helpful way where intervention is to be directed; to identify the causes of the problem (which are nearly always multiple and very rarely stem from simple, destructive intent of a parent which you can see); to focus less on the symptoms of the child than on what problems seemed to lead to those symptoms; to allow one to commit one's resources in such a way as to exert some positive impact on the family's ability to prevent them from happening again.

Each individual medical practitioner, or center, has to work at his own style of management. The model which we have been introducing in Children's Hospital over the last year has a basic idea, *i.e.,* to come to grips with the complexity of each case and to tackle its specific important components directly. There is, of course, an important relationship between the personnel who are providing care and those who are receiving it.

It may be that effective, lasting intervention is less a function of successful treatment relationships than a matter of defining and resolving specific problems of parents' lives, problems such as poor health, inadequate housing, no child care, and legal and monetary difficulties. Our primary function may be improving, to the extent that we can determine, what Julius Richmond (*American Journal of Public Health, 60:* 23, 1970) has called "a family's ecology of health." This means, for a physician, a somewhat different professional role from his customary one. It means, for us at the Children's Hospital, becoming advocates for these children and families. It means cooperating constructively with our colleagues in public and voluntary agencies to reach the objective which concerns us all, enhancing a family's capacity to care for its children.

For us, creating an interagency, multi-disciplinary consultation group with weekly meetings at the hospital has worked well. We meet together to explore the needs of the three to five children who are referred to us each week bearing physical symptoms of severe family distress. We try to help families function better by finding services which will make a difference in their ability to be parents. These services include medical, dental, social services, legal help, child care, homemaker services, psychiatric treatment, and, very often, haggling on their behalf, with landlords, the police, and the welfare department.

Our ability to intervene effectively is challenged by many situations where one cannot simply offer services, but where one has to go out, find the people, and effectively change the environments where they live before they can come to grips with their problems of nurturing their children. The ethical and political implications of this kind of professional activism have been explored in the recent social work literature by Martin Rein (*Social Work, 13:* April 1970) and in the medical literature by Julius Richmond (*Pharos, 35:* 17, 1972).

Even when more adequate resources become available, many of the current problems of management will persist. Not the least of these are the exceeding difficulties which public welfare departments are having in coping with dramatically ncreasing numbers of reported cases. In Boston, for example, the inflicted injury unit of our Division of Child Guardianship, at the time of this writing, has an uncovered backlog of thirty-five new cases. And in Massachusetts under current law, only bona fide battered babies get reported by doctors. This is a situation which will grow worse when we have better reporting laws.

In New York, the problem was utterly out of control until a few spectacular murders galvanized the community to action. Mayor Lindsay appointed a task force, the report of which is available from his office. Inasmuch as Mayor Lindsay's task force report underlines the need for 24-hr. intervention, a child abuse registry and adequate coordination between public and private agencies, this report is a useful document. Many of its recommendations were heeded, with a resulting upsurge in case reports, as well might be expected. Still, however, the New York City Mayor's Task Force Report pins the blame on the parents and touts the old "battered child," "inflicted injury" jargon as the key to the understanding and control of the problem of children in jeopardy in their own homes.

Governor Sargent's committee report, on the other hand, emphasizes that the way to prevent such a tragic symptom of family distress as child abuse is to strengthen family life. Its recommendations include a dial-a-parent hotline for families in crisis, the coordination of human services with a view to maintaining physical and emotional health, as opposed to treating artifacts of disease, as well as other specifically "protective" services such as a registry, legal services, and more action-oriented case workers.

Functions of welfare departments in child protection are unfortunately tarred by the same brush as their relief and medicaid functions when the time comes for legislative scrutiny of budgets. There is also more than a suggestion that their child protection activities may convey many of the same values toward the poor, or toward people in trouble, as do their relief policies, such as taking their children away as the final "protective" service.

Two superb, book-length analyses of welfare have come out recently, and a citation from each one may help us see how the agencies to whom we physicians have to report cases of child abuse may themselves be part of the problem, which in my view is a profound deficiency in our public policy toward children and families who need help.

G.Y. Steiner, whose book *The State of Welfare* (Brookings Institution, 1971) has a brilliant chapter called "Tireless Tinkering with Dependent Families," makes it plain that Welfare Departments mess around with some aspects of poverty but have an investment in maintaining it. He quotes Representative Martha Griffiths describing a mother's life on welfare:

"Can you imagine any conditions more demoralizing than those welfare mothers live under? Imagine being confined all day every day in a room with falling plaster, inadequately heated in the winter and sweltering in the summer, without enough beds for the family, and with no sheets, the furniture falling apart, a bare bulb in the center of the room as the only light, with no hot water most of the time, plumbing that often does not work, with only the companionship of small children who are often hungry and always inadequately clothed—and, of course, the ever-present rats. To keep one's sanity under such circumstances is a major achievement, and to give children the love and discipline they need for healthy development is superhuman. If one were designing a system to produce alcoholism, crime and illegitimacy, he could not do better.

One could also do no better to design a system to make parents fail. Insofar as our established "service" structure in public welfare departments allows these conditions to persist, Steiner demonstrates, our human service system is implicated in many cases of child abuse and neglect.

F.F. Piven and R.A. Cloward's *Regulating the Poor* (Pantheon, 1971) develops a historical argument to show that "relief policies are cyclical—liberal or restrictive, depending on the problems of regulation in the larger society with which government must contend . . . this view clearly belies the popular supposition that government social policies, including relief policies, are becoming progressively more responsible, humane and generous." The authors document several situations where the threat of applying "protective services" has been used to intimidate welfare rights demonstrators. This is a scary and impressive scholarly work to which we professionals interested in salvaging families and protecting children should attend.

We physicians face a dilemma with respect to cases of child abuse. We have an ethical obligation to intervene in situations where a child's life may be in danger. Yet the technologic tools of intervention can be imcompetent or destructive. Fortunately, there is evidence that specific, vigorous activity directed at the causes of an individual family's particular crisis can make a difference in the safety of a child in jeopardy.

Physicians and medical institutions can work toward making public agencies' activities with regard to children more adequate to the task of sustaining families. Just as I think we should reject the punitive taxonomy of illness which fixes the blame for a child's injuries on his parent (because it makes no scientific sense and doesn't help in case management) I think we can offer cooperation, consultation, and support to the personnel in public protective agencies. This could lead, ultimately, to a coherent and humane approach to the control of child abuse. The crux of the matter is that child abuse is a complex phenomenon which requires the investment of diverse and coordinated professional energies. It is a symptom of distress in a complicated family ecosystem with many interacting variables. To recognize and act appropriately on the really important ones requires more than simple definitions and isolated professional activities.

3

Knowledge and Epidemiology of Child Abuse: A Critical Review of Concepts

Eli H. Newberger and
Jessica H. Daniel

By identifying and clarifying concepts underlying present knowledge of child abuse, this article may provide the reader with critical tools for understanding it. We shall focus on the magnitude of the problem and probe the meaning of present data and practice.

There is reason to question the nature and quality of knowledge about child abuse. Formal recognition of an age-old phenomenon, demonstrated by an enormous increase in the number of official case reports annually since the mid-1960s, has created a difficult dilemma for medical professionals. Notwithstanding a century's experience in the American child welfare movement and more recent medically based contributions from Kempe and others, we have a service system that, despite humane rhetoric, is unable to promote the safety and well-being of many children. This is in large part due to a paucity of such essential family supports as counseling, medical, homemaker, child-care, and nursing services and to a heavy reliance on foster-home care. A tightfisted social policy toward families and children ($2.5 billion for child welfare each year since 1972 in the face of two-digit inflation and expanding demands for service) means, simply, that when a professional person files a child-abuse case report, the services that follow may be incapable of dealing with the needs of family and child.

Inadequate or incomplete service is only part of the problem. Our basis for practice is flimsy. We have a commonly accepted humane philosophy (if not in reality programs that can translate that philosophy into humane action): to protect parents and children from repeated physical consequences of family crisis. But because we lack a solid theoretical and practical understanding of the origins of child abuse, our clinical work is at best intuitive and kind, at worst reflexive and mean. We read a literature in each of the professions characterized by homilies, bromides, and few scientific investigations of substance. And we look at child abuse as a phenomenon originating in the psychology of individuals, frequently ignoring the social and cultural realities that frustrate our treatment of particular families and impose formidable obstacles to the prevention of child abuse.

Because of the contradictions between philosophy and practice and our

Reprinted by permission of Insight Publishing Co., Inc. from *Pediatric Annals* (March 1976).

incomplete knowledge, we find ourselves wondering whether the following are unanswerable questions when cases of child abuse are identified: Is the child at risk? Can the family be helped? Are competent intervention resources available? Will I do more harm than good by reporting the case?

We do not mean to suggest that the clinician should throw up his hands in despair when the next case of child abuse is brought in. Within the framework of existing knowledge and resources, possible answers and helpful clinical guidelines can be drawn up, and these are the subject of a recent review.[1] By presenting a glossary of concepts and pertinent current data in this article, we would like to help foster an informed and more logical response to child abuse.

"Child Abuse," "Child Neglect," and "Accidents"

Definitions of child abuse vary, from Kempe's "battered child syndrome,"[2] which identifies injuries inflicted by care givers; through Fontana's "maltreatment syndrome,"[3] which includes child neglect; to the current Office of Child Development model reporting statute,[4] which embraces many physical and emotional symptoms attributable to parental failure; and to Gil's concept of any force that compromises a child's capacity to achieve his physical and psychologic potential.[5] Virtually all definitions identify the child as victim, and most identify parent or family as perpetrator.

Important *value* concepts are built into the vocabulary, and in the words themselves are postulated etiologic mechanisms that logically imply diagnostic and intervention procedures. The names "battered child syndrome" and "maltreatment syndrome" have strong implications. They indicate that a child's injuries were caused by his care giver, either actively or passively.

To make such "diagnoses" requires an investigation to determine whether or not there is parental culpability. Inquisitions of parents to ferret out the facts have been characterized by some as clinically unhelpful, ethically absurd, and intellectually unsound.[6,7] Faced with ambiguous data, conflicting accounts of how the child may have received his injuries, and a need to make a definitive diagnosis, the clinician may find himself playing a detective game for which he is professionally unprepared.

Stoked by the strong feelings that child-abuse cases promote in all of us, the diagnostic process may further alienate an isolated, frightened, and confused family and fulfill the preconception of parental failure: aggressive inquiry eliciting evasive response, angry affirmation of suspicion leading to confirmed diagnosis, and subsequent estrangement of family from clinician and separation of child from family.

Different professional people respond in different ways to the personal and ethical conflicts imposed by contact with troubled families. Some physicians find it difficult to believe that parents could injure children. Many characterize all children's injuries as "accidents" (the term connotes an isolated, random event).

Although traumatic injury to children is the major cause of morbidity and mortality after the first year of life[8] and is predictably associated with familial and child developmental crises,[9-11] the nature and organization of child health practice do not usually permit exploring and acting on the causal antecedents of childhood "accidents." Physicians and nurses may not have the time to interview parents or to make detailed child development observations, and such backup diagnostic services as social work and psychiatry are most often situated in separate institutions and practice settings. No treatment other than of the presenting symptom is implied by the diagnosis of an "accident."

Further, because of the onerous significance of making a judgment that a particular family is "abusive" or "neglectful," it is often easier to ignore these "diagnoses." The finding that the great number of reported victims of child abuse are poor[12] and disproportionately represent ethnic minority groups suggests that the more heavily value-laden diagnoses for childhood traumatic injuries (child abuse and neglect) are made more easily when the clinical setting is public and there is great social distance (social class or ethnic discrepancy) between clinician and family.

We clearly need a more scientific taxonomy of childhood "social illness," one that would organize clinical data in such a way as to stimulate helpful and effective practice. Until we have it, however, we shall have to labor with the existing words.

Child-Abuse Epidemiology

The number of annual child-abuse case reports in the United States has jumped from about 7,000 in 1967[12] to over 200,000 in 1974.[13] To understand the significance of this impressive increase for clinical practice requires the explanation of a few simple concepts.

Incidence. This is the number of events in a defined interval or, for purposes of the present discussion, in a year.

Prevalence. This is the number of phenomena that exist at a particular time.

Duration. This is the length of the phenomenon.

A simple equation expresses the relationship of incidence, prevalence, and duration: Prevalence (P) varies as incidence (I) times duration (D) or, more simply, $P = ID$.[14] (This assumes constant flow of information, or a "steady state," into the system.) Although we are accustomed to thinking of the magnitude of the child-abuse problem in terms of the number of new case reports received each year, it is well to remember that these reports flow to human-service institutions (generally welfare departments) with finite capacities to deal with them. The prevalence of cases already "on the books" is a principal reason why the system bogs down.

Suppose, for the sake of discussion, that the duration of the typical child-abuse case, from diagnosis to resolution of the family problem, is 2.5 years. (This figure obscures the great variety of family situations that present as child abuse and, to be sure, minimizes the continuing, developmental impact of child abuse recently emphasized by Martin and his colleagues.[15] Also, protective-service agencies follow few cases for this long. Take it as an arbitrarily selected number.) For 1967, then, an estimate of the prevalence of child abuse is 7,000 × 2.5 = 17,500. For 1974, the prevalence may be estimated as 200,000 × 2.5 = 500,000.

These estimates may bear little relation to reality, but in the unfortunate absence of reliable data on actual recorded prevalence,* they provide an impression of the extraordinary burden that child welfare institutions are now shouldering. In the face of a rising number of case reports and the essentially fixed ability of the service structure to deal with them, there is an unavoidable risk that a case may not be acted on. Or, perhaps worse, precipitous, uninformed protective-service action may separate a child from his family unnecessarily in the interest of his physical protection. So, when one sees a case of child abuse, one must assure that the case report is followed by sustained, helpful action.

Sampling Bias

Some people are much more likely than others to be discovered as child abusers. Members of ethnic or economic minorities are particularly susceptible. This fact skews the findings of any survey or study towards the attributes associated with the group to be studied. Poor families and ethnic minorities appear with special frequency in child-abuse case rosters and studies. This has in part to do with the dynamics of practice, as was pointed out above.

The pertinence of the findings of any investigation to the experience of the general population from which the study subjects are drawn depends on the investigator's ability to account for whatever selective forces operate to include some and not other members of the population.

Our increasing comprehension of the personal and ethical dilemmas that go into making a diagnosis of child abuse inclines us to believe that as long as we persist in studying phenomena with such negative labels as "child abuse" and "neglect," we will not be able to control the biases favoring the selection of poor ·

---

*It is hoped that this situation will soon be remedied by the new National Center on Child Abuse and Neglect in the Office of Child Development in Washington, which has a specific Congressional mandate under Public Law 93-247 to report annually on the size of the child-abuse problem.

and minority families in our samples. (The foregoing is not to deny the extent to which the exigencies of poverty are associated with physical and psychologic stress in families, which in turn may be expressed in violence or neglect toward children.[17,19])

Confounding

Here, because of the investigator's inability to control an intervening, perhaps unforeseen, variable, a spurious association is mistaken for a causal relationship.

Confounding can be reduced (although seldom completely avoided) by controlling studies with matched comparison groups. A striking example of confounding in the recent child-abuse literature is found in the British study by Smith and colleagues.[20] The authors noted an impressive increase in the prevalence of psychologic problems in the parents of abused children. This finding, however, may be an artifact of the different socioeconomic groups from which the cases and "controls" were drawn. Since social class and psychologic symptoms are associated,[21] one cannot assert that there is a primary relationship between psychologic symptoms and child abuse. This finding is "confounded" by social class. The confounding would have been reduced by "matching" cases and controls on social class. This would "control" the confounding variable.

The concepts of sampling bias and confounding are of particular importance in regard to the postulated association between child abuse and later adult deviant behavior, which Schmitt and Kempe have underlined vividly in the most recent edition of Nelson's *Textbook of Pediatrics*. *Logical problem*

> If the child who has been physically abused is returned to his parents without intervention, 5 per cent are killed and 35 per cent are seriously reinjured. Moreover, the untreated families tend to produce children who grow up to be juvenile delinquents and murderers, as well as the child batterers of the next generation.[22]

The truth of such assertions will have to be weighed by a careful consideration of the data from which they derive. Those socially marginal people who are most susceptible to having their children's injuries characterized as having been "abusively" or "neglectfully" obtained are also those whose adult behavior is most likely to be labeled "criminal."

This is not to minimize the importance of the developmental sequelae of child abuse. Rather, we urge critical and serious attention to the meaning of our professional language and knowledge, the better to develop a vocabulary of words and tools that will more adequately help children and families in distress.

References

1. E.H. Newberger and J.N. Hyde. "Child Abuse: Principles and Implications of Current Pediatric Practice," *Pediatric Clinics of North America* XXII (August, 1975):695-715.

2. C.H. Kempe et al., "The Battered Child Syndrome," JAMA CLXXXI (July 7, 1962):17-24.

3. V.J. Fontana, *The Maltreated Child: the Maltreatment Syndrome in Children,* 2nd ed., Springfield, Ill: Charles C. Thomas, Publisher, 1971.

4. National Center on Child Abuse and Neglect. Office of Child Development, U.S. Department of Health, Education and Welfare. *Model Protective Services Act with Commentary,* July 7, 1975.

5. D.G. Gil. "Unraveling Child Abuse," *American Journal of Orthopsychiatry* XLV (April, 1975):346-356.

6. E.H. Newberger. "The Myth of the Battered Child Syndrome," *Current Medical Dialog* XXX (April, 1973):327-334. Reprinted in S. Chess and A. Thomas, eds., *Annual Progress in Child Psychiatry and Child Development, 1974.* New York: Brunner/Mazel, 1975, pp. 569-573.

7. C.B. Pollock and B.F. Steele, "A Therapeutic Approach to the Parents," in C.H. Kempe and R.E. Helfer, eds., *Helping the Battered Child and His Family,* Philadelphia: J.B. Lippincott, 1972, pp. 3-21.

8. *Lengthening Shadows.* Evanston, Ill.: American Academy of Pediatrics, 1970. p. 45.

9. G.S. Gregg and E. Elmer, "Infant Injuries: Accidents or Abuse?" *Pediatrics* XLIV (September, 1969):434-439.

10. R. Sobel, "Psychiatric Implications of Accidental Poisoning in Children," *Pediatric Clinics of North America* XVII (October, 1971):653-657.

11. J.C. Holter and S.B. Friedman, "Child Abuse: Early Case Finding in the Emergency Department," *Pediatrics* XLII (July, 1968):128-138.

12. D.G. Gil, *Violence Against Children,* Cambridge, Massachusetts: Harvard University Press, 1970.

13. V. DeFrancis (Children's Division, American Humane Society), personal communication.

14. B. MacMahon and T.F. Pugh, *Epidemiology: Principles and Methods.* Boston: Little, Brown and Company, 1970.

15. H.A. Martin et al., "The Development of Abused Children," in I. Schulman, ed., *Advances in Pediatrics,* XXI. Chicago: Year Book Medical Publishers, 1974. pp. 25-73.

16. E.H. Newberger, "Review of *Violence Against Children* by D.B. Gil," *Pediatrics* XLVIII (December, 1971):688.

17. R. Light, "Abused and Neglected Children in America: A Study of Alternative Social Policies," *Harvard Educational Review* XLIII (November, 1973):556-598.

18. B. Lauer, E. TenBroeck, and M. Grossman, "Battered Child Syndrome: Review of 130 Patients with Controls," *Pediatrics* LIV (July, 1974):67-70.

19. E.H. Newberger et al., "Toward an Etiologic Classification of Pediatric Social Illness: A Descriptive Epidemiology of Child Abuse and Neglect, Failure to Thrive, Accidents and Poisonings in Children Under Four Years of Age." Paper presented at the meeting of the Society for Research in Child Development, Denver, Colorado, April, 1975. Published in expanded form as "Pediatric Social Illness: Toward an Etiologic Classification," *Pediatrics* LX (August, 1977):178-185.

20. S.M. Smith, R. Hanson and S. Noble, "Parents of Battered Babies: A Controlled Study," *British Medical Journal* IV (November, 1973):388-391.

21. A.B. Hollingshead and F.C. Redlich, *Social Class and Mental Illness.* New York: John Wiley and Sons, 1958.

22. B.D. Schmitt and C.H. Kempe, "Neglect and Abuse of Children," in V.C. Vaughan and R.J. McKay, eds., *Nelson Textbook of Pediatrics*, 10th ed. Philadelphia: W.B. Saunders Company, 1975.

4

Child Abuse: Principles and Implications of Current Pediatric Practice

Eli H. Newberger and
James N. Hyde, Jr.

This paper summarizes data and experience with child abuse pertinent to child health practice. Because of the complex origin of child abuse, and because of institutional and social changes that will have to accompany excellent practice if child abuse is to be treated and prevented, issues of program and policy development are also addressed.

What Is Child Abuse?

The classic paper of Kempe and colleagues defined "the battered child syndrome" as "a term used by us to characterize a clinical condition in young children who have received serious physical abuse, generally from a parent or foster parent."[1] For the medical profession especially, which previously had not recognized a phenomenon centuries old, the impact of the paper was considerable.[2] The concept of child abuse as inflicted injury in the Kempe paper was admittedly narrow and was associated with constricted definitions of child abuse in the state child abuse reporting statutes which proliferated after the paper's publication.

Fontana proposed a more broadly defined "maltreatment syndrome," where the child "often presents itself without obvious signs of being battered but with the multiple minor evidences of emotional and, at times, nutritional deprivation, neglect and abuse. The battered child is only the last phase of the spectrum of the maltreatment syndrome."[3]

Underlying both narrow and broad definitions of child abuse are implicit concepts of parental fault, which are vividly underlined in chapter 1 of the second edition of Fontana's book *The Maltreated Child:* "Today . . . the important battle continues between the child murderer and the child saver."[4]

Such strong and angry responses to child abuse are not rare in the

Reprinted with permission from *Pediatric Clinics of North America* (August 1975):695-715, *passim.*

Presented in part at the Conference on Research on Child Abuse, National Institute of Child Health and Human Development, Bethesda, June 1974. Supported in part by a grant from the Office of Child Development, Department of Health, Education and Welfare (Project OCD-62-141).

27

professional literature and in journalistic treatments of the subject. They derive in part from the intense feelings which cases of child abuse evoke in everyone and in part from our limited understanding of a complicated problem with multiple causes and many manifestations in child, adult personality, family, environment and culture.

Our understanding of the problem of child abuse is advanced by several recent descriptive reports which demonstrate that childhood accidents and child abuse are temporally associated,[5] that the parents of abused children are rarely neurotic or psychotic,[6] and that the developmental sequelae of child abuse and neglect are serious.[7] Child abuse has also been observed to be associated with poverty, low birth weight, parental alcohol and drug abuse, crime, social isolation, marital stress, and unemployment.[8] There are also data which suggest that the coordinated interdisciplinary management of child abuse can reduce the toll of reinjury while children stay in their own homes.[9]

A helpful integrating concept in the diagnosis and treatment of child abuse is the family's capacity to protect its child, either from the consequences of their own angry feelings toward him, or from the hazards of his nurturing environment. Whether or not an injury is intentionally inflicted is of interest and possibly of importance, but understanding its origin and identifying what can be done to strengthen the child's environment might better be the goals of diagnosis of child abuse.[10]

This is not to say that a parent's anger, expressed actively or passively toward a child, is not primary in many child abuse cases. Steele and others have drawn attention to abusing parents' excessive and premature expectations of their children.[11] Often, the angry feelings of which the child's injury is a symptomatic expression appear to derive from the violent circumstances or deprivation of the parent's own upbringing, and they may reflect a deep disappointment that the child has not been able adequately to fulfill the parents' own nurturing needs.[12] This last phenomenon has been called "role reversal" in the psychiatric literature.[13] It is indeed important in one's conversations with parents to ask about their feelings toward the child and to find out about what their own childhoods were like. A particularly sensitive chapter on how to approach parents of an abused child is found in "Helping the Battered Child and His Family."[14]

In the development of a program to help a family better to protect its offspring, one needs to identify *strengths* in a family which can be built upon and *resources* which can operate effectively to integrate child and parent safely.

Application of the Protective Concept in Diagnosis and Initial Intervention

Case 1. *Drugs, Injury and Denial.* A 10 month old boy was brought to the emergency room by his mother, a 19 year old unkempt woman who on arrival said that she had recently been taking illegal psychoactive drugs. Physical examination showed a stuporous child with a massive hematoma overlying the left orbit. On inspection the right eye was deviated leftward. The mother volunteered that she had been in the child's room where quite by chance a broom had fallen over a shoe. She inadvertently stepped on the shorter side of the broomstick, which, with the shoe as a fulcrum, catapulted the broom into the child's crib, hitting him on the head and causing his injury.

This blatantly fabricated explanation for the child's injury might be taken by a physician or nurse, angered by such a grievously injured baby, as an intentional falsification. One might be tempted to hammer away at the proffered story in an effort to make a definitive diagnosis of the "battered child syndrome." This might expiate some of one's own angry feelings, but it might actually harm the prospects for the establishment of professional relationships in order that both mother and child can receive the treatment they desperately need.

The mother's story should be accepted for the moment, and it should be construed by the professionals managing the case as representation of how profoundly threatening to the mother's sense of herself is the reality that she has been so unable to protect her baby. Her denial of this reality may be seen as a desperate attempt to hold herself together, and there may be a conscious effort to conceal the facts of the injury for fear of legal, punitive reprisal. Shorn of her defenses by an interrogatory diagnostic approach, she might resort to a more primitive ego defense, such as resistance to talking about the problem at all, blaming the hospital for the injury, or taking the child and running from the hospital.

One needs to give the child the necessary emergency treatment and protection and to attend to the parent's distress at the same time. It is appropriate to emphasize to the parent the need for the child's treatment and protection and to express one's ability and interest in helping the parent through the crisis. This is a difficult and vexing process for doctors and nurses, who can be overcome with anger toward abusing or neglectful parents. It is well to keep in mind the need to form a *helping relationship* which will lay the groundwork for future intervention to strengthen the protective ability of the mother and her tie to her child. This long-term management goal can be identified and kept in mind from the outset, notwithstanding the implicit or explicit efforts of the parent to obscure the true instrument, timing and circumstance of the child's injury, the parents' social status or personal attractiveness, and one's own angry feelings toward the parent.

Case 2. *Poverty, Depression and Severe Neglect.* An 8 month old child came to the emergency room with her mother, who complained of her inability to gain weight. The mother was poorly dressed and obviously depressed. Physical examination showed a tiny, emaciated child who did not respond to play. There were moderate hip and elbow contractures. Her weight and length were well below the third percentile. The mother was unmarried, and the patient was the fourth child of a fourth father. The mother was born and raised in North Carolina, where she left her oldest child on coming to Boston a year before to find work as a domestic. Both maternal grandparents were seriously ill in North Carolina. She had no child care for her two older preschool children. Mother and children were supported by Aid to Families with Dependent Children; the stipend was about $235 a month, of which $115 went for rent. The mother said her teeth ached constantly, but she had been unable to get to a dentist. She also complained of back pain, fever and listlessness, and a urinary tract infection was shortly discovered.

In this case, a young, depressed mother failed abjectly in her wish to settle her family in an alien metropolis. She could not get child care, dental care, decent employment or health care, including contraceptive services. Her child's neglect was not taken to be her fault, and a compassionately conducted family assessment permitted identifying a management program which enabled the child to thrive in her care. On discharge from the hospital, a homemaker came three days a week, a visiting nurse on alternate days. Weekly clinic visits were scheduled. Preschool services were found for her two older children. A social worker gave weekly counseling, which was associated with an increase in the mother's self esteem. Dental and medical treatment, along with the other elements in the management plan, were coordinated by the social worker.

At a five year follow-up the patient was physically and psychologically normal. Her family, including a new younger brother, were happy and healthy.

Were one so inclined, one could, on the basis of medical criteria alone, argue successfully in virtually any district, juvenile or family court in the United States that this child was in need of care and protection and should be found by the court to be dependent on the State. Such a practice, which occurs regularly, could aptly be characterized as a form of "blaming the victim."[15] Here, both mother and child can be seen as victims of a social system which distributes jobs, goods, and child health and development resources unequally.

Homemaker, child care, counseling and dental[16] services are frequently expensive and difficult to obtain. The long-term effects on child and family of foster home placement, however, are known from recent studies both to be psychologically and financially costly.[17] It is essential that medical personnel invest the necessary time and energy to assure that, when possible, families can stay together. To do so may involve, as it did in this case, time-consuming conferences with the welfare department, letters requesting homemaker and nursing services, purposeful and systematic efforts to engender a relationship of confidence and trust with a parent who has no previous successful experience with helping services, and convincing one's skeptical colleagues that staying with the family may be in the child's best long-term interest.

The arguments advanced in the recent book *Beyond the Best Interests of the Child* have been influential in framing discussions of the management of individual cases. In this book, distinguished figures in psychiatry and law propose that the traditional criterion for decision-making in child welfare cases ("the best interest of the child") is insufficient. One would often do better, they note, to choose "the least detrimental alternative."[18] Such a concept provides a yardstick to measure for the child in question the impact on his development of a decision affecting his family.

At the time the critical judgment was made to invest professional resources in this fragile family, one could not have been sure that the decision to send the child home with her mother was "the least detrimental alternative." Now it appears to have been. The capacity to *predict* the differential outcome of various interventions is limited. This is a provocative and helpful book for medical personnel concerned with child abuse and neglect, although a superficial reading of it may arm one's colleagues (if not oneself) with apparently simple and unitary formulas for complicated clinical problems with multiple causes. These demand flexibility and creativity in deploying intervention tools appropriate to each case.

Case 3. *New Year's Eve and a "Battering Sibling."* A 2 1/2 year old girl was brought by the police to the emergency room in a blanket after having been found unconscious on the grass outside a housing project on New Year's Eve. The outdoor temperature was in the low thirties. Physical examination showed a semicomatose child whose skin revealed a 3 cm. linear laceration of the left buttock and poor general physical hygiene, including tatoos of dirt on the plantar surfaces of both feet.

The child's mother arrived at the hospital within the hour and informed the physician that she had left the patient in the care of her 5 year old sibling. According to the sibling, the two had been running naked in the apartment, when the older child, angered at the patient, took a knife and chased her, managing to lacerate her buttock before she climbed upon the window ledge, and in her desperation to escape from her sister, opened the window and jumped from the sixth floor.

Further interview disclosed that the patient's mother became pregnant with the older sibling, whose behavior had previously been noted by a local health center to be distressed, when she was a resident at a training school for girls, to which she was sent by the juvenile court after *her* mother asked that she be declared a stubborn child. By virtue of her child's birth, she became an emancipated minor. She was liberated to live with her child in a housing project on an Aid to Families with Dependent Children stipend, estranged from her mother and family and alienated from the social "services" which had so clumsily intervened in her own young life.

One might look on this case as an example of the "battering child" syndrome and simply attribute the child's abuse to a different "perpetrator" than the parent customarily identified as the cause of the child's injury. Similarly, a more penetrating and accurate formulation might address the obvious failure of the mother to protect her two year old from her predatory sister. Both "diagnoses" are correct, in the sense that they address proximal causes of the presenting lesions. Unfortunately, however, the roots of the problem extend deeper. One may look on this patient's injuries as symptoms of more complex familial and social problems, which challenge one's capacity as a medical worker to cure the individual case or to prevent future similar cases.

The origins of the two year old's injury are at least two generations back, from the distressed relationship between her mother and grandmother. The court action which led to the mother's placement in a training school—in reality a prison for children—may have been the only way that the grandmother was able to get help for her problems with her teenaged daughter. This is an example of how so often, as Bronfenbrenner aptly noted, American service institutions are divisive rather than integrative of families.[19] Additionally, one might observe that the services which society made available to this young mother when she was a child, the court and the delinquency "program," could neither anticipate her future nor provide adequate services when she became a mother. Other social institutions, the welfare "service" system, the Boston public housing "program," and the child health services which were equipped only to do minimal health promotion, conspired passively to let her not inconsiderable personal and psychological problems take their toll on her offspring.

It was only when her child was abused that a systematic and coordinated effort to provide counseling, child care, health care, homemaker and better housing began. Ironically, and tragically, it was necessary to invoke the authority of the same juvenile court which committed her as an adolescent to force her to accept these services. It was impossible to convince this mother that we meant to help her better to care for her children. Her experience with "helping" services had been unrewarding or punitive, and she had no basis for trust.

As medical practice is currently organized, it is often impossible to operate effectively on the causes of individual child abuse cases such as this one. To prevent future such cases will require attention to the distribution and quality of such social services as housing, health and counseling, the courts, schools, as well as opportunities to compete for the essential goods of society.

The disturbing question of whether our culture actually *needs* child abuse has been raised by Gil and by Gelles.[20] Simply summarized, the question is whether the sensational nature of the problem conveniently obscures its true social determinants (Gil uses the provocative metaphor "smokescreen" of public and professional interest), both because of society's need to obscure its neglect of so many of its young by depriving them of the resources necessary for them to grow in families whose basic needs for goods and services are met, and because of individual families' needs to make acceptable their own violent parenting practices.

These three cases give a general impression of the complexity of child abuse. Its diagnosis requires more than a comfortable reconciling of symptoms with parent explanation; its management includes tools not found in the medical clinician's own office; and its prevention shall involve addressing cultural traditions, social values and economic realities which exert a deleterious impact on a family's ability to protect its offspring.

The next case raises another complex set of questions, including the mental illness of a parent and the problems associated with the reporting of middle-class families where child abuse has occurred.

Case 4. *A Professional Person's Child.* A 3 week old boy was brought to the emergency room by his mother, who promptly informed the staff that the child had received his injury, a hand-shaped ecchymosis over the left temporoparietal area, at the hands of his father, a professional person who worked in another hospital in the Boston area. The professional staff was reluctant to report the case, as mandated by law, to the Department of Public Welfare. The father was seen by a social worker and psychiatrist, who noted a severe personality disorder, with paranoid features and poor impulse control. He associated the birth of his first child with a sense of abandonment by his wife.

In the present case, the issue of primary adult psychopathology is raised. The findings in the psychiatric and psychological literature are somewhat in conflict on this point. One controlled study of the personalities of abusing parents indicates no definite pattern of neurosis, drawing attention to severely frustrated dependency needs and serious parental inabilities to empathize with their children.[21] Another larger study, where the cases were of significantly lower social class than the controls, indicated a high prevalence of parental personality disorders and neuroses.[22] Here, the psychiatric consultant's perceptions and recommendations were helpful in treating the problem.

It is well known that professional personnel are frequently reluctant to report child abuse cases from middle and upper-class homes. Surveys of the private practitioners who care for the children of more affluent families indicate that they are seeing many more cases than they report.[23] And the 1965 poll of a representative sample of ordinary American citizens conducted by the National Opinion Research Center as part of Gil's national study of child abuse in the late 1960s led to a national incidence extrapolation for which the 95 percent confidence interval was 2.5 to 4.03 million cases, at a time when fewer than 7000 cases were reported each year.[24] The data suggest that child abuse is more prevalent among middle and upper-class families than case reports indicate.

The same survey also posed the intriguing question, "Could you injure a child in your care?" to which six of ten respondents gave an affirmative reply.

A disproportionate number of families who are poor or nonwhite appear in case series of child abuse and in registers of child abuse case reports. To what extent do the circumstances of poverty contribute to this apparently greater frequency of the phenomenon among poor people? And to what extent does the preferential selection for reporting of impoverished families make it appear that poor people abuse their children more? Recent research findings suggest that certain environmental and social stresses are importantly associated with child abuse.[25] These may be experienced disproportionately—but not exclusively— among the poor.

Implications of Child Abuse Reporting Statutes for Clinical Practice and Social Policy

An accepted tenet of child abuse management tells professionals to be compassionate and to convey to parents their interest in helping to maintain the integrity of the family unit. On the other hand, child abuse reporting laws force physicians and others to make judgments about families which they and the family may feel are onerous and heavily value-laden. Additionally, the perceived effect of reporting is to bring to bear a quasi-legal mechanism which, while in theory nonpunitive in orientation, may be the opposite in practice. In such states as Virginia and California, parents may be jailed as a result of the mandated case report.

One may thus be torn between one's legal responsibility to report and one's clinical judgment which may suggest that reporting itself may jeopardize the opportunity to develop a satisfactory treatment program for the family. Often this conflict is expressed in reticence to inform families that they are being reported, or reluctance and even frank refusal to report cases of abuse and neglect.

While there are no cut and dried rules which resolve this conflict definitively, two simple guidelines make it easier for the mandated professional to come to terms with legal responsibility and clinical judgment:

1. The family must be told that a report is being filed. Much of the apprehension which may surround the receipt of this information can be alleviated by explaining to the family what the reporting process is and is not; it does not necessarily mean that the child will be taken away or that a court hearing will be held. The reporting process can best be presented to the family as a referral of the family for services, and an explicit acknowledgment that they have a serious problem in protecting their child which others, including the reporting practitioner, can help to solve.

2. The mandated reporter can also explain to the family that the report represents an obligation on the part of the practitioner which he or she is bound by law to fulfill.

Often, rather than reacting in a hostile or angry way, families will greet the news with relief. The reporting process may produce help which they have been seeking for a long time, and they may be relieved to hear that the suspicions others have had about them and their parenting are finally out in the open where they can be dealt with in a straightforward manner.

While such an approach to child abuse case reporting may palliate the anxiety of reporter and family, it does not remove the real, inherent labeling and stigmatizing aspects of the reporting process as it exists in most of the states today. Unfortunately, this is a problem that cannot be alleviated simply by a revision of reporting itself; it is rather an aspect of our society's perception of child abuse and the abusing parent. So long as child abuse is viewed as a form of radically deviant behavior, and as a symptom of pathology and sickness in others, the stigmatizing process will continue. All concerned to prevent and treat child abuse have, therefore, a responsibility to demythologize the problem: to recognize that the potential to act in ways which we identify as deviant is in all of us. Until attitudes and policies change toward troubled families, where children may bear physical signs of their distress, we shall have to work within the prevailing legal framework and to assure to the extent possible that children and families are helped—not harmed—by it.

All state statutes abrogate privileged communication when it involves a case of known or suspected child abuse. In reporting to mandated state agencies, the reporter should identify the facts as they are known; hearsay and secondary source information can be labeled as such. At least forty-four states have provisions in their statutes for central registers, which may become repositories for information both founded and unfounded, depending on the expungement provisions of the individual statutes. Who has access to this information is left up to the individual states, and it is well to remember that information that is submitted in such reports may be used at some later date to raise the issue of competency of a family or the risk to a child.

The principle on which most prevailing statutes are built is that services should be made available to families in which child abuse has been reported as a problem. The reality in most states is that the actual funds available for the implementation of these statutes nowhere nearly approximates the existing demand for services. This problem has been seriously exacerbated recently by expanding reporting criteria and lists of professionals mandated to report cases of abuse and neglect.

Even in the presence of an efficient system for identifying families where child abuse had occurred, budgetary constraints may make it impossible for adequate services to be provided except in the most critical of cases. This makes it incumbent on the individual reporting a case not simply to view the report as a referral for service which will go forth with or without the professional's continued involvement in its management, but rather to *assure* that help will be given and that the family will not fall between the cracks of the service structure.

The essential elements of child abuse and neglect emergency management are summarized in table 1.

Model Systems

Translating these complex and sophisticated clinical practices into effective programs for large numbers of children and families is a challenge not to be

Table 1

Emergency Management of Child Abuse and Neglect

Diagnosis

Is this child at risk? If his presenting complaint arouses suspicion, act on it forthrightly and compassionately. Protect the child and help his family.

Intervention

Is it safe to send the child home?

Admission to the hospital considered in suspected cases and often when the diagnosis of abuse or neglect is established.

Social worker called.

Assessment

General medical history and physical examination. "Who did it?" is not the issue. Avoid the third degree.

Initial interview and assessment of the family by a social worker; development of understanding of family's strengths and resources.

Nursing evaluation of child's development, parent-child relationship, and family's participation in community health structures.

Honest explanation of the legal responsibility to report the case to the welfare department by the physician.

Report to the public agency mandated by law to receive reports of cases of child abuse and neglect.

Photograph and skeletal survey if indicated.

Appropriate consultations, especially psychiatry, as indicated.

Communication among physician, social worker, and nurse to decide program of care.

Intervention Program

Initiation of rehabilitative efforts for both child and family.

Mobilization of hospital and community resources which may be available for the family, e.g., child care, foster placement, community family service and health agencies.

Follow-up

Primary medical care arranged.

Social service follow-up—community service or public agency, as indicated.

Nursing follow-up as indicated.

taken lightly. In closing we should like to propose fourteen attributes of model systems for the prevention and control of child abuse and neglect. These general programmatic principles would apply at various levels of scale, from individual medical practice to hospital to community service agency to state.

1. Child abuse seen as a symptom of *family crisis*, with professional services oriented to making families stronger.

2. Recognition of the community context in which child abuse occurs: attention to the values of the community, its indigenous techniques of problem solving, its traditions of child rearing, its resources and its leadership, in both the development of programs to help families, and in the approach to preventing child abuse on a larger social scale.

3. Services should be able to respond creatively to individual families' problems with services suited to their needs, to include:(a) social work counseling, liaison with other services and structures; (b) medical and psychiatric consultation and, where necessary, treatment; (c) advocacy; (d) child development services, including education, child care and psychological intervention; (e) legal services; (f) temporary foster home care; and (g) round-the-clock emergency services, such as homemaker services, to prevent family break-up and continued child abuse or neglect.

4. Protection of information about people; consistent and rigorous identification of the rights of children and their parents; and advocacy at all levels of intervention action to assure that fundamental civil liberties are not violated.

5. Regular evaluation of the effectiveness of intervention on several levels: for the individual case, both to assure continued physical protection and the promotion of health and psychological growth; and for the program in general, to assure the adherence to the highest principles of human service.

6. It would identify who is responsible to whom for what; minimize to the extent possible uninformed, reflexive and precipitous action on the part of intervention personnel; maximize the career development possibilities for these personnel in the context of the program structure; integrate into the career development program a systematic method for recruiting and training professional personnel from minority groups; and allow for the acknowledgment and reward of successful work.

7. Services would be provided 24 hours a day.

8. There would be an adequate commitment of resources to assure that a successful program would be able to continue.

9. It would assure adequate legal representation for all parties in any court proceeding relating to child abuse; and active and high-level advocacy to assure judicial determinations consonant with the high standards of modern family law. Its goal would be to integrate families rather than to punish parents; to use the authority of the court, when necessary, to force family change; and, as a last resort when families utterly and completely fail, to allow children who are dependent on the state maximal opportunities for growth in homes they can identify as their own.

10. Administrative organization allowing both flexibility in staff development, supervision, and assignment and at the same time high-level access to the human services leadership, in order most effectively to promote collaboration, constructive and mutual program planning, and, ultimately, the evolution of a human service system which would identify the *family* as the unit of practice, rather than as, at present, to fragment health, social and psychological problems into discrete program units.

11. It would incorporate child advocacy (as defined in the report of the Joint Commission on the Mental Health of Children) and child development education.

12. Systematic attention to the development of public policies which strengthen family life, based on what is already known about family strength and stress.

13. Citizen supervision of professional policies and practices through community-based councils for children.

14. The program should be population based: all people should be eligible for service. Neither a small-scale pilot program nor a major undertaking focusing only on the protection of the children whose cases happen to be reported, it should identify the dimensions of the problem and all possible avenues of individual and larger-scale intervention, as well as recruit and sustain the interest and participation of competent and varied providers of service. Emphatically, it should not be identified as a poor people's program, although it is certain that many children of the poor will be reported, partly but not exclusively because of the circumstances of poverty which may lead their families to fail. It should be a program to which private medical practitioners and voluntary family service agencies, as well as suburban school systems, would feel comfortable in reporting cases, because its services would be helpful and its orientation toward keeping families together and toward preventing child abuse.

References

1. C.H. Kempe et al., "The Battered Child Syndrome." *JAMA* CLXXXI (July 7, 1962):107-112.

2. S.X. Radbill, "A History of Child Abuse and Infanticide," in *The Battered Child,* 2nd ed., ed. by R.E. Helfer and C.H. Kempe. (Chicago: University of Chicago Press, 1974).

3. V.J. Fontana, *The Maltreated Child: The Maltreatment Syndrome in Children,* 2nd ed. (Springfield: Charles C. Thomas, 1971), p. 4.

4. Ibid., p. 4.

5. S.B. Friedman and C.W. Morse, "Child Abuse: A Five-year Follow-up of Early Case Finding." *Pediatrics* LIV (October, 1974):404-410; C.S. Gregg and E. Elmer, "Infant Injuries: Accidents or Abuse?," *Pediatrics* XLII (July, 1969):128-138; J.C. Holter and S.B. Friedman, "Child Abuse: Early Case Finding in the Emergency Department," *Pediatrics* XLII (July, 1969):128-138.

6. B. Melnick and J. Hurley, "Distinctive Personality Attributes of Child Abusing Mothers," *Journal of Consulting Clinical Psychiatry* XXXIII (June, 1969):746-749.

7. E. Elmer, *Children in Jeopardy: A Study of Abused Minors and Their Families.* (Pittsburgh: University of Pittsburgh Press, 1967); H.A. Martin, et al., "The Development of Abused Children," in *Advances in Pediatrics* XXI, ed. by I. Schulman. (Chicago: Year Book Medical Publishers, 1974), pp. 25-73.

8. R. Gelles, *The Violent Home: A Study of Physical Aggression Between*

Husbands and Wives. (Beverly Hills, California: Russell Sage, 1974); D.G. Gil, *Violence Against Children* (Cambridge: Harvard University Press, 1970); M. Klein and L. Stern, "Low Birth Weight and the Battered Child Syndrome," *American Journal of the Diseases of Children* CXXII (July, 1971):15-18; B. Lauer, E. Ten Broeck, and M. Grossman, "Battered Child Syndrome: Review of 130 Patients with Controls," *Pediatrics* LIV (July, 1974):67-70; R. Light, "Abused and Neglected Children in America: A Study of Alternative Policies," *Harvard Educational Review* XLIII (November, 1973):556-598; L.B. Silver et al., "Agency Action and Interaction in Cases of Child Abuse," *Social Casework* (March, 1971):164-171; S.M. Smith et al., "Parents of Battered Babies: A Controlled Study," *British Medical Journal* IV (1973):338-391.

9. M.R. Burt and R. Balyeat, "A New System for Improving the Care of Neglected and Abused Children." *Child Welfare* LIII (March, 1974):167-179; E.H. Newberger et al., "Reducing the Literal and Human Cost of Child Abuse: Impact of a New Hospital Management System," *Pediatrics* LI (May, 1973):840-848.

10. E.H. Newberger, "The Myth of the Battered Child Syndrome," *Current Medical Dialog* XXX (1973):327-330.

11. R. Galdston, "Observations on Children Who Have Been Physically Abused and Their Parents," *American Journal of Psychiatry* CXXII (January, 1965):440-443; B.F. Steele and C.B. Pollock, "A Psychiatric Study of Parents Who Abuse Infants and Small Children," in *The Battered Child*, 2nd ed. ed. by R.E. Helfer and C.H. Kempe. (Chicago: University of Chicago Press, 1974), pp. 89-133.

12. I. Kaufman, "Psychiatric Implications of Physical Abuse of Children," in *Protecting the Battered Child* (Denver: American Humane Association, 1962), pp. 17-22; M. Klein and L. Stern, "Low Birth Weight and the Battered Child Syndrome," *American Journal of the Diseases of Children* CXX (July, 1971):15-18.

13. M.G. Morris and R.W. Gould, "Role Reversal: A Concept in Dealing with Neglect-Battered Child Syndrome," in *The Neglected-Battered Child Syndrome* (New York: Child Welfare League of America, 1973).

14. C.B. Pollock and B.F. Steele, "A Therapeutic Approach to the Parents," in *Helping the Battered Child and his Family*, ed. by C.H. Kempe and R.E. Helfer (Philadelphia: J.B. Lippincott Co., 1972), pp. 3-21.

15. W. Ryan, *Blaming the Victim* (New York: Pantheon, 1971).

16. D.G. Gil, "A Holistic Perspective on Child Abuse and its Prevention," (paper presented at the Conference on Child Abuse, National Institute of Child Health and Human Development, June, 1974); reprinted in shortened form as "Unraveling Child Abuse," *American Journal of Orthopsychiatry* VL (April, 1975):346-356.

17. D. Fanshel and E.B. Shinn, *Dollars and Sense in the Foster Care of Children: A Look at Cost Factors* (New York: Child Welfare League of America, Inc., 1972).

18. J. Goldstein et al., *Beyond the Best Interests of the Child* (New York: Free Press, 1973).

19. U. Bronfenbrenner, *Two Worlds of Childhood* (New York: Russell Sage, 1970).

20. R. Gelles, "The Social Construction of Child Abuse," *American Journal of Orthopsychiatry* XL (April, 1975):363-371; D.G. Gil, *op. cit.*

21. B. Melnick and J. Hurley, *op. cit.*

22. S.M. Smith et al., *op. cit.*

23. D.J. Besharov and P.B. Duryea, "Report of the New York State Assembly," in *The Battered Child,* 2nd ed., ed. by R.E. Helfer and C.H. Kempe (Chicago: University of Chicago Press, 1974), pp. 226-257.

24. D.G. Gil, *op. cit.*

25. E.H. Newberger et al., "Toward an Etiologic Classification of Pediatric Social Illness: A Descriptive Epidemiology of Child Abuse and Neglect, Failure to Thrive, Accidents and Poisonings in Children Under Four Years of Age," (Paper presented at the meeting of the Society for Research in Child Development, Denver, April 1975). Published in expanded form as "Pediatric Social Illness: Toward an Etiologic Classification," *Pediatrics* LX (August, 1977):178-185.

5

A Follow-up Study of Traumatized Children

Elizabeth Elmer

In the last few years the burst of activities related to child abuse has been nothing short of astonishing. In 1961, when the Children's Bureau framed the first suggested model law, some professional persons were concerned at the amount of attention being paid to a phenomenon that seemed quite rare. By 1967 all the states had laws concerning the reporting of abuse. These have been constantly expanded as to the types of mistreatment to be reported and the range of professionals mandated to report; the volume of reports has climbed each year. Light[1] estimates that one in one hundred children in the United States is abused, sexually molested, or neglected. And one eminent authority, Douglas Besharov, predicts that, in the near future, 1 million cases of suspected mistreatment will be reported each year in the United States.[2] It is impossible, of course, to determine whether the increase is due to more incidents of abuse, more effective identification, or expansion in the reporting requirements themselves.

Since the establishment in 1974 of the National Center on Child Abuse and Neglect, demonstration and research programs have sprung up on every side. Hot lines, Parents Anonymous, and many varieties of special projects abound. Among the objectives of these programs, three stand out: identification of high-risk families, identification and reporting of actual cases, and services to children and their families.

Curiously, comparatively little attention has been paid to the subsequent development of abused children. It is reasonable to speculate that children exposed to parental rage and violence will sustain damage in a range of developmental areas. Unfortunately there are few hard data to support this possibility. Although a small number of follow-up studies have been published,[3-6] none of these studies employed a matched comparison group. The findings of the four studies tended to support each other, *i.e.,* abused children suffered disabilities in physical development, personality development, and intellectual achievement. Because of the lack of suitable comparison groups, however, these findings might have been due to uncontrolled variables such as social class.

A five-year follow-up study by Friedman and Morse[7] compared suspected abuse, suspected neglect, and accident cases. However, it was not possible to match the three study groups on demographic characteristics, and there was no comparison group from the general population, a drawback recognized by the authors.

The purpose of this paper is to report the results of a follow-up study of abused and accidentally injured children, utilizing matched comparison groups. Aside from medical care and placement in substitute homes of some abused children, the traumatized children received no specific treatment.

Summary of the Base Study

The traumatized children were first studied as infants of 12 months or less after their referral to the Department of Radiology, Children's Hospital of Pittsburgh, because of an impact event.[a] Each mother was interviewed at home to determine the circumstances of the index event; then the infant was brought to the outpatient department of the hospital for a pediatric and a developmental assessment. These initial data were the basis for a judgment of abuse or accident, which was made jointly by the pediatrician, the social work interviewer, and the author. A child was judged abused if one or more of the following criteria were present: report or admission of abuse of the patient or a sibling; injuries incurred more than once; or history conflicting or inadequate to explain the child's condition. Judgments of abuse had to be unanimous, otherwise the child was considered an accident victim.

Subsequent procedures in the Infant Accident Study included additional home visits, observations of mother-baby interaction, a mailed questionnaire, and a final evaluation of the baby in the outpatient clinic. The concluding procedure was a staff review of the original judgments (abuse or accident) in the light of the data gathered during the one-year investigation. New criteria were added concerning possible indicators of abuse such as marks on the body and observations of extremely harsh physical discipline. At the end of the study twenty-four children were judged abused and seventy-seven were judged accident.

The Follow-up Study

Subject Selection

The follow-up study was conducted approximately eight years after the base study. Abused children were matched to accident children on age, race, sex, and socioeconomic status; seventeen matching pairs could be identified and studied.

[a]"Impact event" means an accident or injury caused by an exchange of energy, *e.g.,* a fall or a blow. It excludes other types of accidents such as burns or ingestions.

In each group there were nine blacks (seven boys and two girls) and eight whites (five boys and three girls). The children were largely lower-class (classes IV and V) according to the Two-factor Index of Social Position.[8]

The comparison children had not been studied before. They were selected from hospital populations and were matched to the traumatized children on the same demographic variables. In addition we required that there be no history of abuse according to Child Welfare Services records and no history of accident resulting in referral to a hospital before the age of twelve months.

Many of the traumatized children had been hospitalized before age twelve months because of their injuries. Since hospitalization implies separation from the mother, and since very young children are considered especially vulnerable to such separation, it seemed possible that any group differences found between traumatized and untraumatized children might be attributable to differences in hospital experience during infancy. To avoid such a possibility, we decided to control for this variable.

The members of nine pairs of traumatized children were similar as to infantile hospitalization, *i.e.,* either both had been inpatients or neither had been. For each of these pairs we selected one untraumatized comparison child who was matched on early hospital experience as well as on the relevant demographic variables. The members of eight pairs of traumatized children were dissimilar as to infantile hospitalization. For each of these pairs we selected two comparison children. One matched the abused child as to infantile hospital experience and the other matched the accident child. The condition leading to inpatient care of comparison children had to be acute illness, not trauma.

To control for hospitalization, a total of twenty-five comparison subjects were chosen. The analyses to be described compare (1) abused children and untraumatized children, matched as to infantile hospital experience; (2) accident children and untraumatized children, matched as to infantile hospitalization; and (3) abused children and accident children. In the latter comparison, history of hospitalization could not be controlled as nine of the seventeen abused children but only five of the seventeen accident children had been inpatients before the age of twelve months.

Hypotheses

The hypotheses were that the abused would fall below the nonabused children in (1) height and weight, (2) language development, (3) self-concept, and (4) intellectual functioning; and that the abused would score higher than the nonabused children as to (5) impulsivity, (6) aggression, and (7) the number of interim illnesses and accidents. Children no longer in the abusive environment, *i.e.,* in foster or adoptive homes, were expected to function at a higher level than those who had remained with the abusive caretakers.

Procedures

The care-takers of all thirty-four traumatized children were located. At the time of follow-up, eight abused children were living with foster or adoptive families. Mothers were interviewed at home to gather demographic data and information about maternal health, perception of the child, and methods of reward and punishment. Black mothers were seen by a black female interviewer and white mothers by a white female interviewer.

Each child was brought to the laboratory for a half-day of evaluations. All clinicians were blind to the child's group identification (abuse, accident, or comparison).

Health was assessed by means of a pediatric examination that included history, anthropometric measures, systems review, and attention to behavioral symptoms and gross neurological signs. Anthropometric measures were later converted into percentiles for age and sex. Well-child care was assessed by examining the immunization record, last visit to the dentist and dental appearance, and physical care, *e.g.,* cleanliness of skin, hair, and clothes. Health data were rated on a five-point scale by a physician and a research assistant, both blind to the children's classification, working in concert.

An experienced speech pathologist performed the language evaluation, which consisted of ratings of articulation during testing[9] and during conversation. Expressive language was judged from the child's responses to the Blacky cards and from five stories that the child made up.

All the child's productions were recorded; articulation during testing and conversational articulation were judged from audio tapes and expressive language from transcripts. Both articulation and expressive language were scored on a five-point scale from 1, very poor, to 5, very good. Other communication disorders, *e.g.,* excessive nonfluency or voice deviations, were noted by the clinician during the testing.

Test-retest reliability was calculated after two months, using the tapes of twelve children and the transcripts of twelve others. For articulation during conversation the reliability was .89 and for expressive language, .96. Reliability with each of two other judges was .88 and .90 for articulation and the same for expressive language.

Self-concept was evaluated by means of the Piers-Harris Children's Self-concept Scale.[10] This is a paper-and-pencil test yielding numerical scores of self-concept in relation to six areas: behavior, intelligence, appearance, anxiety, popularity, and happiness. The overall score is the sum of the six subscales. The test has been widely used for children of approximately the same age as our subjects.

Intellectual standing was assessed by analyzing the entire school record of each child, including results of tests administered in school, grades, and grade placement. A senior psychologist who was familiar with the different school systems involved, and also with the tests commonly used, examined the de-identified data for each child. Achievement and ability were rated separately as either less than average or average. The ratio of achievement to ability was calculated.

A pre-coded teacher questionnaire modeled on that used by Werner *et al.*[11] was designed to obtain systematic data on all children concerning school behavior and attitudes.[b] Each item of the questionnaire was analyzed separately by assigning a numerical score of 0 to 2. Total scores were added to estimate the teacher's overall impressions of each child.

Impulsivity and aggression were assessed by means of a dramatic role-play procedure administered by an expressive arts clinician. The child verbalized and used puppets to act out stories in response to five stimulus situations described by the clinician. A sixth story was entirely spontaneous.

The stories were transcribed, separated, and numbered according to a random table in order to scramble subjects and stories. Two judges independently rated the stories for each of the variables, using a scale that had previously been tested on the story productions of twenty other children. Reliability figures for the 354 stories (six stories for each of the fifty-nine subjects) were impulsivity, .83 and aggression, .98.

Groups of children were compared as to the mean score for each behavioral quality on each story and across all stories, and on the difference between ratings for each behavior for story five minus story one, and for story six minus story 1. The purpose was to assess possible changes in impulsivity and aggression as the child got into increasing fantasy material. Analysis of variance was used to assess changes in patterns between groups.

Several months after the conclusion of testing, all available record material concerning the child's behavior, past and present, was summarized in writing for each child. Possible comments about abuse were deleted as were all identifying data. The material formed the basis for clinical assessments of behavior by a senior psychiatrist, an experienced social worker, and a professional mental health worker with children. The children were rated on control of aggression: under, over, or about average; and on probable degree of disturbance using a five-point scale: 1, very disturbed, to 5, no apparent disturbance. References to nervous mannerisms were collected from teacher questionnaires and pediatric data.

Results

Although material is available for the families, in this paper the focus will be the children. All statistical tests are based on two-tailed estimates of probability.

Anthropometric measures for the children were compared by means of *t*-tests of the percentiles for height, weight, and head circumference. The only

---

[b]A copy of the teacher questionnaire is available from author on request.

difference was in weight: the seventeen abused children weighed significantly more than their nonabused comparisons (t_{32} = 2.010; $P < .05$).

Assessment of well-child care showed that immunizations and physical child care were adequate for the entire sample. The abused children were receiving poorer dental care than their comparison group but this was not a significant difference.

Data for injuries and illnesses showed that the abused children had had a greater number of such occurrences than their untraumatized comparisons, while the accident children exceeded both their untraumatized comparisons and the abused children. The only difference that was significant, however, was accident vs. untraumatized (χ^2 = 9.14; df = 2; $P < .05$). No differences appeared as to ratings for systems review or operations and hospitalizations.

An interesting serendipitous finding was the extent of allergies in the sample. Twenty-four percent of all the children were subject to one or more of a long list of allergies or allergic manifestations, e.g., asthma, hay fever, hives, or sensitivity to foods or plants. Asthma was a problem for seven children or 12 percent of all subjects. (Asthmatic children were also counted among those with allergies.) This contrasts with a figure of 2.8 percent reported for school children in Houston, Texas.[12] Since asthma has been categorized as a disease with strong emotional overtones, we compared the children with and without asthma on clinical ratings of aggression, estimated degree of disturbance, and tallies of nervous mannerisms. None of these showed any association with the disease.

Ratings of neurological findings showed that five abused and four accident children were at the lower points of the scale (poor or very poor). One of the comparison children for the abuse group also had a rating of poor. However, there were no significant differences between any of the major groups.

The groups were compared as to articulation in conversation, expressive language, other communication disorders, and combinations of these problems. No differences were found among the major groups. The surprising finding was the extent of language difficulties across all subjects. Seventy percent of the fifty-six children who could be rated had one or more language problems. Fifty-seven percent were poor or very poor in articulation; 39 percent were poor or very poor in expressive language; and 45 percent demonstrated other communication disorders, e.g., stuttering or intermittent aphonia. The last figure is of particular interest since such problems are widely believed to be associated with tension and anxiety.

Abused children in foster or adoptive homes, compared to those in their natural homes, had a significantly greater number of problems in articulation ($P < .025$, Fisher's Exact Probability) and in combinations of communication problems ($P < .025$, Fisher's Exact Probability), and also tended to be poorer in expressive language. Goldfarb[13] noted that children placed away from a noxious environment recovered in most respects but did not improve substantially in language. Another possible explanation is that the difference in language skills were due to social status and ethnic differences. Foster/adoptive children and natural home children were of course not matched. Six of the eight children in substitute care were lower-class black children, while six of the nine children in natural homes were white; four of these were middle-class. Analyses of expressive language and conversational articulation among all the study children according to socioeconomic status showed that both skills were significantly associated with class: more children in the lower classes (four and five) were rated poor or very poor on expressive language (χ^2 = 8.32; $P <$ .01), and also on articulation (χ^2 = 8.77; $P <$ .01). Other investigators, for example Bernstein,[14] have also found that poorer language skills are a concomitant of lower class. In our sample, analyses of the same skills by ethnic origin indicated that whites had significantly better expressive language (χ^2 = 6.93; $P <$ .01). Although ratings of articulation favored whites, the difference was not significant. Thus, the only significant differences in language were between two subgroups of the major abuse group. In these comparisons the direction of the differences was contrary to expectations. (We expected that children in foster homes would perform better.)

Analysis of the Piers-Harris self-concept material showed no group differences on any of the subscales or on the overall scores.

School achievement ratings, combining the untraumatized comparison groups, are shown in table 1.

Although the proportion of less-than-average achievers was comparatively high in the abuse group, this was not significantly different. Ratings of ability showed even fewer differences: ten children, 16 percent of all subjects, were assessed as less than average in ability. Four of these were abused, three in the accident group, and three in the comparison group. No group differences appeared in the ratio of achievement to ability.

The range of scores on the teacher questionnaire was twelve to thirty-eight. Analysis of the results showed a tendency toward lower (less favorable) scores for the seventeen abused children compared to their accident matches, but this was not a significant difference. Item analysis produced no differences between the major groups. Thus, teachers of the abused children appeared to perceive them as more troubled in general but there was no specific area that could be pinpointed.

Table 1
School Achievement Ratings

	Group		
Rating	Abuse	Accident	Comparison
< average	9	5	7
⩾ average	8	12	18

Mean ratings of the children's scores for impulsivity and aggression were obtained for six stories for each child. There were no group differences on either of these variables considering either the mean score for each story of means across all stories. Further analyses of the ratings produced only three significant differences, all comparing the abused children with the matched accidents. One result showed a greater increase in aggression among abused children between stories one and six $(P < .05)$, and one an increase in impulsivity among abused children between stories one and five $(P = .03)$. Finally, analysis of variance showed that the abused group had a significantly different pattern of impulsivity from story one to six $(P = .04)$.

These results are difficult to interpret. On one hand, marked increases in aggression and impulsivity under the pressure of ongoing provocative stimuli could well be one of the differences between abused and nonabused children; the consistency of the findings would seem to support this possibility. On the other hand, no differences appeared between the abused group and its untraumatized comparisons. Also, the percentage of significant findings was small compared to the number of tests on this material. The conclusions must therefore be considered equivocal: the findings may represent a fertile lead for exploration with a larger number of children but they also may be no more than chance findings.

Nervous mannerisms were assessed by means of pediatric data and also through systematic inquiry on the teacher questionnaire. These mannerisms included behaviors such as thumb-sucking, tics, biting fingers or nails, etc. The group with the fewest nervous mannerisms was the abused group (29 percent). More than one half the children in each of the other groups were listed as having one or more nervous mannerisms but comparisons with the abused group were not statistically significant. A plausible explanation is that the abused child might act out more and therefore have less need for this type of symptom. Neither the clinical assessment of behavior nor the ratings of impulsivity and aggression according to the dramatic role play stories supported this possibility.

Judgments based on the total behavioral history of the child concerned control of aggression and estimated degree of disturbance. Only five children (8 percent) were seen as dealing with aggression adequately. Twenty-one children (36 percent) were judged either variable or undercontrolled and thirty-three (56 percent) overcontrolled. The majority (58 percent) showed some degree of disturbance. Comparisons between the groups showed no differences for any of these ratings but the number of individual children with one or more behavior problems was obviously high.

Several clinicians observed a pronounced feminine identification among each of three abused black boys. During the speech evaluation one of these children began to imitate a girl's voice. When the clinician recognized verbally what he was doing, the child placed a towel over his head, calling it a wig, and continued to talk for the rest of the period in a high falsetto voice. He said that he enjoyed pretending to be a girl at home, and his foster mother confirmed this interest.

One can do no more than speculate about the meaning of these boys' feminine interests. In each case the natural mother was thought to be the abuser, which suggests as explanation a form of identification with the aggressor. Another possible explanation is that all three children were responding to their perception of the world as a matriarchal society. Until recent years one frequently encountered such an analysis of family structure among blacks, although the validity of this formulation has been disputed.[15]

To summarize the follow-up findings: when pertinent demographic variables were taken into account, few overall differences were found between abused, accident, and comparison children. Among the characteristics where no differences were detected were health, language development, intellectual status in school, self-concept, and behavior. The abused differed significantly from their peers only in weight (abused were heavier) and in a few measures of impulsivity and aggression. Each of these differences was in relation to *either* accident or untraumatized children, not to both groups, a fact that tends to weaken the results.

Differences were found in relation to certain subgroups. For example, ratings of language development favored abused children in their own homes compared with abused children in foster/adoptive homes. These findings, however, may stem from differences in social status or ethnicity.

Some differences were also found between another abused subgroup and its matched comparisons. Since this subgroup was characterized by gross neglect as well as abuse, these analyses are not included in this presentation.

Discussion

The absence of substantial differences between the abused children and their matched comparisons was strengthened by our clinical impressions concerning the families. No one group of families stood out: the majority appeared chaotic and poorly organized; many parents relied upon drugs or alcohol; and most were living in circumstances of daily violence. One mother described a recent break-in of her home which had caused her to shoot at the unknown intruder. Another woman talked of a neighborhood shoot-out when she and her children were forced to take refuge under beds and in stairwells. There were reports of fathers pushing mothers downstairs, women beating their children for minor infringements, and children attacking each other with knives and other deadly weapons.

Examples of violence were by no means confined to the abusive group but appeared equally in both the accident and the comparison groups. In one comparison family, the mother reported an incident when she had lunged at the father with a butcher knife. The father retaliated by breaking her arm and knocking out her front teeth. The same man had attacked his teen-age son with a knife because the boy crossed the street against orders. By the time we evaluated the eight-year-old, the parents had separated and scenes of violence were presumably reduced. But the mother had been on massive amounts of tran-quilizers for six years, without medical supervision; she spoke of herself as a zombie who scarcely knew what was going on.

The examiners' clinical impressions of the children were alike in disbelief that so many could appear so handicapped psychologically. Overall, the children had an air of depression, sadness, and anxiety. One accident child voiced suicidal wishes. As part of many spontaneous stories told to the examiners, great concern was shown by the children that they might become the victims of attack. Most children of this age are involved with fantasies of witches, devils, and monsters that will eat up others or set fire to them, etc. These children, by contrast, linked their fears of injury or mutilation to real persons, not fantasy figures. The other persons might be parents, older children, or school teachers. Six of the black boys talked about being paddled in school.

Several children produced stories or fantasies that seemed to be associated with personal mistreatment. One child spent five minutes explaining and demonstrating with materials at hand just how a child might be tied with a lamp cord so he could be beaten.

One of the examiners observed that the terms used by Steele and Pollock[16] to describe abusive families match those used by Pavenstedt[17] to describe impoverished lower-class families: emotional problems, impoverished communi-cation, isolation, self-devaluation, vulnerability to criticism, and separation anxiety. The majority of this study sample were identified with the lower classes (IV and V) and might be described in the same way.

The question remains why no systematic differences were found between abused children and their matched comparisons. Several explanations are possible. All but one of the children in the sample lived in the Greater Pittsburgh Metropolitan Area; all were known to a hospital; and the majority were identified with the lower classes. The first possible explanation concerns place of residence: perhaps children living in Pittsburgh are subjected to poorer methods of child-rearing than their peers living in other communities. Although this hypothesis appears unlikely, it cannot be disputed without studies of other children matched on the relevant variables and reared in other locations.

A second possible explanation for the absence of differences between abused and other study children is the fact that all came from hospital populations: their parents may therefore have utilized exceptionally harsh child-rearing methods. Like the first hypothesis, this one also seems unlikely. If social class is held constant, no valid reason exists to postulate a difference between hospital clients and non-hospital clients as to the use of aggression in child-rearing.

A third possibility is that the entire sample, not just the abused children, had been repeatedly subjected to uncontrolled aggression at the hands of their care-takers, who used such methods because of their lower-class membership. No conclusive data presently exist to confirm such an explanation.

The last hypothesis is that identification of a family with the lower classes may be as potent a factor as abuse for the development of a child. In a ten-year study, Werner et al.[11] found that the most powerful influence on development was social class membership. Whether or not the child is the target of physical insults, as part of the family he is inevitably caught up in the stress and privation to which his family is prey.

Any one of these explanations could account for the high proportion of children in our sample with developmental problems and also for their prevailing mood of sadness and anxiety. Validation of the results of this study await similar controlled investigations of children living in other communities, and from a range of socioeconomic status. The use of matched comparison groups to evaluate the outcome for abused children does offer a means to correct conclusions based on the study of abused children alone.

References

1. R. Light, "Abused and Neglected Children in America: A Study of Alternative Policies," *Harvard Educational Review* XLIII (November, 1973):556-598.

2. "Child Neglect an Epidemic, Study Says," *New York Times*, November 30, 1973.

3. E. Elmer, *Children in Jeopardy* (Pittsburgh: University of Pittsburgh Press, 1967).

4. L.B. Silver et al., "Does Violence Breed Violence? Contributions from a Study of the Child Abuse Syndrome," *American Journal of Psychiatry* CXXVI (September, 1969):404-407.

5. C.W. Morse et al., "A Three-year Follow-Up Study of Abused and Neglected Children," *American Journal of Diseases of Children* CXX (November, 1970):439-446.

6. H.P. Martin et al., "The Development of Abused Children," in *Advances in Pediatrics*, ed. I. Schulman (Chicago: Year Book Medical Publishers, 1974).

7. S.B. Friedman and C.W. Morse, "Child Abuse: A Five-year Follow-up of Early Case Finding in the Emergency Department," *Pediatrics* LIV (October, 1974):404-410.

8. A.B. Hollingshead, *Two Factor Index of Social Position.* Unpublished manuscript, 1956.

9. J. Fudala, *Arizona Articulation Proficiency* Scale, rev. (Los Angeles: Western Psychological Services, 1970).

10. E.V. Piers and D.B. Harris, *The Piers-Harris Children's Self-concept Scale* (Nashville: Counselor Recordings and Tests, 1970).

11. E.E. Werner et al., *The Children of Kauai: A Longitudinal Study from the Prenatal Period to Age Ten* (Honolulu: University of Hawaii Press, 1971).

12. J. Smith, "Incidence of Atopic Disease," *Medical Clinics of North America* LVIII (1974).

13. W. Goldfarb, "Effects of Psychological Deprivation in Infancy and Subsequent Adjustment," *American Journal of Psychiatry* CII (1945):18-43.

14. B. Bernstein, "A Public Language: Some Sociological Implications of a Linguistic Form," *British Journal of Sociology* X (1959):311-318.

15. E.E. Baughman, *Black Americans: A Psychological Analysis* (New York: Academic Press, 1971).

16. B.F. Steele and C.G. Pollock, "A Psychiatric Study of Parents Who Abuse Infants and Small Children," in *The Battered Child*, ed. R.E. Helfer and C.H. Kempe (Chicago: University of Chicago Press, 1968).

17. E. Pavenstedt, ed., *The Drifters: Children of Disorganized Lower-class Families* (Boston: Little, Brown, 1967).

Violence Toward Children in the United States

6

Richard J. Gelles

This paper reports on the incidence, modes, and patterns of parent to child violence in the United States. Despite the considerable attention that has been focused on the issue of child abuse and neglect, and the significant and lengthy discussions concerning the physical punishment of children, valid and reliable data on the incidence and prevalence of the use of violence and aggression on children by their parents are almost nonexistent. The statistics that are available on child abuse and physical punishment do not report on the numerous violent acts that are neither routine physical punishment nor abusive. The wide range of acts between spankings and grievous assault have largely gone unnoticed and unresearched by social scientists.

Available data are often flawed by conceptual, definitional, sampling, and measurement problems. Moreover, the available statistics are usually general estimates of incidence which do not give even the crudest breakdown by age, sex, or demographic characteristics of the children or parents. Nevertheless, the figures on violence and aggression between parents and children do shed *some* light on the scope of the phenomenon.

Physical Punishment

The most comprehensive research on the use of physical force on children are the studies of physical punishment. Between 84 percent and 97 percent, of all parents use some form of physical punishment on their children.[3,9,23] The advantage of these data is that they are typically based on nationally representative surveys. The disadvantages are that they do not provide age specific rates nor do they examine specific acts of force.

Child Abuse

A variety of research strategies have been employed to investigate the incidence of child abuse in America.

Presented to the American Association for the Advancement of Science, February 1977, in Denver. The research is part of a program on intrafamily violence supported by grants from the National Institute of Mental Health (MH27557) and the National Center of Child Abuse and Neglect, Office of Child Development (90-C-425).

Reprinted with permission from the *American Journal of Orthopsychiatry* 48 (October 1978):580-592. Copyright 1978 by the American Orthopsychiatric Association, Inc.

Official Statistics. Investigations of official reports of child abuse provide varying degrees of the yearly incidence of abuse. Gil's 1968 survey yielded a figure of 6000 abused children.[16] One problem with the Gil survey is that all fifty states did not have mandatory reporting laws for the period Gil studied. The Children's Division of the American Humane Society documented 35,642 cases of child abuse in 1974, which were reported to its clearinghouse for child abuse and neglect reports.[1] However, only twenty-nine states reported to the clearinghouse.

Estimates derived from official reports suffer from various problems. First, official reports do not cover all possible states and localities. Second, states and localities do not employ uniform definitions of "child abuse." Third, official reports represent only a fraction of the total number of children who are abused and battered by their parents.

Household Surveys. In 1965, the National Opinion Research Corporation and David Gil collaborated on a household survey of attitudes, knowledge and opinions about child abuse. Of a nationally representative sample of 1520 individuals, forty-five, or 3 percent of the sample, reported knowledge of forty-eight different incidents of child abuse. Extrapolating this finding to the national population, Gil estimated that between 2.53 and 4.07 million adults knew of families involved in incidents of child abuse.[16] Light,[20] by applying corrective adjustments to Gil's data and considering possible overlap of public knowledge of incidents, revised the estimate to be approximately 500,000 abused children in the United States during the survey year.

Survey of Community Agencies. Nagi[21] attempted to compensate for the shortcoming of estimates of child abuse based on official records by surveying a national sample of community agencies and agency personnel to ascertain how many cases of child abuse they encountered annually. Nagi's estimate of child abuse was arrived at by extrapolating from reporting rates which would be expected on a national basis using presumed "full reporting rates" found in Florida. Nagi's estimate is that 167,000 cases of abuse are reported annually, while an additional 91,000 cases go unreported.[21]

Statistical Projection. Estimates of the incidence of child abuse have also been based on projections from regional, state, city, or single agency samples. The range of these estimates is quite wide. DeFrancis estimated that there are between 30,000 and 40,000 instances of "truly battered children" each year.[28] Fontana[10] proposed that there may be as many as 1.5 million cases of child abuse each year. Kempe[19] set the figure closer to 60,000 cases. Cohen and Sussman[8] used data on reported child abuse from the ten most populous states and projected 41,104 confirmed cases of child abuse in 1973.

Deaths of Children by Violence

Just as estimates of the incidence of child abuse vary, so do estimates of the number of children killed each year by parents or guardians. Fontana[10] provided a conservative estimate of 700 children killed each year. Helfer[28] has stated that, if steps are not taken to curb child abuse, there will be over 5000 deaths a year over the next ten years. *Pediatric News*[22] reported that one child dies each day from abuse—a yearly incidence of 365. Gil[16] cited data from the U.S. Public Health Service, which reported 686 children under fifteen died from attacks by parents in 1967.

Summary of Research

Perhaps the most accurate summary of the research on the incidence and extent of child abuse is provided by Cohen and Sussman,[8] who concluded that:

> the only conclusion which can be made fairly is that information indicating the incidence of child abuse in the United States simply does not exist.

It is evident that most projections of the incidence of child abuse are "educated guesses." Information gleaned from official statistics must be qualified by the fact that they represent only "caught" cases of abuse, which become cases through varied reporting and confirmation procedures.[13] In addition, information on child abuse is difficult to interpret because the term "child abuse" is as much a political concept (designed to draw attention to a social problem) as it is a scientific concept that can be used to measure a specific phenomenon. In other words, child abuse can be broadly and loosely defined in order to magnify concern about this social problem. While some social scientists use the term to cover a wide spectrum of phenomena that hinder the proper development of a child's potential,[17] others use the term to focus attention on the specific case of severely physically injured children.[18]

The lack of valid and reliable data on the incidence of child abuse in the United States led to the inclusion of a clause in the Child Abuse Prevention and Treatment Act of 1974 (PL-93-237) calling for a full and complete study on the incidence of child abuse and neglect. Such a study has already been contracted by the National Center of Child Abuse and Neglect. As an indication of the major problems that arise when one tries to measure the abuse and neglect of children, the contracted study has moved into the third quarter of its two-year existence and no decisions have been made on appropriate definitions of abuse or what research design should be employed in the study.

A Note on Trend Data

It should be pointed out that the problems involved in estimating the incidence of child abuse make the task of interpreting trend data almost hopeless. First, it is impossible to determine if rates of reported abuse are rising due to an actual increase in the true rate of abuse or due to increased sensitivity on the part or professionals who see children and families. Second, the constant change in the definition of abuse and the constant revisions of state child abuse and neglect laws, tend to broaden the definition of child abuse. This means that more families and children are vulnerable to being identified as abusers and abused.

The Need for a Study of Parental Violence

It was after evaluating the available evidence on the extent of force and violence between parents and children that we embarked on a national study of parental and family violence. While physical punishment of children appears to be almost a universal aspect of parent-child relations, and while child abuse seems to be a major social problem, we know very little about the modes and patterns of violence toward children in our society. We know almost nothing about the kinds of force and violence children experience. Are mothers more likely than fathers to hit their children? Who employs the most serious forms of violence? Which age group is most vulnerable to being spanked, slapped, hit with a fist, or "beaten up" by parents? Although answers to these questions will not completely fill in the gaps in our knowledge about child abuse, we see the information we generate in this study as providing an important insight into the extent of force and violence children experience and the numbers of children who are vulnerable to injury from serious violence.

Method

One of the most difficult techniques of studying the extent of parental violence is to employ a household interview that involves the self-reporting of violent acts. Although this technique is difficult and creates the problem of under-reporting, we felt that, because of the shortcomings of previous research on child abuse,[14] this was the only research design we could employ to assess the extent and causes of intrafamily violence.

Sample and Procedures

Response Analysis (Princeton, N.J.) was contracted to draw a national probability sample. A national sample of 103 primary areas (counties or groups of counties) stratified by geographic region, type of community, and other population characteristics was generated. Within these primary areas, 300 interviewing locations (census districts or block groups) were selected. Each location was divided into ten to twenty-five housing units by the trained interviewers. Sample segments from each interviewing location were selected. The last step involved randomly selecting an eligible person to be interviewed in each designated household.

Eligible families consisted of a couple who identified themselves as married or being a "couple" (man and woman living together in a conjugal unit). A random procedure was used so that the sample would be approximately half male and half female.

The final national probability sample produced 2143 completed interviews.[a] Interviews were conducted with 960 men and 1183 women. In each family where there was at least one child living at home between the ages of three and seventeen, a "referent child" was selected using a random procedure. Of the 2143 families interviewed, 1146 had children between the age of three and seventeen living at home. Our data on parent-to-child violence are based on the analysis of these 1146 parent-child relationships.

The interviews were conducted between January and April 1976. The interview protocol took sixty minutes to complete. The questions on parent-to-child violence were one part of an extensive protocol designed to measure the extent of family violence and the factors associated with violence between family members.

Violence: Defined and Operationalized

For the purposes of this study, violence is nominally defined as "an act carried out with the intention, or perceived intention, of physically injuring another person." The injury can range from slight pain, as in a slap, to murder. The motivation may range from a concern for a child's safety (as when a child is spanked for going into the street) to hostility so intense that the death of the child is desired.[15]

We chose a broad definition of violence (which includes spankings as violent behavior) because we want to draw attention to the issue of people hitting one another in families; we have defined this behavior as "violent" in order to raise controversy and call the behavior into question. In addition, our previous research[12] indicated that almost all acts, from spankings to murder, could somehow be justified and neutralized by someone as being in the best interests of the victim. Indeed, one thing that influenced our final choice of a concept was that acts parents carry out on their children in the name of corporal punishment or acceptable force, could, if done to strangers or adults, be considered criminal assault.

---

[a]The completion rate for the entire sample was 65 percent, varying from a low of 60 percent in metropolitan areas to a high of 72.3 percent in other areas.

Violence was operationalized in our study through the use of a Conflict Tactics Technique scale. First developed at the University of New Hampshire in 1971, this technique has been used and modified extensively since then in numerous studies of family violence.[2,6,25] The Conflict Tactics Technique scales were designed to measure intrafamily conflict in terms of the means used to resolve conflicts of interest.[26] The scale used contains eighteen items in three groups: (1) use of rational discussion and argument (discussed the issue calmly; got information to back up your side; brought in/tried to bring in someone to help settle things), (2) use of verbal and nonverbal expressions of hostility (insulted or swore at the other; sulked or refused to talk about it; stomped out of room or house; cried; did or said something to spite the other; threatened to hit or throw something at other; threw, smashed, hit or kicked something), and (3) use of physical force or violence as a means of managing the conflict (threw something at the other; pushed, grabbed, shoved the other; slapped or spanked; kicked, bit, or hit with a fist; hit or tried to hit with something; beat up the other; threatened with a knife or gun; used knife or gun).

Administration of the Conflict Tactics Technique involves presenting the subjects with the list of eighteen items, in the order enumerated above, and asking them to indicate what they did when they had a disagreement with the referent child in the past year and in the course of their relationship.

Reliability and Validity. The reliability and validity of the Conflict Tactics Technique has been assessed over the five-year period of its development and modification. Pretests on more than 300 college students indicated that the indices have an adequate level of internal consistency reliability.[26] Bulcroft and Straus[6] provided evidence of concurrent validity. In addition, evidence of "construct validity" exists, in that data compiled in the pretests of the scale are in accord with previous empirical findings and theories.[26]

Advantages and Disadvantages of the Violence Scale. An advantage of the violence scale, aside from previous evidence of its reliability, "concurrent" validity, and "construct" validity, is that the mode of administration increased the likelihood of the interviewer establishing rapport with the subject. The eight force and violence items came at the end of the list of conflict tactics. Presumably, this enhanced the likelihood that the subject would become committed to the interview and continue answering questions. Our analysis of the responses to the items indicates that there was no noticeable drop in the completion rate of items as the list moved from the rational scale questions to the most violent modes of conflict management.

Two disadvantages of the scale are that it focuses on conflict situations and does not allow for the measurement of the use of violence in situations where there was no "conflict of interest," and that it deals with the *commission* of acts only. We have no idea of the *consequences* of those acts, and thus have only a limited basis for projecting these statistics to the extent of the phenomenon "child abuse," since child abuse normally is thought to have injurious consequences for a child. While we may learn that a parent used a gun or a knife, and we can presume that this has negative consequences for a child, even if the child was not injured, we do not know what the actual consequences were.

Results

As proposed at the outset of this paper, "ordinary" physical punishment and "child abuse" are but two ends of a single continuum of violence toward children. In between are millions of parents whose use of physical force goes beyond mild punishment, but for various reasons does not get identified and labeled as child abuse.

Sixty-three percent of the respondents who had children between the ages of three and seventeen living at home mentioned at least one violent episode during the survey year (1975). The proportion of our sample reporting at least one violent occurrence in the course of raising the child was 73 percent.

As expected, and reported in table 1, the milder forms of violence were more common. Slaps or spankings were mentioned by 58 percent of the respondents as having occurred in the previous year and by 71 percent of the parents as having ever taken place. Forty-one percent of the parents admitted pushing or shoving the referent child in 1975; while 46 percent said pushes or shoves had occurred some time in the past. Hitting with something was reported by 13 percent of the parents for the last year and by 20 percent for the duration of their raising the referent child. Throwing an object was less common— approximately 5 percent of the parents did this in the survey year, while fewer than ten percent had ever thrown something at their referent child.

The more dangerous types of violence were the least frequent. However, extrapolating the data to the population of children three to seventeen years of age living with both parents produces an astoundingly large number of children who were kicked, bitten, punched, beat up, threatened with a gun or a knife, or had a gun or a knife actually used on them. First, looking at the number of parents who reported each type of violence, approximately 3 percent of the parents reported kicking, biting, or hitting the referent child with a fist in 1975; nearly 8 percent stated that these acts had occurred at some point in the raising of the child. Slightly more than 1 percent of the respondents reported "beating up" (operationally defined as more than a single punch) the randomly selected referent child in the last year, and 4 percent stated that they had ever done this. One-tenth of 1 percent, or one in a thousand parents, admitted to threatening their child with a gun or a knife in 1975, while nearly three parents in one hundred said they had ever threatened their child with such weapons. The same statistics were found for parents admitting actually using a gun or knife—one-tenth of a percent for the year, almost 3 percent ever.[b]

---

[b]We do not know exactly what is meant by *using* a gun or knife. It could mean a parent threw a knife at the child, or it could mean attempting to stab or actually stabbing the child; a gun could have been fired without the child being wounded. However, the fact is that these parents admit using the weapon, not just threatening its use.

One can extrapolate these frequencies to estimate how many children were victims of these serious modes of violence in 1975 and how many ever faced these types of violence. There were nearly 46 million children between the ages of three and seventeen years old who lived with both parents in 1975.[7] Of these children, between 3.1 and 4.0 million have been kicked, bitten, or punched by parents at some time in their lives, while between 1.0 and 1.9 million were kicked, bitten, or punched in 1975. Between 1.4 and 2.3 million children have been "beat up" while growing up, and between 275,000 and 750,000 three to seventeen year olds were "beat up" in 1975. Lastly, our data suggest that between 900,000 and 1.8 million American children between the ages of three and seventeen have ever had their parents use a gun or a knife on them. Our figures do not allow for a reliable extrapolation of how many children faced parents using guns and knives in 1975, but our estimate would be something close to 46,000 children (based on an incidence of one in 10,000 children).

An examination of the data on violence used on children in 1975 indicates that violence typically represents a *pattern* of parent-child relations rather than an isolated event. Only in the case of using a gun or knife was the violent episode likely to be a one-time affair. While it is generally accepted that slaps, spankings, and shoves are frequently used techniques of child rearing, we find that even bites, kicks, punches, and using objects to hit children occur frequently in the families where they are employed.

Children at Risk

As stated earlier, our examination of violent acts without information on the consequences of those acts prevents us from accurately estimating how many children incurred physical harm from violence during any one year. Our problem is compounded by the fact that we rely on the subject's own definition of what is meant by "beating up" a child. In addition, we do not know what objects were used to hit the child (a pipe or a paddle?), and we do not know how the guns or knives were deployed. Nevertheless, we felt it was important to generate an estimate of children-at-risk. We chose to compile an "at-risk" index which combined the items we felt produced the highest probability of injuring or damaging the child (kicked, bit, or hit with a fist; hit with something; beat up; threatened with a knife or a gun; used a knife or a gun). Using this index, we found that 3.6 percent of the parents admitted to using at least one of these modes of violence at least once in 1975. Assuming the acts we indexed have a high potential of causing harm to the intended victim, between 1.4 million and 1.9 million children were vulnerable to physical injury from violence in 1975.

A Note on the Incidence Data and Extrapolations

The data on the incidence of physical violence between parents and children, and the extrapolations which produced estimates of the number of children who experienced violence and who are at risk of physical injury, ought to be considered *low estimates of violence toward children.* First, we are dealing with self-reports of violence. Although subjects who reported spanking or slapping their children may constitute accurate estimate of incidence, the desire to give socially acceptable responses is likely to have caused many people to under-report the more serious modes of violence. If one subject in a thousand answered that he used a gun or knife, it might be reasonable to assume that at least another one in a thousand used these weapons and did not admit to it in the interview. Second, we interviewed only "intact" families, where both adult males and females were in the household. If, as some believe, parental violence is more common in single-parent families, then our data will underestimate the number of children experiencing potentially damaging acts from their parents. Third, we examined violence used by only one of the two parents on the referent child. Lastly, our lower than expected response rate might mean that some highly violent families refused to be interviewed; if so, our incidence statistics might again be low estimates of violence toward children.

As a result of the sampling frame used and the methodological problems involved in using self-reports of violence, we see our statistics, although they may seem high to some, as being quite conservative and low estimates of the true level of violence toward children in the United States.

Violence Toward Children by Sex of Parent

Sixty-eight percent of the mothers and 58 percent of the fathers in our sample reported at least one violent act toward their child during the survey year. Seventy-six percent of the mothers and 71 percent of the fathers indicated at least one violent episode in the course of rearing their referent child. Our data on violence in the survey year indicate a small but significant difference between mothers and fathers using violence on their children. It has been frequently argued that mothers are more prone to use violence because they spend more time with their children. We hypothesize that the explanation for mothers' greater likelihood of using violence goes beyond the simple justification that they spend more time with the children. Our future analyses of the information gathered in our survey of violence in the family will examine this relationship from a number of points of view, including family power, coping ability, resources, and personality traits.

Examining the relationship between sex of the parent and various modes of violence used on children (see table 2), we find that, for both the survey year and the duration of the relationship, mothers are more likely to throw something at the child, slap or spank the child, or hit the child with something. There are no significant differences between mothers and fathers with respect to any of the other forms of violence. It is interesting to note that even for the most serious forms of violence (beating up; kicking, biting, punching; using guns or knives), men and women are approximately equal in their disposition to use of these modes of violence on their children. This is important because it suggests that the management of children is one of the only situations in which women are as likely as men to resort to violence.

Violence Toward Children by Sex of the Child

While females are more likely to use violence in parent-child relations, male children are slightly more likely to be victims. Sixty-six percent of the sons and 61 percent of the daughters were struck at least once in the survey year, while 76 percent of the male children and 71 percent of the females were ever hit by their parents.

Why sons are slightly more likely than daughters to be victims of parental violence is open for debate. Some might argue that boys are more difficult to raise and commit more "punishable offenses" than daughters. Another hypothesis is that our society accepts and often values boys experiencing violence because it serves to "toughen them up." The data from the 1968 National Commission on the Causes and Prevention of Violence Survey seem to bear this out in that seven in ten people interviewed believed that it is good for a boy to have a few fist fights while he is growing up.[23] Thus, experiencing violence might be considered part of the socialization process for boys and a less important "character builder" for girls.[24]

Data on violence in the survey year (table 3) show that the only significant difference between boys and girls was whether they were pushed, grabbed, or shoved. The other forms of violence showed no significant differences between the sexes. In the course of growing up, boys are more likely to be pushed, grabbed, shoved, spanked, or slapped.

Violence Towards Children by Age of the Child

The literature on physical punishment and abuse of children presents various hypotheses and findings on the relationship between age and being punished or abused. A number of researchers and clinicians have proposed that the most dangerous period in a child's life is from three months to three years of age.[10,11,18] Bronfenbrenner[4] proposed that the highest rates of child abuse and battering occur among adolescents. Gil[6] discovered that half of the confirmed cases of child abuse were children over six years of age, while nearly one-fifth of the confirmed reports were children in their teens.

Our survey excluded parental relations with children three years of age or younger, since we also studied child-to-parent violence in the interview. Thus, our data cannot be used to infer the rate of violence used on infants.

During the survey year, younger children were most likely to be victims of some form of physical force. Eighty-six percent of children three and four years old had some mode of force used on them in 1975; 82 percent of the children five to nine had been hit; 54 percent of preteens and early teenage children (ten to fourteen years of age) were struck; and 33 percent of the referent children fifteen to seventeen years old were hit by their parents ($\chi^2 \leqslant .01$).

It appears that younger children are vulnerable to a wide range of forceful and violent acts. As shown in table 4, preschoolers and children under nine years old were more likely to be pushed, grabbed, shoved, slapped, spanked, and hit with an object. The older children seemed more vulnerable to the severest types of violence, including being beaten up and having a gun or a knife used on them, although the differences are not statistically significant.

Again, there are a number of reasons why younger children are more frequent victims of parental violence. Parents may perceive difficulties in using reason to punish their younger children. A second reason might be that younger children interfere with their parents' activities more than do older children. Our future analyses of the data will focus on the factors associated with young children's susceptibility to being struck.

Discussion and Conclusions

These data on the incidence of parent-to-child violence only begin to scratch the surface of this very important topic. Our results indicate that violence toward children involves acts that go well beyond ordinary physical punishment and is an extensive and patterned phenomenon in parent-child relations. In addition, we see that mothers are the most likely users of violence, while sons and younger children are the more common victims.

A number of controversial points arise from our presentation. First, disagreement over our nominal and operational definitions of violence may lead some to disagree with our conclusion that violence is widespread in families. If someone views slaps and spankings as acceptable punishment, then they might dispute our statistics as being based on a too broadly constructed definition of violence. Although we believe there are many salient reasons for considering spankings and slaps violent, we would counter this argument by pointing to the statistics for beating up children or using a gun or a knife on a child. If a million or more children had guns or knives used on them in school, we would consider that a problem of epidemic proportions. The fact that these acts occur in the home tends to lessen concern about the impact and consequences. However, the impact and consequences are potentially dramatic, since the child is experiencing violence from those who claim love and affection for him.

A second point that will be raised about our findings is the question of bias and whether our respondents actually told the truth. We have spent seven years developing and testing the instruments used in this study. However, we do not know the actual validity of our findings or whether our subjects "told the truth." The major bias in this study of family violence is likely to be one of underreporting. We doubt that many subjects will report beating up their children or using a gun or a knife on them when they did not. Thus, our statistics are probably underestimates of the true level of parent-child violence in the United States. If one considers the possibility that, for every subject who admitted using a knife or a gun, an additional subject used these weapons but did not admit it, then our estimates of risk could be doubled to produce a true estimate of risk of physical violence.

Another issue that will be pursued after examining our data, and an issue we will examine in later analyses, is the fact that people actually admitted using severe and dangerous forms of physical violence. Our tentative explanation of this is that many of our subjects did not consider kicking, biting, punching, beating up, shooting, or stabbing their children deviant. In other words, they may have admitted to these acts because they felt they were acceptable or tolerable ways of bringing up children. Thus, it may be that one major factor contributing to the high level of parent-child violence we have found is the normative acceptability of hitting one's children.

Despite the methodological problems, this is the first survey of parent-to-child violence based on a true cross-section of American families. Thus, the data presented here probably come closer to describing the real situation of violence toward children in America than anything available until now.

References

1. American Humane Association. 1974. Highlights of the 1974 National Data. American Humane Association, Denver. (mimeo)

2. Allen, C. and Straus, M. 1975. Resources, power, and husband-wife violence. Presented to the National Council on Family Relations, in Salt Lake City.

3. Blumberg, M. 1964. When parents hit out. *Twentieth Century* 173 (Winter):39-44.

4. Bronfenbrenner, U. 1958. Socialization and social class throughout time and space. In *Readings in Social Psychology,* E. Maccoby, T. Newcomb, and E. Hartley, eds. Holt, New York.

5. Bronfenbrenner, U. 1974. The origins of alienation. *Scientif. Amer.* 231:53.

6. Bulcroft, R. and Straus, M. 1975. Validity of husband, wife, and child reports of conjugal violence and power. Presented to the National Council on Family Relations, Salt Lake City.

7. Bureau of the Census. 1975. Estimates of the population of the United States by age, sex, and race: 1970-1975. Current Population Reports, Series P-25, No. 614, Government Printing Office, Washington, D.C.

8. Cohen, S. and Sussman, A. 1975. The incidence of child abuse in the United States. (unpublished)

9. Erlanger, H. 1974. Social class and corporal punishment in childrearing: a reassessment. *Amer. Social. Rev.* 39 (Feb.):68-85.

10. Fontana, V. 1973. *Somewhere a Child is Crying: Maltreatment—Causes and Prevention.* Macmillan, New York.

11. Galdston, R. 1965. Observations of children who have been physically abused by their parents. *Amer. J. Psychiat.* 122(4):440-443.

12. Gelles, R. 1974. *The Violent Home: A Study of Physical Aggression Between Husbands and Wives.* Sage Publications, Beverly Hills, Calif.

13. Gelles, R. 1975. The social construction of child abuse. *Amer. J. Orthopsychiat.* 45 (April):363-371.

14. Gelles, R. 1978. Methods for studying sensitive family topics. *Amer. J. Orthopsychiat.* 48(3):408-424.

15. Gelles, R. and Straus, M. 1978. Determinants of violence in the family: toward a theoretical integration. *In Contemporary Theories About the Family,* W. Burr et al., eds. Free Press, New York.

16. Gil, D. 1970. *Violence Against Children: Physical Child Abuse in the United States.* Harvard University Press, Cambridge, Mass.

17. Gil, D. 1975. Unraveling child abuse, *Amer. J. Orthopsychiat.* 45 (April):364-358.

18. Kempe, C. et al. 1962. The battered child syndrome. JAMA 181 (July 7):17-24.

19. Kempe, C. 1971. Pediatric implications of the battered baby syndrome. *Arch. Dis. Children* 46:28-37.

20. Light, R. 1974. Abused and neglected children in America: a study of alternative policies. *Harvard Ed. Rev.* 43 (Nov.):556-598.

21. Nagi, R. 1975. Child abuse and neglect programs: a national overview. *Children Today* 4 (May-June):13-17.

22. Pediatric News. 1975. One child dies daily from abuse: parent probably was abuser. *Pediat. News* 9 (April):3.

23. Stark, R. and McEvoy, J. 1970. Middle class violence. *Psychol. Today* 4 (Nov.):52-65.

24. Straus, M. 1971. Some social antecedents of physical punishment: a linkage theory interpretation. *J. Marr, Fam.* 33 (Nov.):658-663.

25. Straus, M. 1974. Leveling, civility, and violence in the family. *J. Marr. Fam.* 36 (Feb.):13-30.

26. Straus, M. 1978. Measuring intrafamily conflict and violence: the conflict tactics (CT) scales. *J. Marr. Fam.* (in press).

27. Straus, M., Gelles, R. and Steinmetz, S. 1976. Violence in the family: an assessment of knowledge and research needs. Presented to the American Association for the Advancement of Science, in Boston.

28. United States Senate. 1973. Hearing Before the Subcommittee on

Children and Youth of the Committee on Labor and Public Welfare. United States Senate, 93rd Congress First Session, on S.1191 Child Abuse Prevention Act, U.S. Government Printing Office, Washington, D.C.

Table 1
Types of Parent-To-Child Violence ($N = 1146$)[a] Occurrence in Past Year

Incident	Once	Twice	More Than Twice	Total	Occurrence Ever
Threw Something	1.3%	1.8%	2.3%	5.4%	9.6%
Pushed/Grabbed/Shoved	4.3	9.0	27.2	40.5	46.4
Slapped or Spanked	5.2	9.4	43.6	58.2	71.0
Kicked/Bit/Hit with Fist	0.7	0.8	1.7	3.2	7.7
Hit with Something	1.0	2.6	9.8	13.4	20.0
Beat Up	0.4	0.3	0.6	1.3	4.2
Threatened with Knife/Gun	0.1	0.0	0.0	0.1	2.8
Used Knife or Gun	0.1	0.0	0.0	0.1	2.9

[a]On some items, there were a few responses omitted, but figures for all incidents represent at least 1140 families.

Table 2
Parent-To-Child Violence by Sex of Parent[a]

Incident	In Past Year		Ever	
	Father	Mother	Father	Mother
Threw Something	3.6%	6.8%*	7.5%	11.3%*
Pushed/Grabbed/Shoved	29.8	33.4	35.6	39.5
Slapped or Spanked	53.3	62.5**	67.7	73.6*
Kicked/Bit/Hit with Fist	2.5	4.0	6.7	8.7
Hit with Something	9.4	16.7**	15.7	23.6**
Beat Up	0.6	1.8	4.0	4.2
Threatened with Knife/Gun	0.2	0.0	3.1	2.6
Used Knife or Gun	0.2	0.0	3.1	2.7

[a]Reports of 523 fathers and 623 mothers; figures for all incidents represent at least 520 fathers and 619 mothers.
*$X^2 \leqslant .05$.
**$X^2 \leqslant .01$.

Table 3
Parent-To-Child Violence by Sex of Child[a]

| | In Past Year | | Ever | |
Incident	Sons	Daughters	Sons	Daughters
Threw Something	5.9%	4.4%	10.1%	8.8%
Pushed/Grabbed/Shoved	38.1	24.9**	43.9	30.7**
Slapped or Spanked	60.1	56.1	73.9	67.8*
Kicked/Bit/Hit with Fist	3.8	2.6	8.0	7.3
Hit with Something	14.9	11.2	21.5	18.1
Beat Up	1.6	0.7	4.2	4.0
Threatened with Knife/Gun	0.2	0.0	2.4	3.3
Used Knife or Gun	0.2	0.0	2.6	3.3

[a]Reports on 578 sons (responses reported for at least 574) and 547 daughters (responses for at least 545).
$*X^2 \leqslant .05.$
$**X^2 \leqslant .01.$

Table 4
Parent-To-Child Violence in Past Year by Age of Child

Incident	3-4 Years	5-9 Years	10-14 Years	15-17 Years
Threw Something	5.1%	7.0%	3.6%	5.1%
Pushed/Grabbed/Shoved	39.0	39.1	27.9	20.8*
Slapped or Spanked	84.1	79.9	47.9	23.0*
Kicked/Bit/Hit with Fist	6.2	3.2	2.2	2.5
Hit with Something	19.2	19.7	9.6	4.3*
Beat Up	1.1	0.9	1.1	1.7
Threatened with Knife/Gun	0.0	0.0	0.3	0.0
Used Knife or Gun	0.0	0.0	0.3	0.0
	$(N = 177)$[a]	$(N = 346)$[a]	$(N = 365)$[a]	$(N = 236)$[a]

[a]No more than three responses omitted on any category.
$*X^2 \leqslant .01.$

7 Unraveling Child Abuse

David G. Gil

This paper is an attempt to clarify the sources and dynamics of child abuse and to suggest approaches to its primary prevention. To gain understanding of any social problem one needs to view it in the total societal context within which it evolves, rather than, as is so often done, as an isolated, fragmented phenomenon. Furthermore, one needs to avoid the fallacious tendency of interpreting its dynamics along single causal dimensions such as biological, psychological, social, economic, etc., a tendency which in our society is usually weighted in favor of individual interpretations and which thus leads to ameliorative programs designed to change individuals rather than pathogenic aspects of the social order.

A Value-based Definition of Child Abuse

Understanding and overcoming the dynamics of social problems also requires specification of, and a societal commitment to, certain value premises, and a definition logically linked to such premises. I have suggested such a value-based definition of Child abuse at hearings on the *Child Abuse Prevention Act* (S. 1191 of 1973) before the Sub-Committee on Children and Youth of the U.S. Senate. This definition views child abuse as inflicted gaps or deficits between circumstances of living which would facilitate the optimal development of children, to which they should be entitled, and their actual circumstances, irrespective of the sources or agents of the deficit:

> Every child, despite his individual differences and uniqueness is to be considered of equal intrinsic worth, and hence should be entitled to equal social, economic, civil, and political rights, so that he may fully realize his inherent potential and share equally in life, liberty, and happiness. Obviously, these value premises are rooted in the humanistic philosophy of our Declaration of Independence.

> In accordance with these value premises then, any act of commission or omission by individuals, institutions, or society as a whole, and any conditions resulting from such acts of inaction, which deprive children of equal rights and liberties, and/or interfere with their optimal development, constitute, by definition, abusive or neglectful acts or conditions.

Reprinted with permission from the *American Journal of Orthopsychiatry* 45 (April 1975). Copyright 1975 by the American Orthopsychiatric Association, Inc. An earlier version, "A Holistic Perspective on Child Abuse and Its Prevention," appeared in the *Journal of Sociology and Social Welfare* (Winter 1974).

Analytic Concepts

The definition of child abuse presented above suggests the use of two related analytic concepts for studying the nature of child abuse and for developing effective policies and programs for its prevention. These concepts will be referred to here as "levels of manifestation" and "levels of causation" or "causal dimensions." The levels of manifestation identify the agents and the settings in which children may experience abuse. The levels of causation unravel the several causal dimensions, the interactions of which result in abusive acts and abusive conditions at the levels of manifestation. The distinction implicit in these analytic concepts, between the levels at which abuse occurs and the forces that underlie the occurrences, is important, for these levels and forces are not the same. They do, however, complement each other and interact with each other in multiple ways. Moreover, interaction also takes place among the levels themselves, and among the forces. Clarifying the nature of child abuse means, essentially, tracing these multiple interactions among the levels of manifestation and the causal dimensions.

Levels of Manifestation

Three levels of manifestation of child abuse may be distinguished. The most familiar one is abusive conditions in the home, and abusive interaction between children and their caretakers. Abuse on this level consists of acts of commission or omission by individuals which inhibit a child's development. The perpetrators are parents, permanent or temporary parent substitutes, or others living in a child's home regularly or temporarily. Abuse in the home may be intentional and conscious or unintentional and also unconscious. Abuse may result from supposedly constructive, disciplinary, educational attitudes and measures, or from negative and hostile feelings toward children. Abusive acts in the home may be one-time events, occasional incidents, or regular patterns. So far, child abuse at this level of manifestation has been the dominant focus of scholarly, professional, and public concern with this destructive phenomenon.

A second level at which child abuse occurs is the institutional level. This includes such settings as day care centers, schools, courts, child care agencies, welfare departments, and correctional and other residential child care settings. In such settings, acts and policies of commission or omission that inhibit, or insufficiently promote, the development of children, or that deprive children of, or fail to provide them with, material, emotional, and symbolic means needed for their optimal development, constitute abusive acts or conditions. Such acts or policies may originate with an individual employee of an institution, such as a teacher, child care worker, judge, probation officer, or social worker, or they may be implicit in the standard practices and policies of given agencies and institutions. In the same way as in the home, abusive acts and conditions in institutional settings may also result from supposedly constructive, or from negative and hostile attitudes toward children, and they may be one-time or occasional events or regular patterns.

Institutional child care settings such as schools are often perceived by parents as bearers of cultural norms concerning child rearing practices and discipline. Hence, when schools and other child care settings employ practices that are not conducive to optimal child development, *e.g.,* corporal punishment and other demeaning and threatening, negative disciplinary measures, they convey a subtle message to parents—namely, that such measures are appropriate, as they are sanctioned by educational authorities and "experts." Influence also flows in the other direction, from the home to the institutional level. Teachers and child care personnel will frequently adopt child rearing practices and disciplinary measures similar to those practiced in the homes of children in their care, on the assumption that this is what the children are used to, what they expect, and to what they respond. In this way, methods conducive or not conducive to optimal child development tend to be transmitted back and forth, and reinforced, through interaction between the home and the institution.

When child abuse is viewed as inflicted deficits between a child's actual circumstances and circumstances that would assure his optimal development, it seems to be endemic in most existing institutional settings for the care and education of children, since these settings usually do not facilitate the full actualization of the human potential of all children in their care. Analysis of institutional child abuse reveals that this form of abuse is not distributed randomly throughout the population. Schools and institutions serving children of minority groups, children from deprived socioeconomic backgrounds, handicapped children, and socially deviant children are less likely to facilitate optimal development of children's inherent potential than are schools and institutions serving children of majority groups, "normal" children, and children from affluent families and neighborhoods. However, even settings serving children from privileged backgrounds rarely encourage the optimal development of all children in their care. They, too, tend to inhibit the children's spontaneity and creativity, and to promote conformity rather than critical, independent thought. Only rarely will children in these settings develop all their inherent faculties and their unique individuality.

Worse, though, than the educational system, with its mind-stifling practices and its widespread use of corporal punishment and other demeaning and threatening forms of discipline, is the legally sanctioned, massive abuse of children under the policies and practices of the public welfare system, especially the "Aid to Families with Dependent Children" (AFDC) program. This system of grossly income maintenance—inadequate even by measures of minimal needs as published by the U.S. Bureau of Labor Statistics—virtually condemns millions of children to conditions of existence under which physical, social, emotional, and intellectual development are likely to be severely handicapped.

Similarly destructive versions of legally sanctioned abuse on the institutional level are experienced by several hundred thousands of children living in foster care, in training and correctional institutions, and in institutions for children defined as mentally retarded. That these settings of substitute child care usually fail to assure optimum development for the children entrusted to them has been amply demonstrated,[1] and does not require further documentation here.

It should be noted that the readiness to use force in general, and in adult-child relations in particular, is intimately linked to a society's basic philosophy and value premises, and to its concept of humans and their rights. A non-egalitarian philosophy is much more likely to sanction the use of force than is an egalitarian one, since the use of force against other humans constitutes the strongest possible negation of equality. The use of force toward children is also related to the manner in which childhood, and the rights of children are defined by a society, and in turn tends to reinforce that definition.

As mentioned earlier, the use of force toward children is widespread in our society on the institutional and family level. On this level originate social policies which sanction, or cause, severe deficits between the actual circumstances of children and conditions needed for their optimal development. As direct or indirect consequences of such social policies, millions of children in our society live in poverty and are inadequately nourished, clothed, housed, and educated; their health is not assured because of substandard medical care; their neighborhoods decay; meaningful occupational opportunities are not available to them; and alienation is widespread among them. No doubt, these destructive conditions which result, inevitably, from the normal workings of the prevailing social, economic, and political order, and from the value premises which shape that order and its human dynamics, cannot fail to inhibit severely the development of children exposed to them.

Of the three levels of child abuse sketched here, the societal level is certainly the most severe. For what happens at this level determines not only how children fare on the institutional level, but also, by way of complex interactions, how they fare in their own homes.

Levels of Causation

Before discussing the causal dimensions of child abuse, it should be reiterated that the conventional dichotomy between individual and societal causation of social problems distorts the multidimensional reality of human phenomena. We know that psychological forces which shape individual behavior evolve out of the totality of life experiences in specific historical, cultural, social, economic, and political contexts. Individual motivation and behavior are thus always rooted in a societal force field. Yet societal forces are always expressed, or mediated, through the behavior of individuals, for societies cannot act except through their individual members. Clearly, then, any human phenomenon, at any moment, involves both social and individual elements. In real life, these elements are inseparable. Their separation in theory is merely a product of scholarly, or rather pseudoscholary, abstraction.

Based on this reasoning, child abuse, at any level of manifestation, may be understood as acts or inactions of individuals, on their own or as institutional agents, whose behavior reflects societal forces mediated through their unique personalities.

The most fundamental causal level of child abuse consists of a cluster of interacting elements, to wit, a society's basic social philosophy, its dominant value premises, its concept of humans; the nature of its social, economic, and political institutions, which are shaped by its philosophy and value premises, and which in turn reinforce that philosophy and these values; and, finally, the particular quality of human relations prevailing in the society, which derives from its philosophy, values, and institutions. For, in the final analysis, it is the philosophy and value premises of a society, the nature of its major institutions, and the quality of its human relations that determine whether or not individual members of that society will develop freely and fully in accordance with their inherent potentialities.

To discern a society's basic social philosophy and values and its concept of humans, one needs to ascertain whether it considers everyone to be intrinsically of equal worth in spite of his or her uniqueness and, hence, entitled to the same social, economic, and political rights; or whether everyone in the society considers himself, and those close to himself, of greater worth than anyone else, and hence entitled to more desirable or privileged circumstances. The former, egalitarian philosophy would be reflected in institutional arrangements involving cooperative actions in pursuit of common existential interests. Every individual, and that includes every child, would be considered an equally entitled subject, who could not be exploited and dominated by any other individual or group, and whose right to fully and freely develop his individuality would be assured and respected, subject to the same right of all others. The latter, non-egalitarian philosophy, on the other hand, as we know so well from our own existence, is reflected in institutional structures which encourage competitive behavior in pursuit of narrowly perceived, egotistical interests. Everyone strives to get ahead of others, considers himself entitled to privileged conditions and positions, and views and treats others as potential means to be used, exploited, and dominated in pursuit of his egotistical goals.

Analysis of these contrasting social philosophies, societal institutions, and modes of human relations suggests that full and free development of every child's inherent potential may be possible only in a society organized consistently around egalitarian and cooperative value premises, since the equal right to self-actualization is implicit in an egalitarian philosophy, while such a right is incompatible with a non-egalitarian philosophy. In a society organized on non-egalitarian and competitive principles, full and free development for all children is simply impossible, as, by definition, there must always be losers in such societies, whose chances to realize their inherent potential will be severely limited. Hence, significant developmental deficits for large segments of the population or high levels of socially structured and sanctioned abuse of children, are endemic in such societies.

A second, more specific, level of causation of child abuse may be intrinsic to the social construction, or definition, of childhood prevalent in a society. Obviously, this level is closely related to the first level. How does a society view its children, all its children, and how does it define their rights? How much obedience, submission, and conformity does it expect of children? Does it process children through caste-like channels of socialization into relatively closed and inflexible social and occupational structures, or does it encourage them, within limits of reason, to discover and develop their individuality and uniqueness, and to shape their lives accordingly? Obviously, optimal development of the inherent potential of all children is a function of the extent to which a society's processes of socialization are permeated with a commitment to such self-actualization for all. When this commitment is lacking altogether, or when it varies with such factors as sex, race, and social and economic position of a family, then different children will experience varying deficits in realizing their potential. Presently, in our society, social policies that sustain different levels of rights for children from different social and economic backgrounds are a major, direct cause of many forms of child abuse on the societal and institutional levels, and an indirect cause of abuse on the family level.

A further causal dimension of child abuse is a society's attitude toward the use of force as a legitimate means for attaining ends, especially in imbalanced, interpersonal relations such as master-slave, male-female, guard-prisoner, and adult-child. The tendency to resort to the use of force for dealing with conflicts in our society seems to require no documentation here, not does it seem necessary to document the specific readiness to use force, or the threat of it, as a means to maintain authority and discipline in adult-child relations in the public domain, such as schools and other child care settings, and in the private domain of the family. The readiness to use physical force for disciplinary objectives is certainly endemic in our society.

The massive manifestations of institutional child abuse tend to arouse much less public concern and indignation than child abuse in the home, although the abusive conditions and practices of public education, public welfare, and child placement are endemic to these systems, and are visible to all who care to see. Perhaps the enormity of institutional abuse dulls our sensibilities in the same way in which the fate of inmates of concentration camps tends to arouse a lesser response than does the killing of a single individual with whom we are able to identify.

Institutional child abuse is linked, intimately, to the third level at which child abuse is manifested, namely, the societal levels. Attempts to limit and outlaw it in public institutions have had only limited success so far. It may be noted, in this context, that because of the compatibility between the use of physical force on the one hand, and an inegalitarian philosophy and competitive social, economic, and political institutions on the other, corporal punishment and the threat of it may actually be highly functional in preparing children for adult roles in an inegalitarian and competitive social order. For, were our children reared in a harmonious fashion without threats, insults, and physical force, they might not be adequately prepared and conditioned for adult roles in our inegalitarian, competitive reality.

Whenever corporal punishment in child rearing is sanctioned, and even subtly encouraged by a society, incidents of serious physical abuse and injury are bound to happen, either as a result of deliberate, systematic, and conscious action on the part of perpetrators, or under conditions of loss of self-control. In either case, but especially in the latter, physical attacks on children tend to relieve tensions and frustrations experienced by the perpetrators. Clearly, then, these attacks are carried out to meet emotional needs of the perpetrators rather than educational needs of the victims, as is often claimed by advocates of corporal punishment.

The next causal dimension may be referred to as "triggering contexts." These contexts operate jointly with the societal sanction of the use of physical force in adult-child relations. Adults who use force toward children do not do so all the time, but only under specific circumstances which serve as triggers for their abusive behavior. In general, abusive attacks tend to be triggered by stress and frustration which may cause reduction or loss of self-control. Stress and frustration may facilitate abusive attacks even without causing a reduction or loss of self-control, as long as the appropriateness of the use of force in child rearing is accepted.

One major source of stress and frustration for adults in our society are the multi-faceted deprivations of poverty and its correlates, high density in over-crowded, dilapidated, inadequately served neighborhoods; large numbers of children, especially in one-parent, mainly female-headed households; and the absence of child care alternatives. Having identified poverty and its correlates as an important triggering context of child abuse in the home, we may now note that social policies which sanction and perpetuate the existence of poverty among large segments of the population, including millions of children are thus indirect sources of child abuse in the home. It should be emphasized, though, that poverty, per se, is not a direct cause of child abuse in the home, but operates through an intervening variable, namely, concrete and psychological stress and frustration experienced by individuals in the context of culturally sanctioned use of physical force in child rearing.

Poverty is not the only source of stress and frustration triggering child abuse in the home. Such abuse is known to occur frequently in many homes in adequate, and even affluent, economic circumstances. One other, important source of stress and frustration in our society is the alienating circumstances in most workplaces, be the work manual labor, skilled and unskilled occupations, or administrative, managerial, and professional work through all levels and sectors of business, academic, and government bureaucracies. A recent report by a task force of the U.S. Department of Health, Education, and Welfare[2] documented the seriousness of work alienation experienced by constantly growing segments of the working population. This government report reached conclusions similar to those voiced by many severe critics of our economic system in recent years—that the prevailing competitive and exploitative human relations in the work place, and its hierarchical and authoritarian structures, tend to cause psychological stress and alienation for nearly every working person. These pressures may lead to various forms of deviant behavior, such as alcoholism, drug addiction, mental illness, white collar crime, etc. Perhaps the most frequent locus for discharging feelings of stress and frustration originating in the formal world of work is the informal world of primary relations, the home and the family. Conflicts between spouses are one form this discharge may take. Child abuse in the form of violent physical outbursts is another.

Here, then, we identify once again a triggering context for child abuse on the interpersonal level, which is rooted deeply in societal forces, namely, the alienating quality of our society's economic and productive system complemented by the culturally sanctioned use of physical force in child rearing.

The final causal dimension of child abuse on the interpersonal level in the home and in child care settings is made up of intrapsychic conflicts and various forms of psychopathology on the part of perpetrators. Child abuse literature is largely focused on this dimension and thus little needs to be said here to document it. What needs to be stressed, however, is that psychological disturbances and their manner of expression are not independent factors but are deeply rooted in, and constantly interact with, forces in the social environment of the disturbed individual. To the extent that psychopathology is not rooted in genetic and biochemical processes, it derives from the totality of the life experiences of the individual, which are shaped by continuous interactions between the person and his social setting, his informal and formal relations in primary and secondary contexts. However, it is not only the etiology of intrapsychic conflicts and disturbances that is conditioned, in part, by social forces, but also the manner in which these conflicts and disturbances are expressed in social relations. The symptoms of emotional disturbance and mental illness are not randomly generated phenomena, but derive from normal behavioral traits in a culture. These normal traits appear in exaggerated or negated forms in behavior which is considered deviant, neurotic, and psychotic. Hence, one may assume that in a society in which the use of physical force in general, and toward children in particular, is not sanctioned, intrapsychic conflicts and psychopathology would less often be expressed through violence against children. It follows from these considerations that the "battered baby" syndrome,[3] and other forms of child abuse associated with psychological disturbances of one kind or another, are not independent of societal forces, although the perpetrators of these acts may be emotionally ill individuals. We are thus again led to the conclusion that abusive acts and conditions, irrespective of the level of manifestation, cannot be understood in terms of one specific causal dimension, but only in terms of complex interactions among the several causal dimensions sketched here.

Primary Prevention

According to a general conceptual model, primary prevention proceeds from identification toward elimination of the causal contexts from which specified, undesired phenomena derive. It needs to be realized that the prevention of undesired phenomena may also result in the elimination of other phenomena whenever such other phenomenon derive from, or are part of, the same causal context. The likelihood of simultaneous prevention of several phenomena could lead to serious dilemmas if some of the phenomena are desired, while others are considered undesirable, or when groups in a society differ in their respective evaluation of the desirability of the several phenomena. Decisions concerning primary prevention of social phenomena and of "social problems" are thus essentially political choices.[4]

Turning now to the primary prevention of child abuse, we may begin by summarizing our conclusions so far. Child abuse, conceived of as inflicted deficits on a child's right to develop freely and fully, irrespective of the source and agents of the deficit, was found to occur on several related levels: on the interpersonal level in the home and in child-care settings; on the institutional level through the policies and practices of a broad array of child care, educational, welfare, and correctional institutions and agencies; and on the societal level, where the interplay of values and social, economic, and political institutions and processes shapes the social policies by which the rights and lives of all children, and of specific groups of children, are determined. The causal dimensions of child abuse are, first of all, the dominant social philosophy and value premises of a society, its social, economic, and political institutions, and the quality of human relations to which these institutions, philosophy, and values give rise; other causal dimensions are the social construction of childhood and the social definition of children's rights, the extent to which a society sanctions the use of force in general and, more specifically, in the child rearing context, stress and frustration resulting from poverty and from alienation in the workplace which may trigger abusive acts, and expressions of intrapsychic conflicts and psychopathology which, in turn, are rooted in the social fabric. While child abuse, at any particular level, may be more closely related to one rather than another causal dimension, none of these dimensions are independent, and they exert their influence through multiple interactions with each other.

This analysis suggests that primary prevention of child abuse, on all levels, would require fundamental changes in social philosophy and value premises, in societal institutions, and in human relations. It would also require a reconceptualization of childhood, of children's rights, and of child rearing. It would necessitate rejecting the use of force as a means for achieving societal ends, especially in dealing with children. It would require the elimination of poverty and of alienating conditions of production, major sources of stress and frustration which tend to trigger abusive acts toward children in adult-child interaction. And, finally, it would necessitate the elimination of psychological illness. Because of the multiple interactions among the several causal dimensions, progress in overcoming the more fundamental dimensions would also reduce the force of other dimensions. Thus, transforming the prevailing inegalitarian social philosophy, value premises, and institutions, and the kind of human relations they generate, into egalitarian ones would also result in corresponding modifications of children's rights, elimination of poverty and alienation at work, and rejection of the use of force. It would indirectly influence psychological well-being, and would thus eliminate the processes that now trigger child abuse in interpersonal relations.

Effective primary prevention requires working simultaneously toward the transformation of all the causal dimensions. Fragmented approaches focused on one or the other causal dimension may bring some amelioration, but one should entertain no illusions as to the effectiveness of such piecemeal efforts. Even such important and necessary steps as outlawing corporal punishment in schools and other child care settings would have only limited, though highly desirable, results. There simply is no way of escaping the conclusion that the complete elimination of child abuse on all levels of manifestation requires a radical transformation of the prevailing unjust, inegalitarian, irrational, competitive, alienating, and hierarchical social order into a just, egalitarian, rational, cooperative, humane, and truly democratic, decentralized one. Obviously, this realization implies that primary prevention of child abuse is a political issue which cannot be resolved through professional and administrative measures.

Primary prevention of child abuse would bring with it the prevention of other equally undesirable and inevitable consequences or symptoms of the same causal context, including many manifestations of social deviance. However, it would also result in the complete transformation of the prevailing social, economic, and political order with which large segments of our society are either identified or drifting along, because this order conforms to their accustomed mental sets, and because they seem reluctant, due to inertia, to search actively for alternative social, economic, and political institutions that might be more conducive to human fulfillment for all. Some or many members of our society may even be consciously committed to the perpetuation of the existing order, not realizing how destructive that order may be to their own real interests.

Whatever one's attitude may be toward these fundamental political issues, one needs to recognize and face the dilemmas implicit in them and, hence, in primary prevention of child abuse. If one's priority is to prevent all child abuse, one must be ready to part with its many causes, even when one is attached to some of them, such as the apparent blessings, advantages, and privileges of inequality. If, on the other hand, one is reluctant to give up all aspects of the causal context of child abuse, one must be content to continue living with this social problem. In that latter case, one ought to stop talking about primary prevention and face the fact that all one may be ready for is some measure of amelioration.

References

1. D. Gil, *Violence Against Children* (Cambridge, Massachusetts: Harvard University Press, 1970); A. Schorr, ed, *Children and Decent People* (New York: Basic Books, 1974).

2. Task Force to the Secretary, U.S. Department of Health, Education and Welfare, *Work in America* (Cambridge, Massachusetts: Massachusetts Institute of Technology Press, 1973).

3. R. Helfer and C. Kempe, eds., *The Battered Child* (Chicago: University of Chicago Press, 1968); C. Kempe and R. Helfer, eds., *Helping the Battered Child and His Family* (Philadelphia: J.B. Lippincott Company, 1972).

4. D. Gil, *Unraveling Social Policy* (Cambridge, Massachusetts: Schenkman Publishing Company, 1973).

8

Compassion vs. Control: Conceptual and Practical Pitfalls in the Broadened Definition of Child Abuse

Alvin A. Rosenfeld and
Eli H. Newberger

For more than a century, child welfare agencies have undertaken to assure the safety and well-being of children. This important work began as a concern to provide basic life supports for the children of the immigrant poor and focused on providing homes for the homeless.[1] More recently, it has progressed to a legally mandated intervention on behalf of children who are suffering from physical, sexual, or emotional traumatization in their homes.[2] As the statutory basis for this protection has rapidly evolved in the last two decades, there have developed neither clear-cut legal guidelines for family intervention nor a scientific foundation for protective service work.[3-6] The lack of a rigorous practical and theoretical framework for law and for clinical practice has created a muddled and perplexing situation for professionals concerned with the health and welfare of children.

Historical Background

In 1962, Kempe and his co-workers[7] dramatized the problem of child abuse with the term "the battered child syndrome" in a paper that precipitated public outrage and deep professional concern. Although the phenomenon was hardly new[8] and the existing clinical studies of child abuse were mostly of dubious quality,[9] the time was ripe for action. The concern led to the passage of a child abuse reporting statute in every state. In retrospect, it is of note that these laws were enacted in the 1960s, an era of concern for the rights of the disadvantaged. As they have developed (and broadened) to the present day, these statutes oblige all professionals in contact with children to report any symptoms or serious suspicions of physical, sexual, or emotional abuse. Most laws also require signs of neglect to be reported. In 1974, the passage of a national child abuse act (PL 93-247) that makes available to states modest support for protective service

Reprinted with permission from the *Journal of the American Medical Association* 237 (1977):2086-2088. Copyright 1977, American Medical Association.

work has, through the establishment and administration of federal regulations, effectively expanded the list of reportable conditions.

Since nearly all of the statutes are worded imprecisely, they give the reporter wide latitude in addition to legal immunity. Usually, the department of public welfare or the police are designated to receive the report. Once a report is filed, an investigation may begin to determine whether the child is at risk in his parents' care, and appropriate steps may be taken.

The child abuse statutes are intended to protect children whose lives are in danger and for whom other statutes do not afford protection. They spell out state and professional responsibility toward families who have problems in protecting their children, and state that helpful services (such as counseling, provision of a homemaker, day care, and temporary foster-home care) shall be provided to strengthen family life. Few anticipated the number and variety of cases that would be reported under the child abuse laws. Where in 1967 fewer than 7,000 cases of child abuse came to the attention of the authorities,[10] in 1974 there were more than 200,000 (V. De Francis, JD, personal communication, Feb 13, 1976). No child welfare office had resources remotely adequate to deal with this deluge. For example, when Florida introduced a state-wide hot line for child abuse reporting as the centerpiece of its strategy to deal with the problem, the state was overwhelmed with calls. This led to a rapid deterioration of the method of screening cases for service.[11]

Moreover, the social workers who man these departments, which tender mainly to impoverished children and families, are overworked, underpaid, and poorly supervised, and they have insufficient access to psychiatric, psychological, and medical consultation and treatment.[12,13] Staff turnover in welfare departments is enormous, and the prospects for continuing service to troubled families is small. With few clear-cut guidelines for decisions, action can be taken on the basis of exhaustion, emotionalism, or personal values about child rearing, rather than from attention to statutory or administrative guidelines or to commonly understood standards of sound professional practice. At present, services do not approach the humane rhetoric and intent of child abuse legislation. The system may mete out punishment in the guise of help.

Child Abuse and Later Deviant Behavior

It has been noted that child abuse has a multi-generational pattern: the parents of abused children may themselves have been abused and neglected in childhood.[14] Violent criminals seem often to have suffered abuse as children; for this reason, Schmitt and Kempe[15] strongly suggest that action on the problem of child abuse will prevent crime. The data that form the basis for these conclusions can be accounted for in large part by insufficiently rigorous study design. The studies share a prominent bias that favors poor people. Of the few studies that have comparison groups, nearly none match cases and controls adequately.[5] The single controlled follow-up study that matches cases and controls on social class suggests that the developmental consequences of child abuse can be accounted for on the basis of low social class.[16] Finally, foster-home care, a common protective service intervention, is associated with an unfortunate and predictable psychiatric morbidity of its own.[17]

Compassion vs Control

As laws have been passed broadening the list of conditions mandated to be reported as child abuse, a humane philosophy of clinical treatment has evolved.

Newer knowledge has shown social isolation, illness, and parental psychologic symptoms to be associated with child abuse, and our present orientation also acknowledges current life stresses, including unemployment, marital conflict, crises associated with drugs and alcohol, and inadequate access to essential resources and services.[18]

This broadened understanding of the setting of child abuse enables practitioners to see abusing parents not as evil murderers but as human beings caught in a complex web of personal and social deprivation that inhibits the normal loving relationships between parents and their children. The philosophy of practice has become assertedly humane: Kempe and Helfer's second book[19] is entitled *Helping the Battered Child and His Family*. Behavior that might be characterized by an outside observer as destructive or criminal has come to be seen and interpreted by those involved in its identification and treatment in terms of the psychosocial economy of the family.

The more compassionate understanding of the family has changed expectations of the clinician. He or she is expected to approach each case with both an abundance of human kindness and a nonpunitive outlook on intervention, which should be aimed at strengthening the entire family. Compassionate intervention has created a commonly understood language of child abuse treatment, one in which the abusing parents are frequently seen as victims themselves. They may effectively be relieved of responsibility for their actions by a professional who perceives the social and developmental origins of their behavior.

The clinician may find incompatible the dual role suggested by the two models of intervention that we identify as a consequence of our broadened concept of child abuse and call "compassion" and "control."

The compassionate model derives from the need for insight and the formation of a helpful professional-parent relationship to understand and to improve the functioning of abusing families. In practice, when the abusing parents are seen as sad, deprived, and needy human beings (rather than as cold, cruel murderers), one sympathizes with their plight and may proffer help in the form of counseling and other services, such as provision of a homemaker, health and child care, and other supports. One may contemplate with dread strong intervention on behalf of the child, such as court action on his or her behalf, with or without foster-home placement.

The danger implicit in the compassionate approach is that overidentification with an abusive parent can be paralyzing. We have seen injuries and fatalities that are traceable to a physician's, nurse's, social worker's, or judge's inability to act on perceived danger for want of alienating the parents. Fused with utopian notions about the curative power of love and genuine concern, the compassionate model may also demoralize professionals when the treatment relationship proves hopeless.

One may take it as a personal failure to love sufficiently or appropriately. "Perhaps one more week" or "This time I'm sure she won't do it again. We had a really good talk . . ." are familiar refrains of the professional who has become attached, involved, and overidentified with the family as victim. When an interdisciplinary team approaches a case, there may be reluctance to assume the role of the "bad guy" who will tamper with the therapeutic relationship by taking the drastic step of signing a care and protection petition in the juvenile or family court.

The control model refers to the aggressive use of intervention to limit and, if necessary, to punish deviant behavior. It assumes that an individual must take full responsibility for his actions and the State will hold him accountable.

For several reasons, the human service community may reject the notion of control. First, it is perceived as being in direct conflict with the model of compassion and the ethical mandate to be humane and to refrain from a judgmental posture in one's work. Any threat of force against abusing parents may be seen as cruel. The compassionate approach requires the behaviors of physician and friend, while control requires the action of the not-so-friendly policeman who may blow the whistle on an intolerable situation.

Second, child-care professionals are reluctant to set limits for adults, even if the situation screams for action. Third, the philosophy of helping the family carries in it an implicit standard of professional deportment that does not allow the expression (and for many, we fear, the acknowledged experience) of strong negative feelings towards their clients or patients. The rage that a conscientious professional may feel in a child abuse case cannot be expressed directly. It may be translated to a displacement of anger, so that judges and police who impose criminal sanctions on parents (whose behavior would undoubtedly yield them a long jail sentence if done against an adult) become the villains. Another manifestation of this displacement is the anger that sometimes develops between physicians and social workers on these cases. This can grow so intense that communication and intelligent problem-solving cease. Another way to deflect the rage without acknowledging it is to rationalize it. Thus, under the guise of the child's best interests, a harsh and punitive approach may be used in all cases, with the unspoken motive of punishing the bad parents.

Giving Compassion and Control

In all cases, there is a need for a balance and coordination of compassion and control, and we suggest that because it is not always humanly possible to maintain objective judgment during intensive work with abusive families, we might assign the functions separately. The assessment of a family referred for child abuse might be done by someone expert in deciding whether the case warrants a therapeutic trial, or whether strict legal intervention, such as a care and protection petition, is required. If a primarily compassionate treatment approach is attempted, the person working with the family would not be the one deciding if, when, or what legal intervention is necessary. A professional who has no interest in forming a helping relationship with the family (an administrator, as opposed to a therapist, in the psychiatric model) would be assigned to the case. The administrator's function would be to make the practical decisions about protective intervention on behalf of a child. Were the administrator an experienced and senior person, one would reasonably anticipate in him or her the maturity to decide calmly and to help the clinician define the relative balance of compassion and control. Furthermore, at times, only the authority and oversight of a court may give sufficient leverage (*e.g.,* the threat of a child's being taken away) to make possible a compassionate relationship (or any relationship) between professional and family.

Standard for Decision-Making

There is need for a standard that would guide the choice of the intervention model. While there is no body of empirical data with which to finalize such a standard, we propose six measurements in the form of dualisms to inform professional decisions. No one measurement is sufficient for a decision.

1. Acute vs chronic injury: If the injury is an isolated experience that occurs during situational stress, a more compassionate model might be applicable, whereas recurrent severe injuries might call for intervention more weighted on the side of control.

2. The abusive incident acceptable or unacceptable: A parent who continues to manifest guilt and concern after an isolated episode may be more likely to respond to a more compassionate intervention model, whereas the parent who shows lack of concern about the injury may well require control. Prolonged observation may be necessary accurately to assess a parent's reaction. We warn against casual impressions.

3. Social vs dissocial: This measurement addresses the parent's pattern of behavior in reference to the norms of the culture or subculture. In suggesting it, we acknowledge the inability and reluctance of professionals to make such judgments. The greater the degree of social deviance (isolation, alcoholism, drug abuse, criminality), the more likely the need for control.

4. Love vs hate for the child: Of the various symbolic meanings of a child to a parent, the most pertinent to this discussion is valence, or the subjective parental attitude towards the child. If the child is seen as good, a compassionate approach may be more likely to succeed, whereas a child seen as intrinsically bad may need to be protected by a model that emphasizes control of the parent.

5. The child seen as separate from or fused to the parent: This measurement addresses the parent's ability to conceive of the child as a separate entity with needs of its own. A capacity for empathy and aporopriate parental behavior is supported by this ability, and a more compassionate model may be apt in a case of abuse. A fused perception of parent and child may support a control intervention.

6. Integrated or disintegrated parental ego: A person with demonstrated (or potential) personality strength sufficient to inhibit destructive impulses may more likely respond to a compassionate approach. The desire to quiet a crying child is universal. The impulse to harm the child if necessary to quiet him is prevalent, if not universal.[20] The lack of sufficient ego strength to deflect that impulse into a channel other than abuse may reflect either transient disturbance or serious ego pathology. If it means the latter, at least one aspect of intervention will have to be control.

Obviously there is a great deal of overlap in these measurements, and none provides the answer when or how to employ compassion and control. Child abuse, like other clinical problems, calls for sound clinical judgment. The identification of assumptions implicit in present child protective work and the establishment of a rational basis for future thinking about child abuse will promote the development of a more effective and humane practice.

References

1. A. Kadushin, *Child Welfare Services* (New York: Macmillan, 1967), pp. 36-65.

2. M. Wald, "State Intervention on Behalf of 'Neglected' Children: A Search for Realistic Standards," *Stanford Law Review* XXVII (April, 1975):985-1040.

3. R.J. Gelles, "Child Abuse as Psychopathology: A Critique," *American Journal of Orthopsychiatry* XL (July, 1973):611-621.

4. E.H. Newberger and J.N. Hyde, "Child Abuse: Principles and Implications of Current Pediatric Practice," *Pediatric Clinics of North America* XX (August, 1975):695-715.

5. E.H. Newberger and J.H. Daniel, "Knowledge and Epidemiology of Child Abuse: A Critical Review of the Concepts," *Pediatric Annals* V. (March, 1976):15-25.

6. R. Bourne and E.H. Newberger, " 'Family Autonomy' or 'Coercive

Intervention"? Ambiguity and Conflict in the Proposed Standards for Child Abuse and Neglect," *Boston University Law Review* LVII (July, 1977):670-706.

7. C.H. Kempe et al., "The Battered Child Syndrome," *JAMA* CLXXXI (July 7, 1962):107-112.

8. L. DeMause, "Our Forbears Made Childhood a Nightmare," *Psychology Today* (April, 1975):85-88.

9. N.A. Polansky and N.F. Polansky, "The Current Status of Child Abuse and Child Neglect in this Country," in Report of Task Force I, Joint Commission on the Mental Health of Children, Washington, D.C. (February, 1968).

10. D.G. Gil, *Violence Against Children* (Cambridge, Massachusetts: Harvard University Press, 1970).

11. M. Price, quoted in *Child Protection Report* (Washington, D.C., March 13, 1975), p. 5.

12. S.Z. Nagi, *Child Maltreatment in the United States: A Cry for Help and Organizational Response* (Columbus: Ohio State University Publications, 1976).

13. S. Jenkins, "Child Welfare as a Class System," in *Children and Decent People*, ed. A.L. Schorr (New York: Basic Books, 1974), pp. 3-23.

14. B.F. Steele and C.B. Pollock, "A Psychiatric Study of Parents who Abuse Infants and Small Children," in *The Battered Child*, 2nd ed., ed. R.E. Helfer and C.E. Kempe (Chicago: University of Chicago Press, 1974), pp. 89-133.

15. B.D. Schmitt and C.H. Kempe, "Neglect and Abuse of Children," in *Nelson Textbook of Pediatrics*, 10th ed., ed. V.C. Vaughn and R.J. McKay (Philadelphia: W.B. Saunders, 1975), pp. 107-111.

16. E. Elmer, "A Follow-up Study of Traumatized Children," *Pediatrics* LIX (February, 1977):273-279.

17. D. Fanshel and E.B. Shinn, *Dollars and Sense in the Foster Care of Children: A Look at Cost Factors* (New York: Child Welfare League of America, 1972).

18. E.H. Newberger et al., "Pediatric Social Illness: Toward an Etiologic Classification," *Pediatrics* LX (August, 1977):178-185.

19. C.H. Kempe and R. E. Helfer, eds. *Helping the Battered Child and His Family* (Philadelphia: Lippincott, 1972).

20. N.F. Chase, *A Child is Being Beaten* (New York: Holt, Rinehart and Winston, 1975).

Synopsis: Standards Relating to Abuse and Neglect

Ellen J. Flannery

The Standards for Abuse and Neglect proposed by the Institute of Judicial Administration and the American Bar Association, Joint Commission on Juvenile Justice Standards, delineate specific substantive grounds and procedural requirements designed to circumscribe state intervention in suspected instances of child abuse or neglect. The asserted goals of the Standards are (1) to limit intervention to cases in which it is reasonably probable that coercive intervention will do more good than harm to the child; (2) to ensure that when intervention occurs every effort is made to keep the child with his parents but, if the child cannot safely remain home, then to place the child in a stable living situation; (3) to provide procedures to assure that appropriate decisions are made; and (4) to ensure accountability in decision making (Introduction at 3).

The drafters designed the Standards as a single system with interrelated parts and thus have urged their consideration and enactment in toto (Introduction at 7). Part I outlines the general principles underlying the Standards. The basic premise is that deference should be given to parental autonomy, because such deference is most often consistent with the best interests of children. (*Id.*) However, when these are inconsistent, the child's interests must be recognized as paramount (part 1.5). The statutory grounds for court intervention in part II essentially define the circumstances in which the overriding interests of the child may justify state intervention in the parents' child-rearing decisions. Courts are authorized—but not required—to assume jurisdiction when a child falls within any of five categories of "endangerment."

2.1 Statutory grounds for intervention.

A. a child has suffered, or there is a substantial risk that a child will imminently suffer, a physical harm, inflicted nonaccidentally upon him/her by his/her parent, which causes, or creates a substantial risk of causing disfigurement, impairment of bodily functioning, or other serious physical injury;

B. a child has suffered, or there is a *substantial* risk that the child will imminently suffer, physical harm causing disfigurement, impairment of bodily functioning, or other serious physical injury as a result of conditions created by his/her parents or by the failure of the parents to adequately supervise or protect him/her;

C. a child is suffering serious emotional damage, evidenced by anxiety,

Reprinted from *Boston University Law Review* 57 (July 1977). Used by permission of the Trustees of Boston University.

depression, or withdrawal, or untoward aggressive behavior toward self or others, and the child's parents are not willing to provide treatment for him/her;

D. a child has been sexually abused by his/her parent or a member of his/her household (alternative: a child has been sexually abused by his/her parent or a member of his/her household, and is seriously harmed physically or emotionally thereby);

E. a child is in need of medical treatment to cure, alleviate, or prevent him/her from suffering serious harm which may result in death, disfigurement, or substantial impairment of bodily functions, and his/her parents are unwilling to provide or consent to the medical treatment;

F. a child is committing delinquent acts *as a result of* parental encouragement, guidance or approval (part 2.1). However, a finding that a child has been endangered under one of these categories is not sufficient to confer jurisdiction; the court must also find that intervention is necessary to protect the child from endangerment in the future (part 2.2).

Parts III, IV and V establish three routes by which a suspected case of child abuse or neglect can enter the statutory system of state intervention: reporting of abused children, emergency temporary custody of an endangered child, and initiation of court proceedings (see chart following Synopsis). Part III provides that physicians, health and social workers, law enforcement officials and other designated professionals who have reasonable cause to believe that a child is "abused" must file a report with a "qualified report recipient agency" (part 3.1(A)). For purposes of reporting,

> [a]n "abused child" ... is a child who has suffered physical harm, inflicted nonaccidentally upon him/her by his/her parent(s) or person(s) exercising essentially equivalent custody and control over the child, which injury causes or creates a substantial risk of causing death, disfigurement, impairment of bodily functioning, or other serious physical consequence (part 3.1 (B)).

"Report recipient agencies," which can be either public or private, are designated by the state department of social services (part 3.2). When the agency receives a complaint of child abuse, it must immediately notify the state's central registry, operated by the department of social services. The agency then investigates the complaint and submits a report to the registry. Based upon its findings, the agency can dismiss the complaint, file a petition to initiate court proceedings pursuant to part V, or take emergency temporary custody of the child in accordance with part IV (part 3.3(B)).

Although mandatory reporting under part II is limited to cases of physical abuse that are identified by professionals, a second route toward intervention allows *any* person who suspects a case of abuse or neglect to submit a complaint under part V to initiate court proceedings. Complaints are screened by an "intake processing agency" before they are filed with the court (part 5.1). An intake officer can dispose of a complaint by dismissal, referral of the family to a child protective services agency, or submission of a petition to initiate formal judicial proceedings (part 5.1(B)(1)). However, any party aggrieved by the disposition can appeal directly to the juvenile court.

The final means of entry to the court is through the emergency temporary custody provisions of part IV. Any physician, police or law enforcement official, or agent or employee of a specially designated agency is authorized to take emergency temporary custody of an endangered child when necessary to forestall imminent death or serious bodily injury to the child (part 4.1). The child so removed must be placed in a nonsecure setting under the custody of the designated agency, which is chosen from among the qualified report recipient agencies in the region. Immediately thereafter, the custodial agency must report the emergency action to the court and file a petition to initiate court action pursuant to part V, but without prior screening by the intake processing agency (part 4.2(B)).

The court proceedings themselves (part V) are distinguished by the elaborate procedural protections afforded all parties. Upon filing of a petition, the court must notify the parents and provide them with a copy of the petition. Also, the court must inform the parents that they have a right to be represented by counsel at all stages of the proceedings (part 5.1(D)(3)). If the parents are unable to afford counsel, they are entitled to counsel appointed at public expense (part 5.1(D)(4)). Further, the court must in all cases appoint separate counsel for the child, financed at public expense without regard to the financial resources of child or parents (part 5.1(E)). A separate prosecuting agency designated by the state is responsible for prosecuting the petition against the parents (part 5.1(F)). All parties are entitled to attend all proceedings, except that the child can be excluded if the court determines that attendance would be detrimental to the child.

Under circumstances of emergency temporary custody, the court first holds a hearing to determine whether the agency should retain temporary custody or should return the child to his home (part 4.3(A)). At this hearing, the custodial agency also submits for judicial approval a plan for investigating the child's background and environment (parts 4.3(A), 5.2(B)(2)). In proceedings originated by a complaint filed with an intake processing agency under part V and thus not involving emergency custody, the court first determines whether an investigation of the family is warranted. This determination, made without a hearing unless requested by one of the parties to the proceedings, is based upon the petition filed by the intake agency to initiate court involvement (parts 5.2(A), (B)). If the court finds probable cause for asserting jurisdiction under any of the five categories in part II, it then designates a report recipient agency to conduct an investigation (part 5.2(B)(1)). As under part IV, the investigatory plan must be submitted to the court for approval; however, the court need not hold a hearing on the plan if no party has requested one.

The agency's investigation can include: interviews with the child, parents and family members, and with school and medical personnel; examination of school and medical records; physical and psychological tests of the child and/or parents; and visits to the child's home (part 5.2(D)). The child's attorney must be given adequate notice of and opportunity to attend any interviews with or tests of the child. The parent's attorney has similar due process with regard to interviews with and tests of the parent. If any person refuses to cooperate with the agency's investigation, the court can impose various sanctions (part 5.2(E)). For example, if the parent refuses access to the child, the court can authorize the agency to assume custody of the child during the day for that period necessary to conduct its investigation on the child. If the parents refuse to be interviewed or tested, such refusal is admissible as evidence supporting the allegations against the parents. Following its investigations, the agency prepares a report regarding the specific harms found in a given case—such as physical abuse, neglect, or emotional disturbance—that may justify intervention under part II; the kinds of services or placements necessary to prevent further harm to the child; the availability of proposed services and the agency's plans for providing them to the family; and the estimated time that intervention must be continued (part 5.2(F)(1)). Further, if the agency recommends that the child be removed from his parents, the report must indicate why "in-home treatment programs" were inappropriate, what harms to the child are likely to result from such removal, and how the harms of separation might be minimized (part 5.2(F)(1)(e)). Any party can request a hearing on the report and can petition the court to appoint experts at public expense for an independent evaluation of the agency's recommendations (part 5.3(B)). The determination whether the child is "endangered" (part 2.1) is then made by the court, or by a jury if requested by any party. The prosecuting agency must prove by clear and convincing evidence that the allegations are sufficient to justify intervention; and if a jury is the trier of fact, the verdict must be unanimous (part 5.3(E)).

After a determination of endangerment, the court must convene a hearing with regard to the disposition of the petition under part VI. In selecting a disposition, "the court should choose those services which least interfere with family autonomy, provided that the services are adequate to protect the child" (part 6.4(B)). Among other dispositions, the court can dismiss the case, order informal supervision, order specific social services, or remove the child and place him with a relative, foster family, or residential treatment center (part 6.3(A)). However, the Standards restrict removal to those cases in which the court finds by a preponderance of the evidence that the child was physically abused as defined in 2.1A and can be protected from further abuse only by removal from his home; or, by clear and convincing evidence, that the child was endangered in one of the other ways specified in 2.1, and can be protected from that harm only by removal from his home (part 6.4(C)). In addition to either of these findings, the court must ascertain that a placement outside the home is in fact available for the child. Finally, before removal can be effected, the custodial agency must provide the court with a plan detailing the care for the child and the actions the parents must take to resume custody (part 6.5(B)).

This dispositional hearing does not mark the end of court involvement in the child's case. Part VII requires periodic court reviews to monitor the progress made by the child and the parents. These periodic hearings must be held every six months and can be held earlier at the request of any party. When in-home services are being provided to the family, the court should terminate jurisdiction as soon as it determines that the conditions that prompted intervention no longer exist (part 7.4(A)). In any event, such jurisdiction terminates automatically after eighteen months, unless any party proves by clear and convincing evidence that the child is still endangered or would be endangered if services ended (part 7.4(C)). When the child is in foster care, the court must determine at the first six-month hearing whether to return the child to his home, continue foster custody for six months, or terminate parental rights pursuant to part VIII (part 7.5). If a preponderance of the evidence establishes that a child will not be endangered, the court must return the child to his home. However, if the endangerment still exists at the first six-month hearing, the disposition will depend upon the child's age. For a child who was under three at the time of placement, the court ordinarily should terminate parental rights at this hearing (parts 7.5(A), 8.3). For a child who was over three when placed, the court ordinarily may continue foster care until the second six-month hearing; if endangerment still exists at that hearing, parental rights ordinarily will be terminated. However, the Standards do provide exceptions to these termination rules when termination of parental rights would be detrimental to the child because the parent-child relationship is very close; a relative with whom the child is placed is unwilling to adopt the child; continuation of parental rights will not preclude a subsequent permanent placement of the child; or a child over age ten objects to such termination (part 8.4). When parental rights are terminated, the court should order the most stable living situation available for the child; generally, placing the child for adoption is preferable (part 8.5(A)).

Part IX limits criminal prosecution of parents to those cases in which the juvenile court has determined that such prosecution will not result in undue harm to the child. In contrast to those involuntary placement situations permitted under parts VI-VIII, part X provides standards governing situations in which the parents wish to voluntarily place their child in foster care. To prevent unnecessary placements, the Standards require the parents and custodial agency to enter into a formal agreement specifying the services to be provided and parental involvement in the placement process. Further, to assure that when voluntary placement does occur it is for a temporary period, the Standards limit placement to six months and require the agency to explain to the parents that parental rights might be terminated (pursuant to part VIII) if the child remains in placement for one year (part 10.4).

The drafters do not claim that the Standards represent an ideal system. Rather, they have presented the Standards as a "best effort" to protect the interests of both children and parents in a world of limited social services resources. They freely admit that the definitions, categories and rules specified in the Standards will inevitably exclude from the system of reporting and court-ordered intervention some individual children who do need protection. However, the authors of the Standards believe that, by establishing guidelines that circumscribe the discretion of agencies and courts, the majority of children will be benefited. Moreover, the authors emphasize that the definitions and rules must be dynamic, not static, and should be periodically modified if these Standards subsequently prove to be ineffective or infeasible in practice. Ultimately, the success of the proposed Standards may well depend upon whether juvenile courts strictly construe the statutory grounds for intervention, or instead broadly interpret these provisions with regard to both the statutory purpose and the intentions of the drafters as indicated in the commentary.

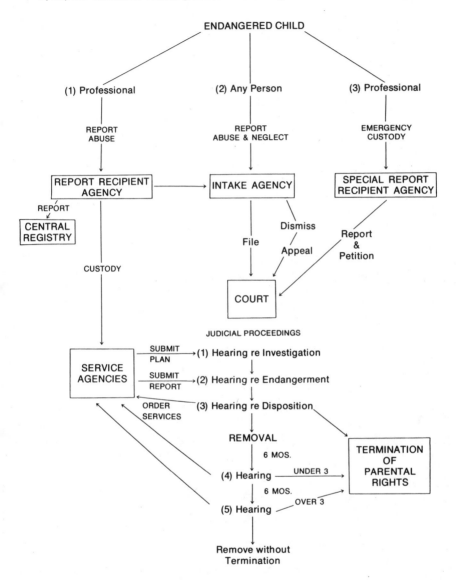

Figure 1. Standards' System of State Intervention.

10 "Family Autonomy" or "Coercive Intervention"? Ambiguity and Conflict in the Proposed Standards for Child Abuse and Neglect

Richard Bourne and
Eli H. Newberger

I. Introduction

Perhaps the strongest and most universal human feeling is the love of a parent for his or her child. Not surprisingly, reaction to the tragedy of a child harmed in the home is equally strong and universal. More subtle, however, is the ambivalent nature of that reaction.[1] Shared notions of parental love and care are deeply offended by a parent who appears not to want his child. The public is puzzled by the parent who loves his child but nevertheless intentionally harms him or fails to protect the child from harm. Public outrage has led the state to intervene in dangerous family situations to guarantee the child's safety. However, American society regards the relationship between parent and child as so precious and so beneficial to the child's growth that the family is protected against all unnecessary state intervention. The specter of unjustified state intrusion into or destruction of this relationship affronts fundamental notions of parenthood.

This ambivalence toward state intervention in harmful family situations clearly influenced the drafters of the *Standards Relating to Abuse and Neglect* (Standards), promulgated by the Juvenile Justice Standards Project of the Institute of Judicial Administration and the American Bar Association.[2] The drafters attempted to accommodate both protection of the child and family independence in the design of every provision of the Standards' comprehensive scheme for state intervention. The Standards suggest model substantive and procedural law concerning reporting of child abuse,[3] emergency temporary custody of endangered children,[4] court-ordered provision of services within the home, removal of a child,[5] criminal prosecution of parents,[6] and voluntary placement of an endangered child.[7] The drafters fashioned the scheme upon three basic principles that underlie the central dilemma of state intervention: deference to parental autonomy, the paramount nature of the child's interests

Reprinted from *Boston University Law Review* 57 (July 1977), *passim.* Used by permission of the Trustees of Boston University.

when in conflict with the parents', and the limitation upon state intervention to remedy only specific harms.

The first principle announced in the Standards codifies a reverence for the family into "a strong presumption for parental autonomy in child rearing."[8] Parental autonomy refers not only to the maintenance of the family unit but also to the insulation from state interference of all parental decisions regarding child management.[9] One purpose of the presumption is to safeguard the parent's traditional right to care, custody and control of his child.[10] Fundamentally, however, the Standards insist upon deference to parental control because it "is most likely to lead to decisions that help children."[11] The Standards assume that a child is most apt to thrive in the custody of those who have cared for him since birth.[12] The bonds of that relationship frequently cannot be fully duplicated by a court-ordered substitute.[13] Thus, the Standards urge proper legal recognition[14] of this long-standing assumption of child development scholarship and practice.[15]

The Standards also acknowledge that deference to parental autonomy may not always be in a particular child's best interests. In that case, the Standards expressly commit the state to protection of the child despite the resulting destruction of and intrusion upon the parent's right to care, custody and control.[16] Thus, the Standards continue the role of the state as *parens patriae*.[17] The commentary to the Standards reiterates the traditional justification that the child's comparatively helpless condition warrants state intervention and protection.[18] In addition, intervention may disrupt the cycle of the abused or neglected child's becoming the abusing or neglecting parent.[19]

The Standards' most innovative precept is the general restriction of the court's power to intervene to only those cases in which the child has suffered *specific* harm.[20] In the past, courts have intervened based upon highly subjective judgments concerning parental unfitness or unpleasant home conditions without any showing that this behavior or these conditions resulted in specific harm to the child.[21] The Standards reflect the widespread disapproval of such overreaching by experts[22] and appellate courts.[23] In effect, the Standards have established a per se rule that the presumption in favor of parental autonomy is rebutted only by a showing of specific harm to the child.

Although these principles provide a sound theoretical basis for a scheme of state intervention, their accommodation and practical application in the Standards are sometimes unsatisfactory. In this article, we will set forth both our criticisms of the present provisions and our suggested revisions. Generally, we conclude that the Standards continually fail to refine the scheme to reflect the different degrees of intrusion upon parental autonomy caused by reporting, court-ordered provision of services in the home and removal. We suggest that legislatures considering reform in child protection laws modify the Standards in order to increase the availability of less intrusive means of state intervention. Accordingly, we believe that the grounds for reporting and for court-ordered provision of services should be significantly expanded. Our experience indicates that the prophylactic and therapeutic nature of early, limited intervention can minimize the instances in which a child must be removed from his parents.[24]

Our criticism generates from our work at Children's Hospital Medical Center in Boston with children who suffer from abuse or neglect as a result of their parents' problems. Our concern in this article will focus upon the impact of the proposed model not only upon children and parents but also upon the professionals who work with them. Throughout the article, we have drawn specific cases from our clinical experience to illustrate the painful choices professionals must make and the inadequacies of the present and proposed systems of child protection.

II. A Grant of Jurisdiction to Order Services

Despite our agreement with the Standards' three basic tenets—deference to parental autonomy, the paramount nature of the child's interests, and the limitation upon state intervention to cases involving specific harm—we fundamentally disagree with the Standards' undifferentiating distrust of all unrequested state intervention into the family.[25] To minimize state intervention, the Standards limit court jurisdiction to only those cases involving *serious* harm to a child.[26] Thus, a flat ban is imposed upon intervention in cases of *nonserious* harm. Moreover, this jurisdictional grant operates without regard to the nature of the intervention sought; it applies equally to courts' power to order removal of the child from the parents and to the power to order less intrusive and potentially less destructive dispositions, such as homemaker services or therapy. To obtain any intervention, the petitioner must show by clear and convincing evidence that the child is "endangered";[27] the child must have suffered, or "there is a substantial risk that the child will imminently suffer, physical harm causing disfigurement, impairment of bodily functioning, or other serious physical injury,"[28] or the child must be suffering "serious emotional damage."[29] Additionally, the petitioner must convincingly demonstrate that intervention is necessary to protect the child from future endangerment.[30] Thus, the same grave level of harm that would justify the removal of a child constitutes the exclusive occasion for all unrequested state intervention.

Two aspects of this jurisdictional scheme are objectionable. First, we disagree with the flat ban upon intervention for nonserious harm. Second, we disagree with the Standards' failure to distinguish between removal and court-ordered provision of services in the threshold requirements for state intervention.[31] Both provisions ignore the difference between the intrusive and potentially harmful effects of removal and the less drastic effects of providing services in the home. Moreover, inherent in this jurisdictional grant is a negative appraisal of the value of services. In denying jurisdiction over cases involving nonserious harm, the Standards have adopted a per se rule that the benefits of services never outweigh the intrusion upon parental autonomy and the risk of harm from intervention.[32] In specifying the prima facie requirements for state intervention in cases of serious harm, the Standards give equal weight to the intrusive effects of the removal of a child from his parents and the unrequested provision of social services.

We urge major revision of this jurisdiction provision. Jurisdiction should be divided into two separate categories: the first, to order services; the second, to order removal.[33] To establish jurisdiction to order services, the petitioner should have to show by clear and convincing evidence that the child has suffered or will imminently suffer physical or emotional harm, serious or nonserious.[34] Once this requirement is satisfied, the burden of proof concerning future harm should shift to the parents. The parents, assisted by counsel, would have to demonstrate that, because future harm is unlikely, intervention is unnecessary. Moreover, we suggest that, if the evidence concerning future harm is inconclusive, the court should be given discretion to consider the therapeutic value of services, presently impermissible under the Standards.

A. Providing Services in Cases of Nonserious Harm

The family situation in which a child suffers nonserious harm is not only not "ideal,"[35] is is quite oppressive, albeit without danger to life and limb of the child. The child will consistently suffer specific, demonstrable physical or emotional harm, even though such harm does not rise to the gravity required by the Standards nor present a "substantial risk that the child will imminently suffer" such severe harm. An example of parental abuse constituting nonserious harm would be a child who regularly receives painful bruises in the course of parental discipline.[36] Nonserious harm attributable to parental neglect would include some "failure to thrive" cases.[37] Commentary accompanying the Standards suggests that court intervention would be permissible if the child suffered "severe malnutrition, extremely low physical growth rate, delayed bone maturation, and significant retardation of motor development." the same or similar symptoms of "failure to thrive" would be outside the court's jurisdiction unless those agencies seeking intervention could prove that more severe harms were imminent.

The Standards' ban upon provision of services in cases of nonserious harm represents one instance of the Standards' deference to the right of parents to rear their children free from state intervention. Several assumptions underlie the prohibition. First, the Standards assume that a meaningful distinction can be made between voluntary and coercive state intervention in abuse and neglect cases. Second, it is assumed that, because parents of children suffering nonserious harm can voluntarily request services, some of these children will be helped. Finally, the Standards assume that coercive provision of services to families in which the child has suffered nonserious harm is more often harmful than beneficial.

1. Voluntary Versus Coercive Intervention. The Standards' reliance upon the distinction between a parent's voluntary request for services and state-coerced intervention is unsound because the distinction is often meaningless or blurred in the context of neglect and abuse cases. An apparently voluntary request, in reality, may be a product of external pressures.[39] For example, the parents may make a "voluntary" request for services because their welfare worker has either expressly or impliedly conditioned continued benefits upon such a request.[40] Conversely, parents may loudly protest intervention while simultaneously making indirect pleas for help.[41] Resistance and denial of guilt are typical reactions of parents when confronted by a social worker's allegations.[42] Yet clinical experience indicates that a parent who harms his child has ambivalent feelings.[43] He wants to hide from the shame and stigma but also wants to stop his abuse or neglect.[44] He is often actually relieved when state authorities have finally concerned themselves with the family's difficulties.[45]

For example, a mother brought her daughter, aged three, to Children's Hospital Medical Center with multiple broken ribs and leg fractures. The mother denied that the injuries were intentionally inflicted and, instead, claimed that they had resulted from her daughter's accidental fall from a bed onto a concrete floor. However, based upon x-rays that revealed varying ages of the fractures, the physicians concluded that the mother's explanation of the cause was inadequate. The mother persisted in her denials and offered arguments and proof in support of her explanation. She displayed a health clinic schedule card to verify that she had taken the child for examinations every few months since birth. She maintained that her evident concern for the child's medical care was inconsistent with a desire to harm her child. She further insisted that the presence of old injuries was impossible because no physician had brought any injuries to her attention at the prior exams. Because of the perceived risk to the child, the Hospital initiated a care and protection petition in juvenile court. Shortly thereafter, the mother admitted her long-term physical abuse of her child. She stated that, for the first time, she was able to verbalize a need for help. Evidently, the petition had provided the structure necessary for such communication. In addition, she explained that her frequent visits to medical clinics had, in fact, been an unstated search for detection and support. Thus, despite her vigorous denials and her failure to request help prior to the court action, the mother apparently desired intervention. However, under the Standards, if this mother had caused only nonserious harm, the Hospital and the court would be forced to ignore urgent but indirectly expressed needs of the family. This case illustrates an additional fallacy in the Standards' distinction between voluntary and coercive intervention. In cases of nonserious harm, the Standards condition the provision of services upon an express request by the parent and forbid any court action. However, in this case, court action was the necessary precondition for the mother's expression of need.

Even if the parent does try to obtain assistance by express request, our experience indicates that this request may go unheeded.[46] For example, a thirteen-month-old infant from a middle-class family was diagnosed by professionals at Children's Hospital as severely retarded with slim developmental prospects. The infant's mother revealed that she was so embarrassed by the infant's condition that she kept him in a back room of the house. She also expressed homicidal tendencies toward the infant. She told the professional staff that, while on a boating excursion with the family, she had held the baby over the side and had actually considered letting go. She sought a voluntary placement of the child through the Department of Public Welfare but was told that no placements were available. Similarly, the Department of Mental Health refused to assist her. Thus, the Hospital physician and protective service social worker were forced to file a care and protection petition in court. Attorneys on behalf of both state agencies argued in court against the petition. Nevertheless, the court granted the petition and placed the child in a hospital for retarded children.

This case starkly illustrates the present practice of both private and public agencies of refusing to expend precious resources unless a court mandates the provision of services.[47] Frequently, the agency will even request a court order simply to justify expenditures to a budget manager. The commentary to the Standards notes, with disapproval, that some state statutes condition financial aid on court supervision of the child. The authors lament the fact that the availability of public housing, for example, will often turn on the issuance of a court order.[48]

Yet, despite this express condemnation, the Standards implicitly give legal sanction to this practice. Because of the scarcity of social services, the Standards effectively legislate their exclusive distribution to cases of serious harm. The commentary justifies the narrow scope of state intervention on the ground that it will channel services to the cases of greatest need and, thus, maximize their effectiveness.[49] However, the Standards and the commentary fail to recognize that, as a result, provision of services at the request of a parent who has caused only nonserious harm may be nothing more than a comforting fiction.[50]

The scarcity of services is further aggravated by the new procedural burdens the Standards impose upon agencies. Under the present draft, a single agency could be called upon to perform an initial investigation of a report of abuse[51] and, if court action ensues, the agency must submit an investigative plan, conduct a detailed investigation, analyze the services available and their possible impact, and submit specific treatment or placement plans and periodic post-disposition reports.[52] Moreover, agency personnel may be required to attend hearings at as many as four stages of the initial proceedings,[53] as well as at periodic reviews of agency provision of services or placement.[54] These procedures are designed to make the agency more accountable to courts.[55] The net result, however, is to so burden the agency that it will be less capable of offering quality services to needy families than it is at present. Unfortunately, the scarcity of services puts even more pressure on both the agency and the court to select less time-consuming, less thoughtful treatment options. For example, the simplicity of removal, although often more costly to the state in the long run,[56] will be more attractive in cases of serious harm than the protracted provision of treatment in the home.[57] Because the processing of each case will exhaust judicial and agency time, the drafters of the Standards evidently felt compelled to narrow the scope of courts' jurisdiction.

The wisdom of drafting the Standards predicted upon the unfortunate present reality of scarce resources[58] is questionable;[59] rather, the Standards should provide for court-ordered services to all families who could benefit from such assistance without regard to the degree of harm or present agency budgets. It would then be incumbent upon any state legislature enacting the Standards into law also to guarantee adequate funding to meet the new state intervention scheme. However, the present draft actually reduces the pressure upon legislatures to expand social service agency budgets to meet the needs and express requests of families.

The Standards' assumption that a sharp distinction exists between voluntary and coercive state intervention underlies the ban upon the provision of services in cases of nonserious harm. Yet our experience indicates that the presence or absence of an express request rarely reflects parents' feelings toward state intrusion into their homes. More importantly, when coupled with the Standards' increased procedural requirements on agencies, the ban may result in the elimination of any assistance to nonseriously harmed children; on the one hand, agencies cannot initiate court action, but, on the other, they often will not expend resources without court approval.

2. The Value of Unrequested Assistance. By conditioning assistance in the home upon parental request, the Standards replace an evaluation of the value of the services to the child and family with an inquiry into whether the parent has requested the state intrusion. If the parent has not waived his right to autonomy, the nonseriously harmed child will be denied access to services.[60] This arrangement appears contrary to the express commitment of the Standards to protect the child's needs in any conflict of interests between parent and child.[61] Additionally, it seems contrary to the Standards' commitment to "strengthen family life"[62] because state-ordered assistance to the family is eliminated. The Standards negate these criticisms by minimizing the value of unrequested assistance. In most cases, court-ordered provision of services to families in which the child has suffered only nonserious harm is assumed not to be in the child's best interests. The commentary suggests that such intervention, at best, would be minimally helpful and, in fact, could even be harmful to the child.[63] The Standards apparently conclude that any minor benefits are outweighed by the loss of parental autonomy.

In another forum, a reporter on the Standards, Professor Michael Wald, has elaborated the bases for this conclusion.[64] He suggests that the effectiveness of any assistance may be significantly reduced if provided on a coercive, as opposed to voluntary, basis. Among the potential dangers of assistance cited, mandatory day care, for example, might weaken the close attachment between parents and child crucial to healthy development. However, as Professor Wald acknowledges, this attachment may already be weak in harmful family situations.[65] Professor Wald also distinguishes between the value of "hard" and "soft" services. He admits that provision of "hard" services—financial aid, medical care and homemakers—would be helpful but adds that such assistance is not usually forthcoming.[66] However, he notes that the effectiveness of the more common "soft" services—such as counseling and parent education—has been disproven.[67] Moreover, Professor Wald maintains that such services can often be harmful if the social worker is inept or injects his middle-class bias into the decisions regarding child care and housekeeping. He fears that the social worker's intervention may result in inconsistent parental behavior that will confuse the child and disturb the child's adjustment to the unhealthy situation. In addition, he postulates that the parent may direct his resentment of the intervention toward the child as the cause of the intrusion.

Studies measuring the effectiveness of services have produced inconclusive results. Some studies have drawn negative conclusions;[68] others, positive.[69] Furthermore, it is generally agreed that measuring the outcome of services on an objective scale is very difficult.[70] It is particularly difficult to design research projects to measure significant improvements in family behavior. Because the Standards maintain the presumption in favor of parental autonomy, failure to prove that services will improve the family situation is dispositive against intervention.[71] This conclusion ignores that the presumption has, to some extent, been rebutted by proof that the parent has caused harm, although not serious. Significantly, Professor Wald has failed to cite studies supporting his thesis that the effectiveness of services turns on whether they are provided on a voluntary or coercive basis.[72] In fact, the intervention of legal authority can enhance a parent's respect for the treatment program and thus increase its effectiveness.[73]

Our experience has been that services provided on an involuntary basis can be helpful. For example, a mother brought her eleven-year-old daughter to Children's Hospital and reported that the child had told her that the father had masturbated in front of the daughter and invited her into his bed. In addition, the mother revealed that three months earlier, fearing her husband's temper, she had fled home and left the child behind with the father. The child denied having mentioned her father's sexual advances. Emergency room physicians were unable or unwilling to make a thorough medical examination because of the child's uncooperativeness and anxiety. The child was admitted for "social reasons" to permit a further evaluation of the family situation and the child's needs. A psychological consultation and social service interview revealed that the child had recently lost bladder and bowel control at night, performed poorly in school, experienced nightmares, gained excessive weight and became increasingly tense. The conclusion drawn from this initial evaluation was that the child was "troubled," even though no clear evidence of serious emotional damage emerged. However, the diagnostic team interpreted the facts that she spoke of a "secret" with her father and mentioned that he had brought her candy during school recess as soft signs of possible sexual abuse. The mother desired help for her daughter but seemed incapable of obtaining assistance herself. She did not know what services were available nor how to use them. However, she did not wish to leave her child in the Hospital for the time required to conduct a full psychiatric examination. Once she even attempted to remove the youngster because of her own fears and loneliness. When the father was interviewed, he denied that any problems existed and expressed strong hostility toward his wife and the Hospital personnel. The Hospital staff attempted, without success, to involve various child protection agencies. The agencies all refused because they either were overcrowded or considered the case "inappropriate." The Trauma-X Group at Children's Hospital—a multi-disciplinary team for treatment of neglect and abuse cries—decided to seek court intervention in this case. At the preliminary hearing, the judge entered a temporary order granting physical custody of the child to a treatment center to conduct further evaluation. The center began diagnosis and therapy and also enrolled the child in a special education program. The mother began weekly counseling with a psychiatric social worker from the same facility. The father, after a court-ordered psychiatric evaluation, agreed to seek help for his depression and drinking problem. Thereafter, the mother and father resumed living together.

This petition would not satisfy either of the relevant grounds for court intervention proposed by the Standards. The commentary indicates that intervention is authorized only when the sexual abuse constitutes a violation of the state penal code.[74] The only hard evidence at the time of the petition had related to the father's exhibitionism and propositions at home, which alone might not constitute criminal violations. The Standards also permit the court to intervene when the child is presently suffering "serious emotional damage."[75] The Trauma-X Group had sought court action before the development of strong manifestations of serious emotional harm because of legitimate concerns about the child's mental status and the adequacy of the mother's caretaking. Additionally, the Group had hoped that early action could prevent the need to remove the child in the future. Although the court would have been forced to dismiss the petition under the Standards, in the actual case the entire family very clearly benefited from the court's intervention. This case and the case of the mother who admitted her abuse only after the court petition was filed also illustrate the therapeutic value of court action itself. In both cases, the court action was the catalyst or vehicle enabling the parents to confront their problems.

Professor Wald's segregation of "hard" and "soft" services, and his respective approval and disapproval, ignores the evolving clinical model and practice of a combined approach to treatment.[76] Based upon evidence indicating that external stress is substantially related to neglect, abuse and other pediatric social illnesses, the treatment of families now focuses upon relieving the external stresses of inadequate housing, health and child care by directly supplying these needs. However, equally important components of this new treatment include "soft" services, such as counseling and education, specifically designed to enable parents to secure resources in the future. A systematic study measuring the effectiveness of this combined approach has not been undertaken. However, the data demonstrating the connection between these external stresses and the incidence of neglect and abuse warrant the inference that treatment directed at relieving these stresses can effectively prevent individual cases of future neglect and abuse and can improve the family's ability to utilize services for the child. Our clinical experience supports this conclusion.[77] Obviously, success on an individual level cannot substitute for efforts to change institutions and correct the inadequacy of resources that affect large numbers of the population.

The fact that this and other novel approaches may not yet be prevalent does not support the narrow grounds for court-ordered services adopted by the Standards. The criticism that was previously leveled with regard to limiting these grounds based upon the present dismal quantity of services applies equally when based upon the present *quality* of services. If enlightened treatment methods would benefit a troubled family, the Standards should permit a court to order such assistance.[78] Concomitantly, professionals must pressure agencies and state legislatures to improve the quality of services through training in modern approaches to treatment of child neglect and abuse. The Standards themselves could be drafted to promote such new approaches to treatment. For example, the Standards could establish citizen-based councils to place continuing pressure on professional groups, agencies and legislatures to increase the quality, as well as quantity, of services.[79] These councils could supply the input of local values, traditions, needs and priorities into the design of treatment models.[80] In addition, the Standards could establish a mechanism to coordinate state departments of child health, mental health, welfare services[81] and employment opportunities for the parents.[82] Through this coordinating mechanism, the Standards would further the goal of a coherent, embracive approach to family problems.[83]

Were we to agree with the Standards' assumption that most nonseriously harmed children are not benefited by court-ordered provision of services, we would nevertheless be unable to support the flat ban upon state intervention. To prohibit all intervention and thus deny assistance to even those children who could be helped does not seem to us the proper resolution of the conflicting interests. The acknowledged trade-off in adopting the ban on intervention for nonserious harm is that cases that warrant intervention must be dismissed in order to prevent unjustified or unproductive intrusions upon parental control in other cases.[84] We are unconvinced that judicial discretion has been so unwisely exercised in the past. Moreover, the instances of useless or harmful intrusions will be reduced by the Standards' limitation upon intervention to cases of specific harm. Courts can thus ensure that the services ordered will closely relate to the nature of the specific harm.[85] Finally, rather than abandoning any attempt to aid the nonseriously harmed child, legislatures should consider proposals, in addition to those suggested in this article, to improve the quality and availability of services.[86]

B. The Future Endangerment Requirement

1. Initial Intervention According to the present draft of the Standards, once a petitioner seeking court intervention has established that a child is "endangered," the petitioner must satisfy the second requirement—demonstrate that intervention is necessary to protect against future endangerment.[87] This requirement applies equally to both services and removal. Objections to this jurisdictional requirement are threefold. First, as in the initial requirement of "endangerment," the petitioner must satisfy the same burden of proof regardless of which disposition is sought. Second, because the likelihood of future harm and the impact of intervention are difficult to prove, placing the burden of proof on the petitioner may be tantamount in many cases to a denial of court jurisdiction. Third, the Standards expressly reject the more discretionary "best interests of the child" test in favor of considering a determination regarding only the prophylactic value of intervention. This latter test, however, excludes a relevant inquiry into the therapeutic value of court-ordered services.

Distinguishing between services and removal is most appropriate in the context of the "necessity of intervention" jurisdictional requirement. Because court-ordered services involve much less drastic interference with the parent-child relationship and much less stigma for the parents than removal, the restraint on court intervention should be significantly less when services are the only disposition requested by the petitioner. Furthermore, services and removal are different in kind, not just in degree. Services most typically involve direct provision of medical care or better housing, training in homemaking techniques, or counseling aimed at emotional and behavioral improvements.[88] These services are directed toward benefiting the entire family. Admittedly, removal sometimes will be accompanied by services to the parents in an effort to reunite the family.[89] However, in general, the curative aspects of removal are less significant than its intrusive effects. Removal is a decision to save the child at the expense of the parents' right to custody. Thus, a distinction between services and removal will be particularly appropriate if the court's jurisdictional inquiry is expanded to include consideration of the therapeutic value of intervention.

The Standards limit the court's inquiry to whether intervention is necessary to prevent future harm. This test, which replaces the prevailing "best interests of the child" test, would guide a court's decision whether[90] and in what manner it should intervene.[91] The drafters of the Standards rejected the prevalent test to avoid the guesswork inherent in its application. For example, in a removal case, the application of the "best interests" test requires a judge to compare the probable consequences of removal with several alternative programs of assistance in the home. The judge's comparative analysis must be based upon predictions about future behavior of each family member in a number of contexts. The judge must also predict the progress the child would make in a foster home. Judicial officers and the adjudication process are particularly ill-suited to make such uncertain predictions about human development.[92] Uncertainty offers opportunities for the court's bias to replace proper criteria.[93] Additionally, when the judgment is, by nature, subject to reasonable differences, appellate court control of the juvenile court becomes minimal.[94]

The Standards' suggested inquiry into the prophylactic value of intervention does not completely avoid the uncertainty inherent in the "best interests" test. The court must still judge the likelihood of future harm based upon predictions about parental behavior. Nevertheless, conditioning intervention on a likelihood of future harm is generally sound. Obviously, if future harm is clearly improbable, a court should not intervene despite a record of past harm; for example, the mother of the injured child may permanently separate from the abusing lover. Theoretically, the presumption in favor of parental autonomy may warrant placing the burden of proof of the likelihood of future harm on the petitioner. However, the petitioner must initially establish in the majority of cases that harm has occurred and, thus, will have rebutted any presumption of parental fitness. In reality, a presumption of future harm arises from past harm because of the nature of child abuse and neglect.[95] A typical pattern of abuse involves a continuing series of assaults, escalating in severity.[96] Neglect is an even more obvious case of a chronic condition.[97] Moreover, placing the burden on the petitioner to show by clear and convincing evidence that intervention is necessary to prevent future harm would effectively preclude intervention in many cases.[98] Because predictive judgments by nature are rarely conclusive, the degree of certainty required by the "clear and convincing evidence" standard of proof may be unattainable.[99]

For the reasons outlined above, we suggest that, in cases in which only court-ordered services are sought, the future endangerment requirement be revised. Once the petitioner has convincingly demonstrated that the child is endangered, the burden of proof concerning future harm should be shifted to the parents. Consistent with the actual nature of child abuse and neglect, the parents, assisted by their attorney, should be required to demonstrate that continuation of the harm is unlikely. Placing the burden of this issue upon the parents is particularly appropriate because the likelihood of future harm entails predictions concerning parental behavior.[100] However, we do not suggest that the parents be required to satisfy the burdensome clear and convincing standard. Rather, in those cases in which evidence concerning future harm is inconclusive, courts should have discretion to expand the inquiry and consider the therapeutic value of services.[101]

In practice, professionals often do not agree on the likelihood of future harm in a particular case but do agree that intervention is warranted. For example, a mother brought her four-month-old daughter to the Hospital, complaining that the child's leg appeared misshapen. An examination revealed a congenital hip deformity. The infant underwent surgery to correct the deformity and had to wear a body cast to allow proper healing. Upon observation of the interaction between mother and daughter in the Hospital, personnel became concerned about the mother's ability to care for the child. The mother occasionally left the bars of the crib down and had difficulty keeping the cast clean. She seemed unable to feed the infant properly and to adjust the frame her daughter required for support. The staff's concern increased because, despite instruction and gentle warning, the mother's behavior did not change after several weeks. In an interview with a social worker, the mother seemed depressed. She denied that she was having difficulty caring for her infant and explained that she needed her daughter because she was "all alone." When the social worker suggested that a home health aide might be helpful after the infant was discharged, the mother protested that she did not want or need any assistance. During the interview, the mother revealed that she had had a poor relationship with her own mother and had been neglected in her childhood. Some members of the Trauma-X Group believed that the infant's need for special care, the mother's inadequate caretaking and her refusal to voluntarily accept assistance placed the child "at risk." While these members advocated court intervention to keep the child out of the home, other members wanted to give the mother a chance to prove herself outside the Hospital. They suggested that the infant could safely be discharged if the Hospital could monitor the child's condition by frequent outpatient visits and if the mother would accept instruction in proper care techniques by a visiting nurse. Although the mother's inattention or carelessness might result in serious injury to the child, no one on the team felt completely comfortable with that prediction. Nevertheless, the entire team advocated intervention based upon shared doubts about the mother's ability to cope with the particular medical problems of the child.

This example suggests the proper criteria by which a court should determine whether to order services. Absent clear evidence that future harm is or is not likely, a court should consider, in addition to the probabilities of future harm, whether the specific services proposed are directed toward and are likely to remedy the particular problem that gave rise to the endangerment and whether the services are beneficial to the family. In the example, the mother's inability to handle the child's treatment gave rise to the endangerment. Services directed toward training and supervising her in the proper care of the child's condition could prevent any future harm that might otherwise occur. Moreover, training in the treatment required by the child's particular condition, as well as in feeding, hygiene and safety generally, could benefit the entire family and improve both the mother's self-image and her relationship with her daughter.

An inquiry into the general therapeutic value of services alone is subject to criticisms similar to those directed at the "best interests of the child" test. Admittedly, a court can find some general benefits in almost any proposed service. Accordingly, we would narrowly limit the court's discretion to consider therapeutic value. A broader inquiry into the therapeutic value of services is triggered only after the petitioner has established a case of endangerment, and then only if the parents' proof that future endangerment is unlikely is insufficient. Moreover, general therapeutic value alone would never be sufficient to justify intervention; proof of specific remedial efforts with regard to the particular endangering problem must be required.

2. Termination of Services. The Standards mandate review every six months regarding "whether the conditions still exist that required initial intervention."[102] Unless the conditions still exist, the court must terminate jurisdiction. If the parents state at the six-month hearing that intervention is no longer necessary, the agency must demonstrate a need to continue.[103] Moreover, at the end of eighteen months of court supervision, the court must terminate jurisdiction unless "there is clear and convincing evidence that the child is still endangered or would be endangered if services were withdrawn."[104] This call for careful, periodic review of the necessity for intervention will help prevent continuances that are based upon perfunctory hearings or that result from forgetfulness of the court or agency.[105] However, by conditioning assistance beyond eighteen months upon "clear proof" of a necessarily uncertain prediction, court jurisdiction may often end before the family situation has stabilized.

The termination provisions retain the unfortunate, narrow focus of the jurisdictional grant for initial intervention. In doing so, the Standards fail to distinguish between the significantly different potential harms caused by initial and continuing intervention. The benefits of continued services in the home will more often outweigh the intrusive effects. The benefits of services often multiply over time as relationships with social workers are strengthened and initial hostility is overcome. As parents develop confidence in their child-caring abilities, their progress will advance more rapidly. Moreover, the intrusive effect of continued supervision is not a multiple of the harm to parental autonomy caused by the initial intervention. The initial outside intervention into the home causes the stigma and most severely undermines parental authority over the child. This shift in the balance justifies a broadened inquiry into the therapeutic value of continued intervention. In fact, therapeutic value is entitled to more weight in the context of termination than was appropriate in the decision whether to intervene initially. Although no intrusion should continue longer than necessary, the determination of necessity in termination hearings should not turn solely upon proof by the intruding party that the child will suffer physical or emotional harm. The mere fact that a child will not be reinjured at the particular moment does not suggest that the family no longer requires judicial monitoring or social welfare intervention. Once the court intervention has begun, jurisdiction should continue until the family can no longer benefit from support and until they have confronted basic problems.[106] In effect, we suggest that the goal of continuing intervention is broader than that of initial intervention. Initial intervention should be primarily, although not exclusively, directed toward protecting against future harm. After the initial intrusion has occurred, continued intervention should be directed toward giving the family the tools to deal with their problems in the remote as well as in the immediate future. Unfortunately, the commentary specifically rejects this broader purpose; the court is directed to continue services only if necessary to protect the child and not solely because services are "useful."[107]

We also disagree with the timing of court review under the Standards. In our clinical experience, we have found that eighteen months is insufficient to cement short-term prophylactic gains into long-term prophylactic and therapeutic benefits for the entire family.[108] For example, the clinic at Children's Hospital examined a girl, aged five, for gross developmental delays and scattered bruises. Her mother had seemed anxious and depressed. Her father had acknowledged enormous rage at his daughter and uncontrollable impulses to harm her. Pursuant to statutory mandate, the Hospital filed a child abuse case report. The report effected neither change in the family's behavior nor advancement in the child's developmental progress. New bruises were evident upon subsequent examinations. The Hospital filed a court complaint, requesting that physical custody remain with the parents while the state was acting to acquire legal custody. The Hospital staff hoped that court supervision would assure that the parents would follow through with a treatment program designed to resolve many of the family conflicts that had apparently culminated in the father's anger toward his child. The court granted the petition. Now, two years after the initial hearing, the parents participate—although somewhat reluctantly—in a family treatment program in the local court clinic. The father receives regular doses of a major tranquilizer. There have been no further incidents of injury to the child. The daughter is making excellent developmental progress with the support of a specially designed academic program. Without court monitoring and services, family decompensation and reinjury might well occur. Moreover, the parents probably would not voluntarily request continued services. For these reasons, and because the family appears to benefit generally from the treatment, the state has recently urged a six-month continuance of the case. Under the Standards, however, the state might well fail to demonstrate by clear and convincing evidence that future harm would occur if court supervision terminated.

III. A Grant of Jurisdiction to Order Removal
for Serious Harm

We share with the drafters of the Standards a distaste for removal of the child from the home. Removal must be a remedy of last resort because of its tremendous potential for harm to the child[109] and its total invasion of the parent's right to custody and control. Thus, we approve of the Standards' narrow jurisdictional grant to order removal. Removal is available only if the child has suffered or there is a substantial risk that he will imminently suffer serious harm *and* if it is necessary to protect against future harm.[110] In addition, removal must be the only means of protecting the child.[111] It is because we concur with these severe limitations upon the court's power to order removal that we have urged significantly broader power to order services. Services should be more available because, as even the commentary suggests, services can often remedy a dangerous family situation and thus prevent the need for removal in the future.[112] Therefore, our criticism of the present draft of the Standards has focused upon the unwise limitations upon the power of courts to order services. However, we do suggest certain amendments to the present removal scheme. First, courts should have the power to remove a child suffering serious physical harm, even though the harm is caused by environmental conditions beyond the parent's control. Second, courts should have the power to extend parental rights to a removed child beyond the termination date required by the Standards, if the agency or the parent presents clear evidence of the parent's progress toward the goal of reunification of the family.

A. Removel in Cases of Serious Physical Harm Caused
by Environmental Conditions

The commentary to the Standards declares that the only purpose of court-ordered intervention is "to protect the child from future harm, not to punish parents or to provide ongoing supervision of families where the child is endangered."[113] To further this purpose, the Standards condition all court intervention primarily upon whether the child has suffered harm. This condition is deliberately intended to shift the focus away from an examination of parental fault.[114] The commentary suggests that a court can intervene when a child has suffered serious physical injuries, even though the cause is unexplained and the parents' responsibility remains unproven.[115] Consistent with this emphasis on harm rather than parental fault, the commentary states that a court may intervene when the child's injuries are a result of the parent's mental illness, alcoholism, or drug addiction. The commentators offer this suggestion with the explicit awareness that these problems are often beyond the parent's control and are a result of social conditions.[116]

There is, however, one instance in which the Standards depart from this principle of intervention for harm without regard to parental fault.[117] A court is specifically prohibited from ordering removal of a child suffering serious harm caused by environmental conditions that are beyond the parents' control.[118] If the parents are willing but unable to remedy such conditions, a court cannot order removal regardless of the quantum of danger to the child. Yet the Standards do permit a court to order *services* in this situation,[119] despite the commentary's general disapproval of any coercive intervention to remedy "societal neglect." The only apparent reason for this inconsistency is that the drafters recognize that a court order may be a necessary precondition to delivery of services requisite to correct dangerous conditions.

We disagree with this departure by the Standards from its own principle of disregard of parental fault.[120] We share the commentators' reluctance to punish parents and invade their fundamental right to raise their child when "societal neglect" is the real culprit. The parents are as much victims of their poverty as are the children. If the Standards had selected punishment as the goal, intervention in cases of faultless parents would be clearly inappropriate. However, because that goal was rejected and protection alone was adopted, such intervention will be warranted in some cases. As unfair as removal is to the parents, failure to remove may cause serious harm, even death, to the child. Thus, failure to remove the child from harm because of the parents' innocence is contrary to the Standards' explicit recognition that the child's interest must supersede the parents'.[121]

The Standards predicate removal on harm to the child and, in general, embrace this principle without regard to the family's socioeconomic level. Children of the poor are no less deserving of state protection to assure their safety than are children of the affluent. Yet, in recognizing the necessity of intervention in cases of serious harm, the Standards concede that such intervention is likely to occur more often in low-income families.[122] Data have established a significant correlation between poverty and neglect[123] and have suggested a more disputed correlation between poverty and abuse.[124] Even if this causal link is refuted, harm to poor children is more likely to be discovered because all aspects of the lives of poor families are subject to the constant scrutiny of public clinics and welfare workers.[125] Intervention because of the parent's mental illness, alcoholism, or drug addiction, which the commentary declares permissible, gives rise to similar class disparities in enforcement. A poor parent laboring under one of these disabilities is more likely to come to the attention of state authorities. Moreover, these disabilities may often be a result of the parent's poverty.[126] Apparently, the Standards tolerate intervention when poverty is an indirect cause of harm but not when it is a direct cause.[127] This distinction is without substance and merely disguises the disturbing reality that the state will continue to intervene more often in poor than nonpoor families.

Situations requiring removal despite the parent's innocence will be extremely rare. In the vast majority of cases, services will solve the problem. In particular, the new approach to treatment that focuses upon the family's external needs is likely to increase the success rate of services.[128] For example, if a child is not receiving proper nourishment because of the parent's meager financial resources, food stamps would provide an easy remedy. If a child is suffering from rat bites or lead paint poisoning, the parents or state housing and health officials could file complaints against the landlord in court;[129] if necessary, new housing could be found.[130] If a child is continually suffering severe beatings at the hands of neighborhood gangs, and if the police were unable to prevent these incidents, the entire family could be moved out of the area.

If parents refuse to move out of an unsafe neighborhood or home, a court has the power to order removal of the child under the Standards. However, even if the parent is willing, no public housing may be available at that time. Even though the child cannot otherwise be protected from very serious physical harm, a court does not have the power to remove the child under the Standards. We suggest that a court should be able to order temporary removal until safe housing is found. We cannot conceive of an analogous case in which permanent removal would be necessary. Removal here is simply a stopgap measure until the inadequacy of the community's provision of shelter is remedied.

In addition to limitations upon the duration of removal in these cases, limitations upon the type of harm triggering removal should be imposed. Obviously, massive relocation of families because their children suffer the typical, terrible harms of urban blight and poverty cannot be achieved under the child protection power. To permit removal on the basis of environmental conditions, the harm must be even more severe than in normal instances of removal. Removal should also be restricted to cases of actual physical harm. Because of the indefinite nature of emotional harm, its identification entails subjective, value-laden judgments,[131] and the attendant danger that removal will become a wholesale weapon against the poor is too great. Similarly, the child must actually be suffering or must recently have suffered serious physical harm; a substantial risk of imminent harm should not be sufficient. The inherent uncertainty of predictive judgments, especially in the absence of past harm,[132] offers too many opportunities for injection of class biases.

Because the Standards predicate removal on whether the harm was caused by parental neglect or by environmental conditions beyond the parent's control, the petitioner would have an additional element to prove.[133] Apparently, the petitioner would have to show either that environmental conditions did not cause the harm, or, if they did, that the parent was unwilling to take the steps necessary to correct them. Unfortunately, the boundaries of parental control are not distinct.[134] Thus, the remedy of removal may be unduly denied in many cases of parental neglect because the petitioner has failed to satisfy his burden of proof.

We offer an illustration from our clinical files of how a single family history may present conflicting evidence of parental control. A mother gave birth seven weeks prematurely to a three-pound nine-ounce son. The infant remained in the Hospital one month because of lack of oxygen at birth, bloody stools and mild jaundice. After discharge from the Hospital, the infant was scheduled to have pediatric follow-up on a biweekly basis, but the mother failed to keep the appointments at a community health center. Two months passed before a visiting nurse found the mother and child at home. During the visit, the mother seemed depressed and complained about poor housing conditions. The nurse wrote in her notes: "Living room was completely dark despite the bright sunshine ... dirty dishes were piled in the sink, dirty clothes on the floor ... roaches were observed in the infant's crib." The nurse further noted that the mother did not interact with her youngster. The mother described herself as a good caretaker and her son as "slow." Examination revealed that the infant's physical development was in fact well below average; on the growth chart, the child was below the third percentile for height, weight and head circumference. The mother continued to miss appointments at the clinic. During the appointments she did keep, the staff observed that the infant seemed apathetic; he offered little response to his social environment and had made few developmental gains. At the clinic, the infant repeatedly drank four to eight ounces of water, an indication of hunger. When questioned about her son's eating habits, the mother replied that baby food and milk were too expensive on her welfare allowance. Although this case would probably not require removal to protect against harm,[135] it manifests the difficulties in discerning whether the poor housing conditions and the child's poor nutrition were a result of the family's inexorable poverty or the mother's neglect. However, the present draft of the Standards would require courts to determine if the mother was at fault. Such an inquiry is not only impractical but also contrary to the Standards' focus upon prevention of harm.

B. Termination of Parental Rights

Once the child is removed, the Standards permit the child's need to achieve stability and continuity in parenting[136] to dominate efforts to reunite the family. The Standards provide for automatic termination of the parents' rights if the child cannot safely be returned home at the end of a specified period of time. The court must terminate parental rights at the end of six months of foster care if the child is under three at the time of placement, and at the end of one year if the child is over three.[137] This represents a reversal of the priorities the Standards mandate for return of the child after shorter periods of removal.

In effect, this termination provision codifies two generalizations. First, the Standards assume that, as time passes, children are likely to form strong new parental attachments while the old ones weaken. Second, the Standards assume that the number of families in which the danger of harm has subsided sufficiently to permit the child's return decreases over time.[138] To limit judicial discretion and avoid unnecessary extensions of this harmful limbo, the Standards select an arbitrary deadline for termination.

The Standards do, however, provide some room for judicial discretion. The parent's rights will not be terminated if the court finds by clear and convincing evidence that the case fits within one of the exceptions provided.[139] The most important exception requires the court to extend the parent's rights if, "because of the closeness of the parent-child relationship, it would be detrimental to the child to terminate parental rights...."[140] Thus, the parents have an opportunity to rebut the first generalization of the Standards concerning the progressive weakening of attachments to the old parents. However, the Standards do not provide a similar opportunity to rebut the second generalization concerning the progressive failure of rehabilitation. Our clinical experience indicates that, because enough instances of rehabilitation occur over periods longer than the Standards recognize, another exception is warranted.[141] Six months to a year is often insufficient time for an agency to induce significant attitudinal and behavioral improvements and for the court and the agency to evaluate the family's caretaking capacity and the potential safety of the home.[142] The agency providing services to the parents or the parents themselves should have an opportunity to submit evidence of substantial progress. If no significant evidence is presented, the court should terminate the parents' rights. This opportunity to rebut the Standards' presumption that the family cannot be safely reunited in the near future is demanded by the Standards' express goal of revitalizing and reuniting the family[143] and by the absolute nature of the court's contemplated action.

Even if this exception for progress in treatment were to be incorporated, there would still be substantial dangers in the termination scheme. Courts will be aware of the possible consequences of a finding of neglect or abuse and of a decision to remove the child. Quite naturally, if one likely consequence is the automatic termination of the parents' rights, courts might hesitate in making the initial finding or in ordering removal even in cases that warrant both steps.[144] Particularly when the substantive rules in this area are by nature elusive, courts will often be able to characterize the same set of facts as either sufficient or insufficient grounds for jurisdiction or removal. Thus, this termination scheme might result in a court finding either that fewer cases are within its jurisdiction or appropriate for removal, or that more cases are within the exceptions to automatic termination. If the former were to occur, many suffering children would be deprived of state protection. If the latter were to occur, the termination provision's limitations upon judicial discretion would amount to a confusing fiction. To avoid these results, the Standards should simply call for review every six months regarding the advisability of continuing the parents' rights and the possibility of return. The Standards should guide the judge's discretion by listing relevant factors, such as the closeness of the natural parents and the child and the progress the family is making toward a safe return. Admittedly, this open-ended review might result in some harmful postponements of the inevitable break.[145] In exchange, however, this arrangement could prevent some untimely and tragic terminations of parental rights.

IV. Revision of the Pre-Court Involvement in the Family: The Reporting Process

The major contemporary reform of the child protection system has been the nationwide enactment of mandatory reporting of child abuse.[146] The Standards have proposed a reporting mechanism that is consistent with the drafters' emphasis upon preventing unwarranted intrusions into the family. The Standards impose a duty upon professionals, including medical personnel, educators, childcare workers, social workers and law-enforcement personnel, to report cases of serious physical abuse.[147] Failure to report by designated professionals constitutes a misdemeanor and gives rise to civil liability.[148] The Standards provide these professionals with immunity from civil and criminal liability in cases in which they report in good faith.[149] Under the reporting scheme, the professional files the report with a designated agency—the report recipient agency.[150] That agency initiates a limited investigation,[151] files notice of the report with a central registry[152] and may file a court complaint.[153]

Surprisingly, the type of harm that must be reported—serious physical abuse—is narrower than the type of harm that constitutes grounds for court intervention. Additionally, the power of the report recipient agency to investigate the report before a complaint is filed in court is more limited than the agency's power to investigate after filing. Thus, the Standards have failed to recognize that outside intervention in the form of reporting is far less intrusive[154] and results in far less stigma to the parents than court action.[155] In adopting this narrow reporting provision, the drafters have again failed to exploit the opportunity to prevent very intrusive state intervention in the future by increasing the availability of less intrusive means of intervention. Reporting can prevent the need to file court action because the agency may discover upon intervention that the child was not abused or that intervention is unnecessary. Moreover, to the extent that it manifests or perhaps prompts the concern of persons outside the home,[156] the report may be the catalyst for voluntary improvements in the family situation.[157] Accordingly, we suggest that the reporting scheme be significantly expanded.

A. Permissive Reporting

The reporting provision of the Standards addresses only mandatory reporting. Nonprofessionals are explicitly exempted from a duty to report. Yet nonprofessionals, such as neighbors, friends, or relatives, have the most intimate, unguarded contact with the family and thus can frequently discover abuse before professionals. The commentary states that the Standards implicitly adopt "permissive" reporting by nonprofessionals.[158] Because of their superior knowledge, these persons must be more actively encouraged to come forward.[159] However, we do not favor mandatory reporting because it would give rise to difficulties in policing and to destructive interference with intimate relationships among friends and relatives. Rather, the Standards should explicitly provide that these persons are encouraged to report, that they will receive a good faith immunity and that their reports will trigger the Standards' agency process.[160] It is important that the Standards clearly establish permissive reporting because the authority of the commentary will vary with the scope of each state's enactment. In addition, explicit recognition of permissive reporting would force the Standards to establish mechanisms to control the increased likelihood of malicious reporting. Presumably, nonprofessionals are more likely than professionals to misuse the reporting system, possibly as a means to malign their acquaintances or relatives. Accordingly, the Standards should establish civil or criminal liability for malicious reports and should require the recipient agency to question the nonprofessional reporter with particular care during the investigation.[161]

B. Reporting Neglect

The present draft limits mandatory reporting to cases involving abuse. Only serious physical harm inflicted nonaccidentally must be reported.[162] Nonphysical, nonabuse categories of "endangerment" that are included in the jurisdictional grant are explicitly excluded from the reporting scheme.[163] Neither the Standards nor the commentary clarify whether permissive reporting of nonabuse endangerment will trigger the advantages of mandatory reporting, including immunity, agency processing and central registry. If the excluded categories of endangerment cannot be processed through the reporting system, the Standards would effectively make filing a complaint in court the exclusive route for bringing these harms to the attention of authorities.

The Standards never explain this apparent preference for processing allegations of nonabuse endangerment through the courts. Indeed, because of the publicity and stigma associated with juvenile courts, this preference seems antithetical to the Standards' concern for the interests of the parents. Under the provisions for court proceedings, anyone may file any complaint of harm[164] and receive good faith immunity.[165] An "intake processing agency" of the court screens the complaint and, without a hearing, orders either dismissal, judicial disposition, or referral to a report recipient agency.[166] Thus, an allegation of nonabuse endangerment is acted upon initially by an intake processing agency rather than a report recipient agency.[167]

We disagree with this utilization of the intake agency in cases of nonabuse endangerment. The qualifications of the intake agency are never articulated in the Standards. In contrast, the Standards institute quality control of the report recipient agency, outlining criteria that an agency must satisfy to become a "qualified" agency and providing for its disqualification if the agency later proves inadequate.[168] The only controls on the intake agency are through the promulgation of guidelines for disposition of complaints[169] and through judicial review.[170] The guidelines do not necessarily guarantee intelligent or competent handling of cases. A report recipient agency, which has direct contact with families and is in the business of providing services and investigating these types of cases, is better able to evaluate the existence and cause of harm and the need for and availability of intervention.[171] An illustration of the incompetency of some intake officials is furnished by an extreme case from our clinical files. A mother brought her eight-year-old child, his body covered with bruises, to Children's Hospital. The mother admitted that she had hit her son and that she still had an uncontrollable urge to hurt him. She asked that the child be temporarily placed outside the home. Because no voluntary foster placement was available, the Hospital attempted to initiate a care and protection petition in court. The clerk refused authorization of the petition because it was Christmas and "every child belongs with his mother."

Clearly, guidelines for and judicial review of the officer's decision would be ineffective to protect the child from immediate harm in the above case. In addition, the scope of judicial review of the intake officer's action may not be broad enough under the Standards to provide adequate safeguards against abuse of discretion. Apparently, the Standards provide for appeal only of an intake officer's disposition of a sufficient complaint—either dismissal, judicial disposition, or referral to an agency. The language of the Standards suggests that no appeal may be taken from an officer's dismissal of a complaint based upon a finding of insufficiency.[172] Given the necessarily ambiguous grounds for court intervention, an officer could easily abuse his power to dismiss complaints because of insufficiency. In that case, the petitioner is left without recourse.

Therefore, we not only urge that the initial screening task be delegated to the more qualified report recipient agency, but also suggest that a person filing a complaint have the right to judicial review of an intake official's determination of insufficiency.

The deliberate omission of neglect from the mandatory reporting system is the most distressing aspect of the Standards' reporting provision.[173] Initially, the commentators cite the systematic bias of reporting against poor and minority families as a justification for the omission.[174] They make the simplistic calculation that the broader the scope of reporting, the greater the effect of this bias. However, the authors themselves note that this bias infects the reporting of abuse.[175] In fact, they admit that no evidence suggests that permitting reporting of neglect has aggravated the class and race disparities of reporting.

The Standards enumerated three additional reasons for refusing to include child neglect among the harms that must be reported. First, the Standards cite the present inadequate availability of services.[176] Second, it is suggested that including neglect within the reporting system potentially damages the opportunity for successful psychotherapy. The final reason advanced in support of the narrow reporting scheme is the fear that reporting will become a legislative "panacea" that merely substitutes for a meaningful commitment of resources.[177] Significantly, none of these justifications applies exclusively to cases involving child neglect; rather, each applies equally to cases involving child abuse. Thus, because the Standards mandate reporting only in cases of abuse, we must conclude that the drafters believe that abuse is more harmful than neglect. In fact, the commentators do imply that abuse is more damaging.[178] No sound distinction can be premised upon supposed differences in the danger to the child in cases of abuse rather than neglect.[179] Indeed, a child's life can be equally, and frequently even more, endangered by parental neglect.[180] If such a distinction is valid, it is surprising that the Standards treat neglect and abuse identically in the jurisdictional grant.[181] Although a child can be removed from his home based upon parental neglect, a professional who becomes aware of that neglect need not report it. Thus, the Standards again seem to encourage the more intrusive form of state intervention.

Because of both the equivalent danger to the child from neglect and the reporting system's potential for avoiding the need for court intervention, we suggest including neglect as a proper subject of mandatory reporting.[182] The Standards should be revised to provide explicitly that a report of neglect will be protected by the good faith immunity, will be recorded in the central registry and will be the subject of prompt agency investigation. As in cases of abuse, nonprofessionals should have the opportunity, but not the duty, to report neglect. Furthermore, the Standards should still impose a duty to report harm resulting from *suspected* neglect. Because of the imprecise nature of neglect, however, professionals should not be subject to criminal liability for failure to report suspected cases. On the other hand, knowing failure to report should subject professionals to civil liability. This modified duty is imposed upon the professional because his repeated contact with these types of cases gives him the expertise requisite to this kind of judgment.

The basic definition of neglect could be imported from the jurisdictional grant and would include harm resulting from "conditions created" by the parents and from the parents' failure to "adequately supervise or protect" the child.[183] For purposes of reporting, neglect could also include failure to provide needed medical treatment, even though the jurisdictional grant only covers the parents' refusal to provide such treatment.[184] By including neglect, the Standards, in effect, would modify the definition of reportable abuse.[185] The Standards presently provide for report of injuries "inflicted nonaccidentally." Conceivably, cases in which the injury was accidental might now be reportable because of the parent's failure to supervise and protect the child against accidents.[186] For example, a one-year-old child ingested a small quantity of bleach from a bottle that the parents had left on the kitchen floor. The youngster was treated at Children's Hospital and released after the staff warned the family of the safety hazards in the home. Less than a month later, the child was again admitted to the Hospital for ingestion of liquid furniture polish "accidentally" left in the living room. The physician filed a report of neglect. This case illustrates the difficulty in drawing the line between accidental and nonaccidental injury.[187] These diagnostic difficulties might well result in many cases in an unwarranted decision not to report.[188] Moreover, the distinction between accidental and nonaccidental injury has no significance with regard to the child's future safety when the accident is part of a pattern of neglect.[189] Thus, the problems involved in reporting only nonaccidental injuries argue in favor of expanding mandatory reporting to include neglect.

C. Expanding the Definition of Reportable Abuse

The Standards require reporting of actual abuse only.[190] Professionals are not required to report cases in which no serious harm has yet occurred, even if there exists a "substantial risk that a child will imminently suffer" serious harm. Thus, mandatory reporting of abuse will occur significantly later in the family history than will court intervention. In addition, the gravity of harm that triggers a report is the same as the gravity required for court intervention; the injury must cause or risk causing "death, disfigurement, impairment of bodily functioning, or other serious physical injury." Both the narrower time factor and the identical level of harm frustrate the primary purpose of reporting and ignore its less intrusive nature. Ideally, reporting should operate as an early warning system. Child abuse can take the form of a single traumatic injury, but a more typical pattern is a series of attacks that escalate in severity.[191] Reporting

should be directed toward identifying the early harbingers of more severe injury
so that agencies can provide assistance on a voluntary basis and avert both the
need for court intervention and the danger of infliction of more serious
harm.[192] Thus, the same reasons for allowing court intervention for nonserious
harm have added force in the context of a warning system.

Ironically, the Standards design a warning system that excludes mandatory
reporting of imminent harm. Apparently, a professional would not even be
required to report an unsuccessful attempt at abuse. We frequently encounter
cases of attempt at Children's Hospital. For example, a mother brought her child
to the Hospital because the father had thrown a glass vase at the toddler.
Fortunately, the child was unhurt, but that fact did not prevent the social
service worker from filing a report. Protection of a child should not hinge upon
his luck.

In fact, the commentary cites the example of an unsuccessful attempt as
reason to include imminent harm in the jurisdictional grant, despite the
increased danger of unwarranted intervention when no actual harm has occurred.[193] A fortiori, these identity dangers are outweighed when the type of
state intervention—reporting—has substantially less intrusive effects upon the
family. In providing a recipient agency with discretion to file a court complaint
based upon a report, the Standards clearly contemplate that reporting will not
necessarily result in court action.[194] Thus, the intrusive nature of reporting is
distinct from that of its possible but not inevitable consequence—court
action.[195] Reporting will involve agency investigation into the allegations and
into the family situation. But, according to the Standards, even that investigation is circumscribed.[196] Any provision of services at this stage would be on a
voluntary basis. Furthermore, public access to the report should be forbidden in
contrast to the guaranteed public access to the courtroom. Privacy is further
safeguarded by the expunction of all unsubstantiated and stale reports.[197] In
sum, this limited intrusive effect is outweighed by the unique opportunity
reporting offers for preventing abuse and court intervention.

We also suggest that only professionals be required to report imminent
harm. A report of imminent harm made by nonprofessionals should not trigger
the provisions for immunity, investigation and notice to the central registry. The
difficult judgment about the likelihood of future harm may be beyond the
competency of most nonprofessionals. Additionally, limiting mandatory reporting of imminent harm to professionals would avoid unwarranted or maliciously
motivated reporting and would avoid overburdening the report recipient agency
with dubious reports.

In one significant respect, the Standards broaden the ground for reporting
abuse beyond that for jurisdiction. Abuse inflicted by the "parent(s) or
person(s) exercising essentially equivalent custody and control over the
child"[198] must be reported, whereas only abuse inflicted by the parent
constitutes grounds for court intervention.[199] If abuse is inflicted by a regular

nonparent caregiver, the court may be able to intervene because of the parent's failure to supervise or protect the child.[200] Because neglect is omitted from the reporting mandate, a more inclusive definition of the perpetrator of abuse was necessary. However, we think the Standards should have gone further and permitted reporting of abuse inflicted by anyone. A reporter may not be in a position to discover who inflicted the harm and whether an abuser's relationship to the child was that of parental equivalent.[201] If the reporter is required to make that threshold determination, he may incorrectly decide not to report if he is uncertain of the identity and status of the perpetrator. Moreover, the Standards' limitation to those exercising parent-like custody and control might exclude many abusers who have regular access to the child. For example, this language may not require reporting of abuse by the mother's boyfriend, a sibling, or a babysitter, who regularly are in the home but do not necessarily exercise parent-like custody and control.[202] Courts may interpret this language to include only permanent nonparent guardians or relatives. Reporting of all harm without regard to the identity of the perpetrator is desirable.[203] If the agency discovers that, because of the status of the perpetrator, future abuse is unlikely, the agency will not proceed with court action.[204] Nevertheless, this difficult determination should be made by the agency based upon investigation and not by the reporter.

D. Expanding the Scope of Agency Investigation

Under the Standards, a report recipient agency may be called upon to conduct an investigation at two stages of a case—after it has received a report,[205] and after a sufficient complaint has been filed and the court has authorized an investigation.[206] The scope of the second investigation is broader than the first in one significant feature; with court authorization, the agency may take temporary custody of the child to facilitate questioning if the parents have denied the agency access.[207] Conversely, an agency investigating a report cannot examine the most crucial witness and evidence[208]—the child—without first obtaining court authorization.[209] Apparently, to obtain this authorization the agency must file a formal complaint with the court.[210] The commentary suggests that the parents' refusal of access would constitute "reason to believe" that the child was abused and that intervention was necessary. Thus, refusal would provide grounds for filing.[211]

This provision sacrifices an important benefit of reporting—avoiding the need for court action. As previously suggested, court action entails greater publicity, stigma and intrusion into the family's life. The advantage of reporting is that, through preliminary investigation and voluntary provision of services, the number of instances in which court action is necessary can be reduced.[212] By limiting the scope of the investigation at the reporting stage, the agency will be

forced to file in order to obtain the informa
court action is appropriate. This dilemma is
information exists in many cases of neglect a
information itself may be a sign of danger. Tl
may be caused by the family's isolation from
agencies, which is a characteristic of abusing and n
tively, the lack of information may suggest that th
avoid detection. The fact that the parents have neve.
outsiders may also indicate that they have not conscic
the reality of their conduct. Thus, the net effect of
investigation will be that the agency will file court actions
if they could have fully investigated prior to filing.

Admittedly, granting the agency power to compel exan.
rary custody of the child without initial court supervision r
to unwarranted intrusions.[214] Great harm to the child may result from
questions implicating the child's parents in mistreatment.[215] However, judicial
control of agency abuse would continue because the agency would still have to
apply to the court for enforcement of its subpoena.[216] Although we concede
that such judicial oversight does not eliminate the potential for harm, we doubt
the efficacy of the Standards' more rigid court supervision. Courts cannot
control the crucial element—the sensitivity of each investigator.[217] In sum, the
necessity and usefulness of increased, initial court control is outweighed by the
advantages of a full-scale investigation preceding court involvement.[218]

V. Conclusion

Our critique of the Standards attempts to preserve the advantages of the present
draft—the focus on harm to the child rather than on the parent's conduct,
respect for the family unit, specificity of the statutory language, and restraint on
the power to remove a child from the home—while expanding the occasions for
state intervention. In our opinion, the Standards fail to appreciate and exploit
the different degrees of intrusion into the family caused by reporting, court-
ordered services and removal. Additionally, the Standards do not recognize and
maximize the prophylactic potential of reporting and the therapeutic potential
of services. To correct these errors, our proposal calls for both reporting of cases
of nonserious harm and court jurisdiction to order services for children suffering
such harm.

The awareness and careful study of the problem of neglected and abused
children over the past fifteen years has culminated in a mandate to legislatures to
enact broad reforms of the system of state intervention. The Standards present
one response. However, the Standards fail to capitalize on this special time when
confident and creative rethinking is both needed and desired. At bottom, the

drafters were so painfully aware of past mistakes and present limitations that they were unwilling to aim for something better in the future. Instead, their effort is directed solely toward minimizing the harm of state involvement rather than toward promoting the benefits. The negative assumptions of the Standards do not keep pace with the advances in understanding, diagnosis and treatment of harmed children and their parents. We believe the essentially defeatist approach of the Standards is both unwise and unnecessary for legislatures contemplating ways to improve the present system.

Notes

1. *Cf.* J. Goldstein, A. Freud & A. Solnit, Beyond the Best Interests of the Child 106 (1973). Public responses to a survey evinced this contradictory reaction: 36 percent of those surveyed favored removal of the child after the first incident of abuse, 53.9 percent of those surveyed favored nonremoval to give the parent a second chance. D. Gil, Violence Against Children 65 (1973).

2. Institute of Judicial Administration & American Bar Association, Joint Commission on Juvenile Justice Standards, Standards Relating to Abuse and Neglect (tent. ed. 1977) (R. Burt & M. Wald, Reporters) [hereinafter cited as IJA/ABA Standards].

3. IJA/ABA Standards pt. III.

4. *Id.* pt. IV.

5. *Id.* pts. II, V-VIII.

6. *Id.* pt. IX.

7. *Id.* pt. X.

8. *Id.* pt. 1.1.

9. Indeed, the Standards refuse to mandate affirmative duties of child care. Instead, the Standards specify only those harms that parents must not cause or permit. Thus, the child has no right to an "ideal" family that will furnish the best opportunity for growth. *See* IJA/ABA Standards, Commentary, p. I, at 37, 38, 42; *Id.,* Commentary, pt. 2.1, at 49 [hereinafter cited as Commentary]. In fact, under the Standards, the child's rights to adequate care and protection are realized only when the parents have committed gross acts of abuse or neglect. *Contra,* IJA/ABA Standards 182 (Nuernberger, dissenting). *See generally* S. Katz, When Parents Fail 55-57 (1971); Fraser, The Child and His Parents: A Delicate Balance of Rights, *in* Child Abuse and Neglect: The Family and the Community 324-29 (R. Helfer & C. Kempe eds. 1976). The Standards refuse to go any further because of a lack of consensus on what constitutes adequate child care and a fear that any consensus would ignore healthy cultural biases. IJA/ABA Standards pt. 1.4; Commentary 44.

10. *See* Stanley v. Illinois, 405 U.S. 645, 658 (1972); Prince v. Massachusetts, 321 U.S. 158, 170 (1944); Fraser, *supra* note 9, at 326.

11. IJA/ABA Standards, Introduction at 3.

12. In some cases, this may not be the "biological parent" but rather the "psychological parent." J. Goldstein, A. Freud & A. Solnit, *supra* note 1, at 19.

13. *See* J. Bowlby, Child Care and the Growth of Love 8 (2d ed. 1965); Burt, Developing Constitutional Rights of, in and for Children, 39 Law & Contemp. Prob. 118, 127 (1975).

14. For a list of state statutes explicitly adopting this preference for the home, see Mnookin, Child Custody Adjudication: Judicial Functions in the Face of Indeterminacy, 39 Law & Contemp. Prob. 226, 243 n.83 (1975).

15. *See* A. Kadushin, Child Welfare Services 257 (2d ed. 1974); S. Katz, *supra* note 9, at 52.

16. IJA/ABA Standards pt. 1.5; *accord,* J. Goldstein, A. Freud & A. Solnit, *supra* note 1, at 7.

17. *See* S. Katz, *supra* note 9, at 4; Mnookin, Foster Care: In Whose Best Interest?, 43 Harv. Ed. Rev. 599, 603 (1973).

18. Commentary 45.

19. *Id.*; J. Goldstein, A. Freud & A. Solnit, *supra* note 1, at 7.

20. IJA/ABA Standards p. 1.2.

21. Commentary 38-39.

22. *See, e.g.,* J. Bowlby, *supra* note 13, at 85.

23. *See, e.g., In re* Roya, 255 Cal. App. 2d 260, 267-68, 63 Cal. Rptr. 252, 256-57 (Ct. App. 1967); *In re* Cager, 251 Md. 473, 479, 284 A.2d 384, 388 (1968); State v. Geer, 311 S.W.2d 49, 52 (Mo. Ct. App. 1958).

24. *See* Burt & Balyeat, A New System for Improving the Care of Neglected and Abused Children, 53 Child Welfare 167 (1974); Newberger, Hagenbuch, Ebeling, Colligan, Sheehan & McVeigh, Reducing the Literal and Human Cost of Child Abuse: Impact of a New Hospital Management System, 51 Pediatrics 840 (1973).

25. IJA/ABA Standards 184 (Polier, dissenting).

26. *Id.* pt. 2.1.

27. *Id.*

28. *Id.* pt. 2.1 (B); *accord, id.* pts. 2.1(A) & (E).

29. *Id.* pt. 2.1(C).

30. *Id.* pt. 2.2.

31. *See id.* at 181 (Nuernberger, dissenting).

32. *See* Commentary 38, 43.

33. One of the co-reporters for the Standards, Professor Robert Burt, has similarly suggested that adjudication and disposition alternatives should not be considered separately. *See* Burt, Forcing Protection on Children and Their Parents: The Impact of *Wyman v. James,* 69 Mich. L. Rev. 1259, 1286 (1971).

34. *See* Daly, Willful Child Abuse and State Reporting Statutes, 23 U. Miami L. Rev. 283, 318, 343 (1969) (favors reporting of nonserious harm).

35. Commentary 49.

36. *Id.* at 53-54. Recent data has shown that, of reported incidents of physical injuries allegedly caused by abuse, 51.3 percent were considered minor and only 2.4 percent constituted major physical abuse. American Humane Ass'n, National Study on Child Neglect and Abuse Reporting 4 (1977).

37. *See generally* Sussman, Reporting Child Abuse: A Review of the Literature, 8 Fam. L.Q. 245, 268 (1974).

38. Commentary 55.

39. Based on clinical experience, some experts have suggested that the parent's voluntary acceptance of intervention may actually represent an unhealthy submissiveness manifested as a psychiatric ego defense. Steele & Pollock, A Psychiatric Study of Parents Who Abuse Infants and Small Children, *in* The Battered Child 125 (2d ed. R. Helfer & C. Kempe 1974).

40. *See* Commentary 167; Levine, *Caveat Parens:* A Demystification of the Child Protection System, 35 U. Pitt. L. Rev. 1, 11-13 (1973).

41. Parents rarely make direct, voluntary requests. Alexander, The Social Worker and the Family, *in* Helping the Battered Child and His Family 22-23 (C. Kempe & R. Helfer eds. 1972); DeFrancis, Child Protection—A Comprehensive Coordinated Process, Fourth National Symposium on Child Abuse, October, 1973, at 8 (The American Humane Ass'n, Children's Div. 1975).

42. *See* Steele & Pollock, *supra* note 39, at 125.

43. Davoren, The Role of the Social Worker, *in* The Battered Child, *supra* note 39, at 138, 144.

44. A. Kadushin, *supra* note 15, at 242.

45. *Id.* at 251, 165, *quoting* C. Hancock, Digest of a Study of Protective Services and the Problem of Neglect of Children in New Jersey 8 (1958).

46. *Accord.* IJA/ABA Standards 185 (Polier, dissenting); Polier & McDonald, The Family Court in an Urban Setting, *in* Helping the Battered Child and His Family, *supra* note 41, at 208, 221; Terr & Watson, The Battered Child Rebrutalized: Ten Cases of Medical-Legal Confusion, 124 Am. J. Psych. 1432, 1438 (1968); Wald, State Intervention on Behalf of "Neglected" Children: A Search for Realistic Standards, 27 Stan. L. Rev. 985, 1000 (1975).

47. Additionally, experts state that the social worker may resist dealing with the abusive side of the parent/patient. Holmes, Barnhart, Cantoni & Reymer, Working with the Parent in Child-Abuse Cases, 56 Social Casework 3, 5-6 (1975). This refusal based on the social worker's own make-up suggests another reason why a court order may be a prerequisite for provision of services.

48. Commentary 54-55.

49. IJA/ABA Standards, Introduction at 4; Commentary 43.

50. The Standards' assumption that services will be provided on a voluntary basis is clear. IJA/ABA Standards pt. 1.1; Commentary 38, 43. In situations in which the services of social workers are in fact only available through court intervention, one distinguished commentator urged early intervention. Paulsen, Law and Abused Children, *in* The Battered Child, *supra* note 39, at 153, 169.

51. IJA/ABA Standards pt. 3.3(A).

52. *Id.* pts. 5.2(C), (F), 6.2, 6.5, 7.1.

53. *Id.* pt. 5.2 (authorization of investigation); *id.* pt. 5.2(C) (approval of investigation plan); *id.* pt. 5.3 (report); *id.* pt. 6.1 (disposition).

54. *Id.* pt. 7.1.

55. *Id.* pt. 1.8; Commentary 47.

56. Select Comm. on Child Abuse, N.Y. State Assembly, Report, April 1972, *reprinted in* The Battered Child, *supra* note 39, at 229, 246 (app. c).

57. DeFrancis, *supra* note 41, at 13.

58. *See generally* DeFrancis, The Status of Child Protective Services, A National Dilemma, *in* Helping the Battered Child and His Family, *supra* note 41, at 127, 131-36.

59. IJA/ABA Standards 184 (Polier, dissenting). *Contra,* Wald, State Intervention on Behalf of "Neglected" Children: Standards for Removal of Children from Their Homes, Monitoring the Status of Children in Foster Care, and Termination of Parental Rights, 28 Stan. L. Rev. 625, 642 (1976) (supporting "realist's" approach).

60. *See* IJA/ABA Standards 186 (Polier, dissenting) ("benign neglect" by state).

61. *Id.* pt. 1.5

62. *Id.*

63. Commentary 42-43.

64. Wald, *supra* note 46, at 996-1000. The author expressly disclaims that the views expressed there are those of the Juvenile Justice Standards Commission. *Id.* at 985.

65. *Id.* at 996-97.

66. *Id.* at 999.

67. *Id.* at 998 n.73.

68. *See, e.g.,* N. Polansky & N. Polansky, The Current Status of Child Abuse and Child Neglect in this Country, Report to the Joint Comm'n on Mental Health for Children (1968), *quoted in* D. Gil, *supra* note 1, at 43-47; The Multi-Problem Dilemma: A Social Research Demonstration with Multi-Problem Families (G. Brown ed. 1968); Fischer, Is Casework Effective? A Review, 18 Social Work 5 (1973); Geismar, Implications of a Family Life Improvement Project, 52 Social Casework 455 (1971).

69. *See, e.g.,* A. Kadushin, *supra* note 15, at 106-15, 269-71; 2 S. White, Federal Programs for Young Children: Review and Recommendations 275-76 (1973); Burt & Balyeat, *supra* note 24; Morse, Hyde, Newberger & Reed, Environmental Correlates of Pediatric Social Illness: Preventive Implications of an Advocacy Approach, 67 Am. J. Pub. Health 612 (1977); Newberger, Hagenbuch, Ebeling, Colligan, Sheehan & McVeigh, *supra* note 24; Steele & Pollock, *supra* note 39, at 131.

70. *See* Wald, *supra* note 46, at 978 n.73.

71. *See* Burt, *supra* note 13, at 127-28; *cf.* Wald, *supra* note 46, at 999 n.86.

72. Professor Wald even concedes that social services are successful despite initial hostility. Wald, *supra* note 59, at 658.

73. Polansky, DeSaix & Sharlin, Child Neglect: Understanding and Reaching the Parent 58 (1972).

74. Commentary 60.

75. IJA/ABA Standards pt. 2.1(C). The Standards further define the specific manifestations constituting serious harm as "severe anxiety, depression, or withdrawal, or untoward aggressive behavior toward self or others." We share one expert's hesitancy to freeze the definition into a statute because of the present state of our knowledge about development. S. Katz, *supra* note 9, at 68. In addition, as the commentary also suggests, the definition must be read in the context of the different stages of development at different ages. Commentary 57. However, fixing specific attributes in the statute may produce static rather than developmental interpretations. For example, courts working with the definition may ignore the fact that what constitutes "untoward aggressive behavior" at one age may be quite normal at another.

76. *See generally* Newberger & Hyde, Child Abuse, Principles and Implications of Current Pediatric Practice, 22 Pediatric Clinics of North America 695 (1975); Newberger, Hagenbuch, Ebeling, Colligan, Sheehan & McVeigh, *supra* note 24.

77. Morse, Hyde, Newberger & Reed, *supra* note 69.

78. *Cf.* Burt, *supra* note 33, at 1285.

79. *See* Select Comm. on Child Abuse, N.Y. State Assembly, *supra* note 56, at 251-52; Edelman, The Massachusetts Task Force Reports: Advocacy for Children, 43 Harv. Ed. Rev. 639 (1973).

80. *See* D. Gil, *supra* note 1, at 147; DeFrancis, *supra* note 58, at 138-39; Holmes, Barnhart, Cantoni & Reymer, *supra* note 47, at 12. *See generally* Joint Comm'n on the Mental Health of Children, Crisis in Child Mental Health; Challenge for the 1970's, at 9-21 (1970).

81. *See* Newberger, Newberger & Richmond, Child Health in America: Toward a Rational Public Policy, 54 Milbank Memorial Fund Q./Health & Soc'y 249 (1976).

82. *See* National Research Council, National Academy of Sciences, Toward a National Policy for Children and Families (1976).

83. Another reason for broadened court intervention to effectuate the coordinated approach to treatment has been suggested by clinicians. Terr & Watson, *supra* note 46, at 1439.

84. IJA/ABA Standards, Introduction at 6; Commentary 50; *cf.* S. Katz, *supra* note 9, at 63-67.

85. D. Gil, *supra* note 1, at 5-6; S. Katz, *supra* note 9, at 64.

86. IJA/ABA Standards 185-86 (Polier, dissenting).

87. *Id.* pt. 2.2. In part 5.3(E)(2), the Standards place the burden on the petitioner to prove by clear and convincing evidence allegations sufficient to support the petition. Presumably, this includes the jurisdictional requirement of future endangerment.

88. *See* Commentary 117-19.

89. *Id.* 119.

90. *See* Mnookin, *supra* note 17, at 614, 627-28.

91. The commentary discusses the replacement of the "best interests" test at the dispositional phase. Commentary 120. However, for both jurisdiction and disposition, the Standards substitute similar tests of the necessity of intervention to protect against future harm. IJA/ABA Standards pts. 2.2 & 6.4. Thus, discussion of the substitution of the "best interests" test is equally appropriate at the jurisdictional phase. For a citation of the states that have adopted the "best interests" test for dispositions in their statutes or case law, see Mnookin, *supra* note 14, at 253 n.81.

92. Commentary 121-22; Mnookin, *supra* note 14, at 249-62; Mnookin, *supra* note 17, at 613-22.

93. Commentary 121; Mnookin, *supra* note 14, at 269.

94. Mnookin, *supra* note 14, at 253-54.

95. *See* Commentary 63.

96. D. Gil, *supra* note 1, at 113; Child Abuse and Neglect Project Educ. Comm'n of the States, National Center for the Prevention and Treatment of Child Abuse and Neglect, Child Abuse and Neglect: Model Legislation for the States 2 (1976); *see* Weston, The Pathology of Child Abuse, *in* The Battered Child, *supra* note 39, at 79-85.

97. *Cf.* Koel, Failure to Thrive and Fatal Injury as a Continuum, 118 Am. J. Diseases of Children 51 (1969).

98. *Cf.* Wald, *supra* note 46, at 1010 n.137.

99. *See* Commentary 113 (similar problems of proof constitute basis for rejecting "beyond a reasonable doubt standard").

100. Although the language of the Standards would support denying jurisdiction unless the petitioner satisfies the burden of proof, the commentary implies a shift of the burden to the parents. Commentary 63-64. The commentary lists examples of when a child may have suffered a specific, serious harm but, nonetheless, intervention is unnecessary to prevent future harm. First, when the abuse represented an isolated moment of anger, future incidents are not as likely. Second, a court should deny jurisdiction when the family situation has undergone material, long-term alteration since the time the petition was filed. For example, the parent's failure to supervise the child while the parent was at work may have been corrected by the provision of day care services on a voluntary basis. Third, when intervention may do more harm than good, the court should not proceed. In effect, the commentary offers examples of instances in which the parents would be able to satisfy the burden of proof that

intervention is unnecessary. The fact that the information required by these examples is more likely within the parents' knowledge provides further reason for placing the burden upon the parents.

101. The commentary's third example of when not to intervene despite a showing of "endangerment"—when intervention may do more harm than good—suggests that inquiry into therapeutic value is appropriate. As an illustration, the commentary refers to a case of sexual abuse in which there is no evidence that future abuse is likely, the counseling resources are limited and the family seems to be handling the problem adequately. *Id.* at 64.

102. IJA/ABA Standards pt. 7.4(A).

103. Commentary 141.

104. IJA/ABA Standards pt. 7.4(C).

105. *See id.* pt. 7.1; Commentary 136.

106. *See* Pollock & Steele, A Therapeutic Approach to the Parents, *in* Helping the Battered Child and His Family, *supra* note 41, at 20.

107. Commentary 141.

108. *See* Pollock & Steele, *supra* note 106; Roth, A Practice Regimen for Diagnosis and Treatment of Child Abuse, 54 Child Welfare 268, 273 (1975). *See also* Kempe & Helfer, Innovative Therapeutic Approaches, *in* Helping the Battered Child and His Family, *supra* note 41, at 46 (success of treatment by visiting nurses never realized before eighth or ninth month).

109. *See* Mnookin, *supra* note 14, at 270-72; Wald, *supra* note 59, at 644-46.

110. IJA/ABA Standards pts. 2.1 & 2.2.

111. *Id.* pt. 6.4(C)(1)(2).

112. Commentary 118; *see* Mnookin, *supra* note 14, at 272; Wald, *supra* note 59, at 647-48.

113. Commentary 63.

114. *Id.* at 39.

115. *Id.* at 53; *see* Paulsen, *supra* note 50, at 157.

116. Commentary 53.

117. *Id.* at 55.

118. IJA/ABA Standards pt. 6.4(C)(4).

119. Commentary 54-55, 128-29.

120. *Accord,* IJA/ABA Standards 183 (Nuernberger, dissenting).

121. *Id.* pt. 1.5; Commentary 45.

122. *See* Dembitz, Child Abuse and the Law—Fact and Fiction, 24 Record of N.Y.C.B.A. 613, 623 (1969); Sussman, Reporting Child Abuse: A Review of the Literature, 8 Fam. L.Q. 245, 262 (1974). Professor Michael Wald, co-reporter of the Standards, has similarly suggested that the system's discrimination against the poor and its failure to provide services pending removal of the child should not prohibit temporary or permanent placement of the child when necessary. Wald, *supra* note 59, at 692 n.269.

123. *See, e.g.,* A. Kadushin, *supra* note 15, at 246-47; S. Katz, *supra* note 9, at 24-25; Boehm, The Community and the Social Agency Define Neglect, 43 Child Welfare 459 (1964).

124. *See, e.g.,* D. Gil, *supra* note 1, at 113, 129, 136 (suggests link between poverty and abuse). *But see* A. Kadushin, *supra* note 15, at 250 (suggests more random distribution, abuse related to personality factors); Light, Abused and Neglected Children in America: A Study of Alternative Policies, 43 Harv. Ed. Rev. 556, 562-67 (1973) (questions validity of Gil's statistics); Newberger & Daniel, Knowledge and Epidemiology of Child Abuse: A Critical Review of Concepts, 5 Pediatric Annals 140 (1976) (same).

125. S. Katz, *supra* note 9, at 28-29; *see* Areen, Intervention Between Parent and Child: A Reappraisal of the State's Role in Child Neglect and Abuse Cases, 63 Geo. L.J. 887, 892-93 (1975) (suggests that professionals may inject social class bias into diagnosis of cause of injury); Paulsen, Juvenile Courts, Family Courts, and the Poor Man, 54 Calif. L. Rev. 694 (1966).

126. S. Katz, *supra* note 9, at 25.

127. For discussion of poverty as an indirect cause of neglect, see Wald, *supra* note 59, at 692 n.268.

128. *See* notes 76-77 and accompanying text *supra.*

129. Morse, Hyde, Newberger & Reed, *supra* note 69, at 5.

130. *See, e.g., id.* at 7.

131. *See* Commentary 56.

132. *See* Wald, *supra* note 46, at 1003-04 & n.109.

133. *See* IJA/ABA Standards pt. 6.4(C)(5) (burden of proof on those advocating removal on all issues).

134. *See generally* Morse, Hyde, Newberger & Reed, *supra* note 69.

135. Removal might be an appropriate remedy in this case even though the Standards' requirement that it be the only means to prevent future harm would not necessarily be satisfied. IJA/ABA Standards pt. 6.4(C)(1)(2); Commentary 123. A combined showing of the distinct possibility of specific harm and the incidence of an acute mental or physical crisis in the parent's life could conceivably justify removal for a very short time limited to the period of crisis. The stress brought on by divorce, death in the family, severe illness—perhaps even the immediate weakened condition of the mother in this case after a difficult birth—may make the parent less able to cope with the demands of child rearing at that time. This added strain, along with a child's illness or the parent's lack of understanding of child development, are all contributing factors to abuse. *Cf.* Holmes, Barnhart, Cantoni & Reymer, *supra* note 47, at 11. However, even a brief period of separation of a child from the mother may disrupt the bond of attachment and result in subsequent development disability. Klaus & Kennell, Mothers Separated from Their Newborn Infants, 17 Pediatric Clinics of North America 1015 (1975); Sameroff & Chandler, Reproductive Risk and the Continuum of

Caretaking Casualty, *in* Review of Child Development Research (F. Horowitz ed. 1975). Thus, temporary removal to relieve the stress of an acute crisis should be the exception and not the rule.

136. IJA/ABA Standards pt. 1.6.

137. *Id.* pts. 8.3(A) & (B).

138. *Cf.* Commentary 155; N. Polansky & N. Polansky, *supra* note 68 (return after abuse, a rare exception).

139. IJA/ABA Standards pt. 8.4.

140. *Id.* pt. 8.4(A).

141. *Accord,* N. Polansky & N. Polansky, *supra* note 68 (predicts years rather than months before a severely neglected child can be safely returned home).

142. Clinicians have noted pseudo-rapid improvement by parents in treatment. Pollock & Steele, *supra* note 106, at 17. This progress could mask the more enduring problems unless observation is continued for an extended period of time.

143. IJA/ABA Standards pt. 1.5.

144. Paulsen, The Legal Framework for Child Protection, 66 Colum. L. Rev. 679, 699-700 (1966); Wald, *supra* note 59, at 675-76.

145. *See* Mnookin, *supra* note 14, at 281.

146. Commentary 65.

147. IJA/ABA Standards pts. 3.1(A) & (B).

148. *Id.* pt. 3.1(D).

149. *Id.* pt. 3.1(C).

150. *Id.* pt. 3.2(A).

151. *Id.* pt. 3.3(A).

152. *Id.* pt. 3.4.

153. *Id.* pt. 3.3(C).

154. For a graphic illustration of the different magnitudes of intrusion resulting from reporting and court intervention, see A. Schuchter, Child Abuse Intervention 74 (1976).

155. Burt, *supra* note 33, at 1270.

156. *See* A. Kadushin, *supra* note 15, at 240-41.

157. *See, e.g.,* S. Katz, *supra* note 9, at 30-33 (case study).

158. Commentary 65.

159. Lucht, Providing a Legislative Base for Reporting Child Abuse, *in* Fourth National Symposium on Child Abuse, *supra* note 41, at 54-55. A survey indicated that 45.6 percent of neighbors that learn of an incident of abuse would report it to the local welfare agency. D. Gil, *supra* note 1, at 63. In a close-knit community, the censure of neighbors, relatives and friends has traditionally operated as the primary tool of social control over parental misconduct. A. Kadushin, *supra* note 15, at 223. The reporting system should promote that social mechanism because it is effective in preventing misconduct and because it incorporates local values.

160. Six states have adopted this combination of mandatory and permissive reporting. *See* V. DeFrancis & C. Lucht, Child Abuse Legislation in the 1970's, at 22-23 (1974). New York explicitly enacted permissive reporting to curb the practice of the state social services agency of refusing to process all nonmandatory reports. Select Comm. on Child Abuse, N.Y. State Assembly, *supra* note 56, at 234. Processing through the reporting system triggers the dual advantages of prompt agency action and filing in the central registry. Admittedly, the utility of the central registry to track families is in dispute. Whiting, The Central Registry for Child Abuse Cases: Rethinking Basic Assumptions, 56 Child Welfare 761, 763 (1977) (not effective). *Contra,* Freedman, The Need for Intensive Follow-up of Abused Children, *in* Helping the Battered Child and His Family, *supra* note 41, at 85. Two recent proposals for reporting legislation have also expressly advocated permissive reporting by nonprofessionals. Child Abuse and Neglect Project Educ. Comm'n of the States, *supra* note 96, p. III; *id.* at 16-17 (commentary); A. Schuchter, *supra* note 154, at 111.

161. Lucht, *supra* note 159, at 54-55.

162. IJA/ABA Standards pt. 3.1(B).

163. Commentary 65-66.

164. IJA/ABA Standards pt. 5.1(A)(1).

165. *Id.* pt. 5.1(A)(3).

166. *Id.* pt. 5.1(B).

167. *See* A. Schuchter, *supra* note 154, at 56 (suggests that public health agency act as the primary screener of reports and that medical institution act as the primary gatekeeper to the courts, rather than relying upon law enforcement or judicial personnel); *cf.* Paulsen, *supra* note 50, at 169.

168. IJA/ABA Standards pts. 3.2(B) & (C); Commentary 71, 75.

169. IJA/ABA Standards pt. 5.1(B)(3).

170. *Id.* pt. 5.1(B)(4).

171. *Id.* pt. 5.1(B)(2)(a)-(c).

172. *Compare id.* pt. 5.1(B)(1) ("disposition" of a sufficient complaint) *with id.* pt. 5.1(B)(4) (appeal of agency's "disposition").

173. Only eleven states do not require reporting of neglect in any form. Katz, Howe & McGrath, Child Neglect Laws in America, 9 Fam. L.Q. 1, 63 (1975).

174. Commentary 66; *see* Levine, *supra* note 40, at 4-5.

175. *See* Areen, *supra* note 125, at 888.

176. Commentary 66-67. It is indeed "foolish business" for legislatures to require reporting but fail to provide adequate funds for services following a substantiated report. Paulsen, Child Abuse Reporting Laws: The Shape of Legislation, 67 Colum. L. Rev. 1, 3, 49 (1967); *see* DeFrancis, *supra* note 41, at 143-45. Rather than designing an inadequate reporting system, however, the Standards' drafters should adopt a comprehensive system that is not circumscribed by meaningless distinctions between neglect and abuse. At the same

time, the system should incorporate in its design a mandate for legislative commitment to services. For example, the Standards could create a right to services in the parents that is triggered by a substantiated report and that is judicially enforceable. In addition, if the report recipient agency failed to respond with the necessary investigation and provision of services within a specified time, a court could order the destruction of the report and any record of it in the central registry.

177. Commentary 66-68.

178. *See id.* at 67 (dangers of abuse sufficient to override risk of harm to therapy relationship between parents and reporter).

179. Paulsen, *supra* note 50, at 164-65 (need to report malnutrition due to parental inattention equivalent to need to report abuse).

180. Note, An Appraisal of New York's Statutory Response to the Problem of Child Abuse, 7 Colum. J.L. & Soc. Prob. 51, 52 (1971). For a horrifying description in words and pictures of deaths of and severe injuries to children due to parental neglect, see Weston, *supra* note 96, at 69-74.

181. IJA/ABA Standards pt. 2.1. However, the Standards do distinguish abuse from nonabuse in the level of proof required to support a disposition of removal. *Id.* pt. 6.4(C)(1) (abuse—preponderance of the evidence); *id.* pt. 6.4(C)(2) (nonabuse—clear and convincing evidence). However, this distinction is based upon the more speculative nature of predictions about future harm in neglect cases and, more importantly, the greater likelihood of successful services intervention in the home. Commentary 126. It is not based upon any false distinction in the severity of harm.

182. *Accord,* Child Abuse and Neglect Project Educ. Comm'n of the States, *supra* note 96, pt. II(2); Lucht, *supra* note 159, at 50 (supports reporting neglect); Paulsen, *supra* note 50, at 164-65 (supports reporting of malnutrition); *see* A. Schuchter, *supra* note 154, at 5 (notes trend toward including neglect in reporting); *cf.* A. Sussman, Reporting Child Abuse and Neglect: Guidelines for Legislation 72 (1975) (notes that recent federal legislation seems to anticipate reporting of both abuse and neglect in state statutes).

183. IJA/ABA Standards pt. 2.1(B).

184. *Id.* pt. 2.1(E).

185. *Id.* pt. 3.1(B).

186. *See* Paulsen, *supra* note 50, at 164 (supports reporting); Sussman, *supra* note 122, at 252 (same).

187. *Cf.* Gregg & Elmer, Infant Injuries: Accidents or Abuse?, 44 Pediatrics 434 (1969).

188. Daly, *supra* note 34, at 319; Paulsen, *supra* note 176, at 49; Wald, *supra* note 46, at 1010 & n.135.

189. *See* V. Fontana, Somewhere a Child is Crying 23-29 (1973) ("maltreatment syndrome"); Newberger, The Myth of the Battered Child Syndrome, 40 Current Medical Dialogue 327 (1973), *reprinted in* Annual Progress in Child

Psychiatry and Child Development, 1974, at 569 (S. Chess & A. Thomas eds. 1975).

190. IJA/ABA Standards pt. 3.1(B).

191. *See* note 96 *supra.*

192. Child Abuse and Neglect Project Educ. Comm'n of the States, *supra* note 96, pts. II(2) & (3); *id.* at 13-14 (commentary); *see* Daly, *supra* note 34, at 318, 343; McCoid, The Battered Child and Other Assaults upon the Family (pt. 1), 50 Minn. L. Rev. 1, 50-51 (1965). *Contra,* Paulsen, *supra* note 50, at 164.

193. Commentary 52.

194. IJA/ABA Standards pt. 3.3(C); Commentary 74-75.

195. *See* note 154 *supra.*

196. IJA/ABA Standards pt. 3.3(B).

197. *Id.* pt. 3.3(D).

198. *Id.* pt. 3.1(B).

199. *Id.* pt. 2.1(A).

200. *See* Commentary 54 (examples three and four).

201. *See* Paulsen, *supra* note 50, at 164 (notes problem of identifying wrongdoer; suggests no duty to report if noncaretaker).

202. Gil's statistics demonstrated that the mother's boyfriend accounted for 17.2 percent of reported injuries and the babysitter for 2.7 percent. D. Gil, *supra* note 1, at 129.

203. Child Abuse and Neglect Project Educ. Comm'n of the States, *supra* ne 96, pt. II(2) (definition of reportable abuse does not specify identity of perpetrator); *cf.* Wald, *supra* note 46, at 1003. *But see* A. Sussman, *supra* note 182, at 67 (reporting of injuries caused by regular caretaker but not occasional paramour).

204. *Cf.* Wald, *supra* note 46, at 1003 n.109.

205. IJA/ABA Standards pt. 3.3(A).

206. *Id.* pt. 5.2(B)(1).

207. *Id.* pt. 5.2(E)(1).

208. *See* Schneider, Pollock & Helfer, Interviewing the Parents, *in* Helping the Battered Child and His Family, *supra* note 41, at 62.

209. IJA/ABA Standards pt. 3.3(B).

210. *See id.* (reference to court authorization pursuant to the filing of a complaint).

211. Commentary 74.

212. *Cf.* Burt, *supra* note 33, at 1283-85 (notes agency's need for widest access to information). *But see* note 214 *infra.*

213. S. Katz, *supra* note 9, at 25; Davoren, *supra* note 43, at 140.

214. For criticism of the Supreme Court's failure to require a warrant for an at-home visit by a welfare worker, Wyman v. James, 400 U.S. 309 (1971), see Burt, *supra* note 33. The author suggests that issuance of warrants in child protection cases be based upon "reasonableness" grounds. *Id.* at 1306-08.

215. *See* Commentary 100; Wald, *supra* note 46, at 1006. Professor Burt, co-reporter for the Standards, has argued against recognition of a fifth amendment privilege against self-incrimination for the child. Burt, *supra* note 33, at 1288-306.

216. The problems of delegation of reporting, investigating and prosecuting powers to private agencies is beyond the scope of this article. The commentary suggests that the Standards provide for sufficient state controls to satisfy delegation requirements. Commentary 72.

217. *See generally* Goldberg, Breaking the Communication Barrier: The Initial Interview with an Abusing Parent, 54 Child Welfare 274 (1975) (techniques for sensitive interviewing).

218. *Cf.* Paulsen, *supra* note 50, at 169. We have similar doubts about the value of tight court control over the investigation after court action has been initiated. The Standards require court approval of a plan of investigation. IJA/ABA Standards pt. 5.2(C). Binding the agency to its initial plan and forcing the agency to come back for authorization of any new avenues of investigation is both unrealistic and a waste of judicial and agency resources. *See id.* at 182 (Nuernberger, dissenting). Typically, an agency will not be able to identify the sources and means of investigation until after it has commenced an investigation. Prior investigations will be available only when court action was initiated by a report recipient agency. Expansion of the present statutory guidelines for the investigation could substitute for close judicial scrutiny.

Another waste of resources is found in the Standards' provision for the appointment of experts, at public expense, at the request of any party. *Id.* pt. 5.3(B). The expert is intended as "an independent evaluation" of the agency's investigation and recommendations. *Id.* Our experience indicates that experts in child protection proceedings are often counterproductive. The courtroom becomes a forum for the experts to do battle over child protection issues of high emotional charge and based upon underdeveloped theories. The discussion will often stray onto irrelevant conflicts of professional turf, status and prerogative. The phenomenon of "cross-sterilization of the disciplines" also may develop. Frankfurter, Introduction, *in* A. Whitehead, The Aims of Education (1949). Rather than fostering a fruitful exchange of information from the many disciplines involved in child protection, each profession too easily resolves its uncertainty by reference to a dubious truth in another. A typical example of cross-sterilization in child protection proceedings is the recommendation of further psychiatric consultation merely to avoid the difficult custody questions before the court. Thus, we suggest that, to avoid the cost of experts, both financial and substantive, the Standards should place more emphasis upon broadening the scope of the agency's investigation; increasing the time, money and care with which the investigation is prepared; and providing for rigorous cross-examination in court of the investigator and his sources of information.

11 The Medicalization and Legalization of Child Abuse

Eli H. Newberger and
Richard Bourne

Child abuse has emerged in the last fifteen years as a visible and important social problem. Although a humane approach to "help" for both victims of child abuse and their families has developed (and is prominently expressed in the title of one of the more influential books on the subject[29]), a theoretical framework to integrate the diverse origins and expressions of violence toward children and to inform a rational clinical practice does not exist. Furthermore, so inadequate are the "helping" services in most communities, so low the standard of professional action, and so distressing the consequences of incompetent intervention for the family that we and others have speculated that punishment is being inflicted in the guise of help.[3,28]

What factors encourage theoretical confusion and clinical inadequacy? We propose that these consequences result, in part, from medical and legal ambiguity concerning child abuse and from two fundamental, and in some ways irreconcilable, dilemmas about social policy and the human and technical response toward families in crisis. We call these dilemmas *family autonomy versus coercive intervention* and *compassion versus control.*

This paper will consider these dilemmas in the context of a critical sociologic perspective on child abuse management. Through the cognitive lens of social labeling theory, we see symptoms of family crisis, and certain manifestations of childhood injury, "medicalized" and "legalized" and called "child abuse," to be diagnosed, reported, treated, and adjudicated by doctors and lawyers, their constituent institutions, and the professionals who depend on them for their social legitimacy and support.

We are mindful, as practitioners, of the need for prompt, effective, and creative professional responses to child abuse. Our critical analysis of the relationship of professional work to the societal context in which it is embedded is meant to stimulate attention to issues that professionals ignore to their and their clients' ultimate disadvantage. We mean not to disparage necessary efforts to help and protect children and their families.

How children's rights—as opposed to parents' rights—may be defined and

Presented, in part, at the Second World Conference of the International Society on Family Law, June 1977, in Montreal. Partially supported by a grant from the Office of Child Development, DHEW (Project OCD-CB-141).

protected is currently the subject of vigorous, and occasionally rancorous, debate.

The *family autonomy vs. coercive intervention* dilemma defines the conflict central to our ambiguity about *whether* society should intervene in situations of risk to children. The traditional autonomy of the family in rearing its offspring was cited by the majority of the U.S. Supreme Court in its ruling against the severely beaten appellants in the controversial "corporal punishment" case (*Ingraham vs. Wright et al.*).[25] The schools, serving *in loco parentis*, are not, in effect, constrained constitutionally from any punishment, however cruel.

Yet in California, a physician seeing buttock bruises of the kind legally inflicted by the teacher in the Miami public schools risks malpractice action if he fails to report his observations as symptoms of child abuse (*Landeros vs. Flood*).[32] He and his hospital are potentially liable for the cost of the child's subsequent injury and handicap if they do not initiate protective measures.[7]

This dilemma is highlighted by the recently promulgated draft statute of the American Bar Association's Juvenile Justice Standards Project, which, citing the low prevailing quality of protective child welfare services in the U.S., would sharply restrict access to such services.[28] The Commission would, for example, make the reporting of child neglect discretionary rather than mandatory, and would narrowly define the bases for court jurisdiction to situations where there is clear harm to a child.

Our interpretation of this standard is that it would make matters worse, not better, for children and their families.[3] So long as we are deeply conflicted about the relation of children to the state as well as to the family, and whether children have rights independent of their parents', we shall never be able to articulate with clarity *how* to enforce them.

The *compassion vs. control* dilemma has been postulated and reviewed in a previous paper,[47] which discussed the conceptual and practical problems implicit in the expansion of the clinical and legal definitions of child abuse to include practically every physical and emotional risk to children. The dilemma addresses a conflict central to the present ambiguity about *how* to protect children from their parents.

Parental behavior that might be characterized as destructive or criminal were it directed towards an adult has come to be seen and interpreted by those involved in its identification and treatment in terms of the psychosocial economy of the family. Embracive definitions reflect a change in the orientation of professional practice. To the extent to which we understand abusing parents as sad, deprived, needy human beings (rather than as cold, cruel murderers) we can sympathize with their plight and compassionately proffer supports and services to aid them in their struggle. Only with dread may we contemplate strong intervention (such as court action) on the child's behalf, for want of alienating our clients.

Notwithstanding the humane philosophy of treatment, society cannot, or will not, commit resources nearly commensurate with the exponentially increasing number of case reports that have followed the promulgation of the expanded definitions. The helping language betrays a deep conflict, and even ill will, toward children and parents in trouble, whom society and professionals might sooner punish and control.

We are forced frequently in practice to identify and choose the "least detrimental alternative" for the child[21] because the family supports that make it safe to keep children in their homes (homemakers, child care, psychiatric and medical services) are never available in sufficient amounts and quality.

That we should guide our work by a management concept named "least detrimental alternative" for children suggests at least a skepticism about the utility of these supports, just as the rational foundation for child welfare work is called into question by the title of the influential book from which the concept comes, *Beyond the Best Interests of the Child.*[21] More profoundly, the concept taps a vein of emotional confusion about our progeny, to whom we express both kindness and love with hurt.

Mounting attention to the developmental sequelae of child abuse[16,33] stimulates an extra urgency not only to insure the physical safety of the identified victims but also to enable their adequate psychological development. The dangers of child abuse, according to Schmitt and Kempe in the latest edition of the Nelson Textbook of Pediatrics,[53] extend beyond harm to the victim:

> If the child who has been physically abused is returned to his parents without intervention, 5 per cent are killed and 35 percent are seriously reinjured. Moreover, the untreated families tend to produce children who grow up to be juvenile delinquents and murderers, as well as the batterers of the next generation.

Despite the speculative nature of such conclusions about the developmental sequelae of child abuse,[6,10,11] such warnings support a practice of separating children from their natural homes in the interest of their and society's protection. They focus professional concern and public wrath on "the untreated families" and may justify punitive action to save us from their children.

This professional response of control rather than of compassion furthermore generalizes mainly to poor and socially marginal families, for it is they who seem preferentially to attract the labels "abuse" and "neglect" to their problems in the public settings where they go for most health and social services.[36] Affluent families' childhood injuries appear more likely to be termed "accidents" by the private practitioners who offer them their services. The conceptual model of cause and effect implicit in the name "accident" is benign: an isolated, random event rather than a consequence of parental commission or omission.[37,38]

Table 1 presents a graphic display of the two dilemmas of social policy (*family autonomy vs. coercive intervention*) and professional response (*compassion vs. control*). The four-fold table illustrates possible action responses. For purposes of this discussion, it is well to think of "compassion" as signifying responses of support, such as provision of voluntary counseling and child care services, and "control" as signifying such punitive responses as "blaming the victim" for his or her reaction to social realities[49] and as the criminal prosecution of abusing parents.

Child Abuse and the Medical and Legal Professions

The importance of a technical discipline's conceptual structure in defining how it approaches a problem has been clearly stated by Mercer:[34]

> Each discipline is organized around a core of basic concepts and assumptions which form the frame of reference from which persons trained in that discipline view the world and set about solving problems in their field. The concepts and assumptions which make up the perspective of each discipline give each its distinctive character and are the intellectual tools used by its practitioners. These tools are incorporated in action and problem solving and appear self-evident to persons socialized in the discipline. As a result, little consideration is likely to be given to the social consequence of applying a particular conceptual framework to problem solving.

> When the issues to be resolved are clearly in the area of competence of a single discipline, the automatic application of its conceptual tools is likely to go unchallenged. However, when the problems under consideration lie in the interstices between disciplines, the disciplines concerned are likely to define the situation differently and may arrive at differing conclusions which have dissimilar implications for social action.

What we do when children are injured in family crises is shaped also by how our professions respond to the interstitial area called "child abuse."

"Medicalization"

Though cruelty to children has occurred since documentary records of mankind have been kept,[9] it became a salient social problem in the United States only after the publication by Kempe and his colleagues describing the "battered child syndrome."[30] In the four-year period after this medical article appeared, the legislatures of all 50 states, stimulated partly by a model law developed under the aegis of the Children's Bureau of the U.S. Department of Health, Education, and Welfare, passed statutes mandating the identification and reporting of suspected victims of abuse.

Once the specific diagnostic category "battered child syndrome" was applied to integrate a set of medical symptoms, and laws were passed making the syndrome reportable, the problem was made a proper and legitimate concern for the medical profession. Conrad has discussed cogently how "hyperactivity" came officially to be known and how became "medicalized."[5] Medicalization is defined in this paper as the perception of behavior as a medical problem or illness and the mandating or licensing of the medical profession to provide some type of treatment for it.

Pfohl[41] associated the publicity surrounding the battered child syndrome report with a phenomenon of "discovery" of child abuse. For radiologists, the potential for increased prestige, role expansion, and coalition formation (with psychodynamic psychiatry and pediatrics) may have encouraged identification and intervention in child abuse. Furthermore,

> ... The discovery of abuse as a new "illness" reduced drastically the intraorganizational constraints on doctors' "seeing" abuse . . . Problems associated with perceiving parents as patients whose confidentiality must be protected were reconstructed by typifying them as patients who needed help . . . The maintenance of professional autonomy was assured by pairing deviance with sickness . . .

In some ways, medicine's "discovery" of abuse has benefited individual physicians and the profession.

> One of the greatest ambitions of the physician is to discover or describe a "new" disease or syndrome.[24]

By such involvement the doctor becomes a moral entrepreneur defining what is normal, proper, or desirable: he becomes charged "with inquisitorial powers to discover certain wrongs to be righted."[24] New opportunities for the application of traditional methods are also found—for example, the systematic screening of suspected victims with a skeletal X-ray survey to detect previous fractures, and the recent report in the neurology literature suggesting the utility of diphenyl-hydantoin[a] treatment for child abusing parents.[46]

Pfohl's provocative analysis also took note of some of the normative and structural elements within the medical profession that appear to have reinforced a *reluctance* on the part of some physicians to become involved: the norm of confidentially between doctor and patient and the goal of professional auton-omy.[41] For many physicians, child abuse is a subject to avoid.[50]

First, it is difficult to distinguish, on a theoretical level, corporal punish-ment that is "acceptable" from that which is "illegitimate." Abuse may be

---

[a]Dilantin, a commonly-used seizure suppressant.

defined variably even by specialists, the definitions ranging from serious physical injury to nonfulfillment of a child's developmental needs.[13,19,30]

Second, it is frequently hard to diagnose child abuse clinically. What appears on casual physical examination as bruising, for example, may turn out to be a skin manifestation of an organic blood dysfunction, or what appear to be cigarette burns may in reality be infected mosquito bites. A diagnosis of abuse may require social and psychological information about the family, the acquisition and interpretation of which may be beyond the average clinician's expertise. It may be easier to characterize the clinical complaint in terms of the child's medical symptom rather than in terms of the social, familial, and psychological forces associated with its etiology. We see daily situations where the exclusive choice of medical taxonomy actively obscures the causes of the child's symptom and restricts the range of possible interventions: examples are "subdural hematoma," which frequently occurs with severe trauma to babies' heads (the medical name means collection of blood under the *dura mater* of the brain), and "enuresis" or "encopresis" in child victims of sexual assault (the medical names means incontinence of urine or feces).

Third, child abuse arouses strong emotions. To concentrate on the narrow medical issue (broken bone) instead of the larger familial problem (the etiology of the injury) not only allows one to avoid facing the limits of one's technical adequacy, but to shield oneself from painful feelings of sadness and anger. One can thus maintain professional detachment and avert unpleasant confrontations. The potentially alienating nature of the physician-patient interaction when the diagnosis of child abuse is made may also have a negative economic impact on the doctor, especially the physician in private practice.

"Legalization"

The legal response to child abuse was triggered by its medicalization. Child abuse reporting statutes codified a medical diagnosis into a legal framework which in many states defined official functions for courts. Immunity from civil liability was given to mandated reporters so long as reports were made in good faith; monetary penalties for failure to report were established; and familial and professional-client confidentiality privileges, except those involving attorneys, were abrogated.

Professional autonomy for lawyers was established, and status and power accrued to legal institutions. For example, the growth in the number of Care and Protection cases[b] before the Boston Juvenile Court "has been phenomenal in recent years . . . four cases in 1968 and 99 in 1974, involving 175 different

[b]Care and Protection cases are those juvenile or family court actions which potentially transfer, on a temporary or permanent basis, legal and/or physical custody of a child from his biological parents to the state.

children."[44] Though these cases have burdened court dockets and personnel, they have also led to acknowledgement of the important work of the court. The need for this institution is enhanced because of its recognized expertise in handling special matters. Care and Protection cases are cited in response to recommendations by a prestigious commission charged with proposing reform and consolidation of the courts in Massachusetts. Child protection work in our own institution would proceed only with difficulty if access to the court were legally or procedurally constrained. Just as for the medical profession, however, there were normative and structural elements within law which urged restraint. Most important among them were the traditional presumptions and practices favoring family autonomy.

If individual lawyers might financially benefit from representing clients in matters pertaining to child abuse, they—like their physician counterparts—were personally uncertain whether or how to become involved.

> Public concern over the scope and significance of the problem of the battered child is a comparatively new phenomenon. Participation by counsel in any significant numbers in child abuse cases in juvenile or family courts is of even more recent origin. It is small wonder that the lawyer approaches participation in these cases with trepidation.[26]

Lawyers, too, feel handicapped by a need to rely on concepts from social work and psychiatry and on data from outside the traditional domain of legal knowledge and expertise. As counsel to parents, lawyers can be torn between advocacy of their clients' positions and that which advances the "best interest" of their clients' children. As counsel to the petitioner, a lawyer may have to present a case buttressed by little tangible evidence. Risk to a child is often difficult to characterize and impossible to prove.

Further problems for lawyers concerned with child abuse involve the context of intervention: whether courts or legislatures should play the major role in shaping practice and allocating resources; how much formality is desirable in legal proceedings; and the propriety of negotiation as opposed to adversary confrontation when cases come to court.

Conflicts Between Medical and Legal Perspectives

Despite the common reasons for the "medicalization" and the "legalization" of child abuse, there are several areas where the two orientations conflict.

1. *The seriousness of the risk.* To lawyers, intervention might be warranted only when abuse results in serious harm to a child. To clinicians, however, *any* inflicted injury might justify a protective legal response, especially if the child is very young. "The trick is to prevent the abusive case from becoming the

terminal case."[14] Early intervention may prevent the abuse from being repeated or from becoming more serious.

2. *The definition of the abuser.* To lawyers, the abuser might be defined as a wrongdoer who has injured a child. To clinicians, both the abuser and child might be perceived as victims influenced by sociological and psychological factors beyond their control.[17,35]

3. *The importance of the abuser's mental state.* To lawyers, whether the abuser intentionally or accidentally inflicted injury on a child is a necessary condition of reporting or judicial action. So-called "accidents" are less likely to trigger intervention. To clinicians, however, mental state may be less relevant, for it requires a diagnostic formation frequently difficult or impossible to make on the basis of available data. The family dynamics associated with "accidents" in some children (*e.g.*, stress, marital conflict, and parental inattention) often resemble those linked with inflicted injury in others. They are addressed with variable clinical sensitivity and precision.

4. *The role of law.* Attorneys are proudly unwilling to accept conclusions or impressions lacking empirical corroboration. To lawyers, the law and legal institutions become involved in child abuse when certain facts fit a standard of review. To clinicians, the law may be seen as an instrument to achieve a particular therapeutic or dispositional objective (*e.g.*, the triggering of services or of social welfare involvement) even if, as is often the case, the data do support such objectives legally are missing or ambiguous. The clinician's approach to the abuse issue is frequently subjective or intuitive (*e.g.*, a *feeling* that a family is under stress or needs help, or that a child is "at risk"), while the lawyer demands evidence.

Doctoring and Lawyering
the Disease

These potential or actual differences in orientation notwithstanding, both medicine and law have accepted in principle the therapeutic approach to child abuse.

To physicians, defining abuse as a disease or medical syndrome makes natural the treatment alternative, since both injured child and abuser are viewed as "sick"—the one, physically, the other psychologically or socially. Therapy may, however, have retributive aspects, as pointed out with characteristic pungency by Illich:

> The medical label may protect the patient from punishment only to submit him to interminable instruction, treatment, and discrimination, which are inflicted on him for his professionally presumed benefit.[24]

Lawyers adopt a therapeutic perspective for several reasons. First, the rehabilitative ideal remains in ascendance in criminal law, especially in the juvenile and family courts which handle most child abuse cases.[1]

Second, the criminal or punitive model may not protect the child. Parents may hesitate to seek help if they are fearful of prosecution. Evidence of abuse is often insufficient to satisfy the standard of conviction "beyond all reasonable doubt" in criminal proceedings. An alleged abuser threatened with punishment and then found not guilty may feel vindicated, reinforcing the pattern of abuse. The abuser may well be legally freed from any scrutiny, and badly needed social services will not be able to be provided. Even if found guilty, the perpetrator of abuse is usually given only mild punishment, such as a short jail term or probation. If the abuser is incarcerated, the other family members may equally suffer as, for example, the relationship between spouses is undercut and childrearing falls on one parent, or children are placed in foster home care or with relatives. Upon release from jail, the abuser may be no less violent and even more aggressive and vindictive toward the objects of abuse.

Third, the fact that child abuse was "discovered" by physicians influenced the model adopted by other professionals. As Freidson[15] noted:

Medical definitions of deviance have come to be adopted even where there is no reliable evidence that biophysical variables "cause" the deviance or that medical treatment is any more efficacious than any other kind of management.

Weber, in addition, contended that "status" groups (*e.g.*, physicians) generally determine the content of law.[45]

The Selective Implementation of Treatment

Medical intervention is generally encouraged by the Hippocratic ideology of treatment (the ethic that help, not harm, is given by practitioners), and by what Scheff[52] called the medical decision rule: it is better to wrongly diagnose illness and "miss" health than it is to wrongly diagnose health and "miss" illness.

Physicians, in defining aberrant behavior as a medical problem and in providing treatment, become what sociologists call agents of social control. Though the technical enterprise of the physician claims value-free power, socially marginal individuals are more likely to be defined as deviant than are others.

Characteristics frequently identified with the "battered child syndrome," such as social isolation, alcoholism, unemployment, childhood handicap, large family size, low level of parental educational achievement, and acceptance of severe physical punishment as a childhood socializing technique, are associated with social marginality and poverty.

Physicians in public settings seem, from child abuse reporting statistics, to be more likely to see and report child abuse than are those in private practice. As poor people are more likely to frequent hospital emergency wards and clinics,[36] they have much greater social visibility where child abuse is concerned than do people of means.

The fact that child abuse is neither theoretically nor clinically well defined increases the likelihood of subjective professional evaluation. In labeling theory, it is axiomatic that the greater the social distance between the typer and the person singled out for typing, the broader the type and the more quickly it may be applied.[48]

In the doctor-patient relationship, the physician is always in a superordinate position because of his or her expertise; social distance is inherent to the relationship. This distance necessarily increases once the label of abuser has been applied. Importantly, the label is less likely to be fixed if the diagnostician and possible abuser share similar characteristics, especially socioeconomic status, particularly where the injury is not serious or manifestly a consequence of maltreatment.

Once the label "abuser" is attached, it is very difficult to remove; even innocent behavior of a custodian may then be viewed with suspicion. The tenacity of a label increases in proportion to the official processing. At our own institution, until quite recently, a red star was stamped on the permanent medical record of any child who might have been abused, a process which encouraged professionals to suspect child abuse (and to act on that assumption) at any future time that the child would present with a medical problem.

Professionals thus engage in an intricate process of selection, finding facts that fit the label which has been applied, responding to a few deviant details set within a panoply of entirely acceptable conduct. Schur[53] called this phenomenon "retrospective reinterpretation." In any pathological model, "persons are likely to be studied in terms of what is 'wrong' with them," there being a "decided emphasis on identifying the characteristics of abnormality"; in child abuse, it may be administratively impossible to return to health, as is shown by the extraordinary durability of case reports in state central registers.[58]

The response of the patient to the agent of social control affects the perceptions and behavior of the controller. If, for example, a child has been injured and the alleged perpetrator is repentant, a concensus can develop between abuser and labeler that a norm has been violated. In this situation, the label of "abuser" may be less firmly applied than if the abuser defends the behavior as proper. Support for this formulation is found in studies by Gusfield,[22] who noted different reactions to repentant, sick, and enemy deviants, and by Piliavin and Briar,[42] who showed that juveniles apprehended by the police receive more lenient treatment if they appear contrite and remorseful about their violations.

Consequences of Treatment for the Abuser

Once abuse is defined as a sickness, it becomes a condition construed to be beyond the actor's control.[39] Though treatment, not punishment, is warranted, the *type* of treatment depends on whether or not the abuser is "curable," "improvable," or "incurable," and on the speed with which such a state can be achieved.

To help the abuser is generally seen as a less important goal than is the need to protect the child. If the abusive behavior cannot quickly be altered, and the child remains "at risk," the type of intervention will differ accordingly (*e.g.*, the child may be more likely to be placed in a foster home). The less "curable" is the abuser, the less treatment will be offered and the more punitive will society's response appear. Ironically, even the removal of a child from his parents, a move nearly always perceived as punitive by parents, is often portrayed as helpful by the professionals doing the removing ("It will give you a chance to resolve your own problems," etc.).

Whatever the treatment, there are predictable consequences for those labeled "abusers." Prior to diagnosis, parents may be afraid of "getting caught" because of punishment and social stigma. On being told of clinicians' concerns, they may express hostility because of implicit or explicit criticism made of them and their child-rearing practices yet feel relief because they love their children and want help in stopping their destructive behavior. The fact that they see themselves as "sick" may increase their willingness to seek help. This attitude is due at least in part to the lesser social stigma attached to the "sick," as opposed to the "criminal," label.

Socially marginal individuals are likely to accept whatever definition more powerful labelers apply. This definition, of course, has already been accepted by much of the larger community because of the definers' power. As Davis[8] noted:

> The chance that a group will get community support for its definition of unacceptable deviance depends on its relative power position. The greater the group's size, resources, efficiency, unity, articulateness, prestige, coordination with other groups, and access to the mass media and to decision-makers, the more likley it is to get its preferred norms legitimated.

Acceptance of definition by child abusers, however, is not based solely on the power of the labelers. Though some might consider the process "political castration,"[43] so long as they are defined as "ill" and take on the sick role, abusers are achieving a more satisfactory label. Though afflicted with a stigmatized illness (and thus "gaining few if any privileges and taking on some especially handicapping new obligations"[15]) at least they are merely sick rather than sinful or criminal.

Effective social typing flows down rather than up the social structure. For example, when both parents induct one of their children into the family scapegoat role, this is an effective social typing because the child is forced to take their definition of into account.[48] Sometimes it is difficult to know whether an abusive parent has actually accepted the definition or is merely "role playing" in order to please the definer. If a person receives conflicting messages from the same control agent (*e.g.*, "you are sick and criminal") or from different control agents in the treatment network (from doctors who use the sick label, and lawyers who use the criminal), confusion and upset predictably result.[56]

As an example of how social definitions are accepted by the group being defined, it is interesting to examine the basic tenets of Parents Anonymous, which began as a self-help group for abusive mothers.[29]

> A destructive, *disturbed* mother can, and often does, produce through her actions a physically or emotionally abused, or battered child. Present available *help* is limited and/or expensive, usually with a long waiting list before the person requesting help can actually receive *treatment* . . . We must understand that a problem as involved as this cannot be *cured* immediately . . . the problem is *within* us as a parent . . . [emphasis added]

To Parents Anonymous, child abuse appears to be a medical problem, and abusers are sick persons who must be treated.

Consequences of Treatment for the Social System

The individual and the social system are interrelated; each influences the other. Thus, if society defines abusive parents as sick, there will be few criminal prosecutions for abuse; reports will generally be sent to welfare, as opposed to police, departments.

Since victims of child abuse are frequently treated in hospitals, medical personnel become brokers for adult services and definers of children's rights. Once abuse is defined, that is, people may get services (such as counseling, child care, and homemaker services) that would be otherwise unavailable to them, and children may get care and protection impossible without institutional intervention.

If, as is customary, however, resources are in short supply, the preferred treatment of a case may not be feasible. Under this condition, less adequate treatment strategems, or even clearly punitive alternatives, may be implemented. If day care and competent counseling are unavailable, court action and foster placement can become the only options. As Stoll[56] observed,

... The best therapeutic intentions may be led astray when opportunities to implement theoretical guidelines are not available.

Treating child abuse as a sickness has, ironically, made it more difficult to "cure." There are not enough therapists to handle all of the diagnosed cases. Nor do most abusive parents have the time, money, or disposition for long-term therapeutic involvement. Many, moreover, lack the introspective and conceptual abilities required for successful psychological therapy.

As Parents Anonymous emphasizes, abuse is the *abuser's* problem. Its causes and solutions are widely understood to reside in individuals rather than in the social system.[5,17] Indeed, the strong emphasis of child abuse as an individual problem means that other equally severe problems of childhood can be ignored, and the unequal distribution of social and economic resources in society can be masked.[20] The child abuse phenomenon itself may also increase as parents and professionals are obliged to "package" their problems and diagnoses in a competitive market where services are in short supply. As Tannenbaum[57] observed in 1938:

> Societal reactions to deviance can be characterized as a kind of "dramatization of evil" such that a person's deviance is made a public issue. The stronger the reaction to the evil, the more it seems to grow. The reaction itself seems to generate the very thing it sought to eliminate.

Conclusion

Dispelling the Myth of Child Abuse

As clinicians, we are convinced that with intelligence, humanity, and the application of appropriate interventions, we can help families in crisis.

We believe, however, that short of coming to terms with—and changing—certain social, political, and economic aspects of our society, we will never be able adequately to understand and address the origins of child abuse and neglect. Nor will the issues of labeling be adequately resolved unless we deal straightforwardly with the potentially abusive power of the helping professions. If we can bring ourselves to ask such questions as, "Can we legislate child abuse out of existence?" and, "Who benefits from child abuse?," then perhaps we can more rationally choose among the action alternatives displayed in the conceptual model (table 1).

Although we would prefer to avoid coercion and punishment, and to keep families autonomous and services voluntary, we must acknowledge the realities of family life and posit some state role to assure the well-being of children. In making explicit the assumptions and values underpinning our professional actions, perhaps we can promote a more informed and humane practice.

Because it is likely that clinical interventions will continue to be class and culture-based, we propose the following five guidelines to minimize the abuse of power of the definer.

1. *Give physicians, social workers, lawyers, and other intervention agents social science perspectives and skills.* Critical intellectual tools should help clinicians to understand the implications of their work, and, especially, the functional meaning of the labels they apply in their practices.

Physicians need to be more aware of the complexity of human life, especially its social and psychological dimensions. The "medical model" is not of itself inappropriate; rather, the conceptual bases of medical practice need to be broadened, and the intellectual and scientific repertory of the practitioner expanded.[12] Diagnostic formulation is an active process that carries implicitly an anticipation of intervention and outcome. The simple elegance of concepts such as "child abuse" and "child neglect" militate for simple and radical treatments.

Lawyers might be helped to learn that, in child custody cases, they are not merely advocates of a particular position. Only the child should "win" a custody case, where, for example, allegations of "abuse" or "neglect," skillfully marshaled, may support the position of the more effectively represented parent, guardian, or social worker.

2. *Acknowledge and change the prestige hierarchy of helping professions.* The workers who seem best able to conceptualize the familial and social context of problems of violence are social workers and nurses. They are least paid, most overworked, and as a rule have minimal access to the decision prerogatives of medicine and law. We would add that social work and nursing are professions largely of and by women, and we believe we must come to terms with the many realities—including sexual dominance and subservience—that keep members of these professions from functioning with appropriate respect and support. (We have made a modest effort in this direction at our own institution, where our interdisciplinary child abuse consultation program is organized under the aegis of the administration rather than of a medical clinical department. This is to foster, to the extent possible, peer status and communication on a coequal footing among the disciplines represented—social work, nursing, law, medicine, and psychiatry.)

3. *Build theory.* We need urgently a commonly understandable dictionary of concepts that will guide and inform a rational practice. A more adequate theory base would include a more etiologic (or causal) classification scheme for children's injuries, which would acknowledge and integrate diverse origins and expressions of social, familial, child developmental, and environmental phenomena. It would conceptualize strength in families and children, as well as

pathology. It would orient intervenors to the promotion of health rather than to the treatment of disease.

A unified theory would permit coming to terms with the universe of need. At present, socially marginal and poor children are virtually the only ones susceptible to being diagnosed as victims of abuse and neglect. More affluent families' offspring, whose injuries are called "accidents" and who are often unprotected, are not included in "risk" populations. We have seen examples of court defense where it was argued (successfully) that because the family was not poor, it did not fit the classic archetypes of abuse or neglect.

The needs and rights of all children need to be spelled out legally in relation to the responsibilities of parents and the state. This is easier said than done. It shall require not only a formidable effort at communication across disciplinary lines but a serious coming to terms with social and political values and realities.

4. *Change social inequality.* We share Gil's[20] view that inequality is the basic problem underlying the labeling of "abusive families" and its consequences. Just as children without defined rights are *ipso facto* vulnerable, so too does unequal access to the resources and goods of society shape a class hierarchy that leads to the individualization of social problems. Broadly-focused efforts for social change should accompany a critical review of the ethical foundations of professional practice. As part of the individual's formation as doctor, lawyer, social worker, or police officer, there could be developed for the professional a notion of public service and responsibility. This would better enable individuals to see themselves as participants in a social process and to perceive the problems which they address in their work at the social as well as the individual level of action.

5. *Assure adequate representation of class and ethnic groups in decision-making forums.* Since judgments about family competency can be affected by class and ethnic biases, they should be made in settings where prejudices can be checked and controlled. Culture-bound value judgments in child protection work are not infrequent, and a sufficient participation in case management conferences of professionals of equal rank and status and diverse ethnicity can assure both a more appropriate context for decision making and better decisions for children and their families.

References

1. Allen, F. 1964. *The Borderland of Criminal Justice.* University of Chicago Press, Chicago.

2. Becker, H. 1963. *Outsiders: Studies in the Sociology of Deviance.* Free Press, New York.

3. Bourne, R. and Newberger, E. 1977. 'Family autonomy' or 'coercive intervention?' ambiguity and conflict in a proposed juvenile justice standard on child protection. *Boston Univ. Law Rev.* 57(4):670-706.

5. Conrad, P. 1975. The discovery of hyperkinesis: notes on the medicalization of deviant behavior. *Soc. Prob.* 23(10):12-21.

6. Cupoli, J. and Newberger, E. 1977. Optimism or pessimism for the victim of child abuse? *Pediatrics* 59(2):311-314.

7. Curran, W. 1977. Failure to diagnose battered child syndrome. *New England J.* 296(14):795-796.

8. Davis, F. 1975. Beliefs, values, power and public definitions of deviance. In *The Collective Definition of Deviance.* F. Davis and R. Stivers, eds. Free Press, New York.

9. Demause, L., ed. 1974. *The History of Childhood.* Free Press, New York.

10. Elmer, E. 1977. A follow-up study of traumatized children. *Pediatrics* 59(2):273-279.

11. Elmer, E. 1977. *Fragile Families, Troubled Children.* University of Pittsburgh Press, Pittsburgh.

12. Engel, G. 1977. The need for a new medical model: a challenge for biomedicine. *Science* 196(14):129-136.

13. Fontana, V. 1964. The Maltreated Child: The Maltreatment Syndrome in Children. Charles C. Thomas, Springfield, Ill.

14. Fraser, B. 1977. Legislative status of child abuse legislation. In *Child Abuse and Neglect: the Family and the Community*, C. Kempe and R. Heifer, eds. Ballinger, Cambridge, Mass.

15. Freidson, E. 1970. *Profession of Medicine: A Study of the Sociology of Applied Knowledge.* Dodd, Mead, New York.

16. Galdston, R. 1971. Violence begins at home. *J. Amer. Acad. Child Psychiat.* 10(2):336-350.

17. Gelles, R. 1973. Child abuse as psychopathology: a sociological critique and reformulation. *Amer. J. Orthopsychiat.* 43(4):611-621.

18. Gelles, R. 1978. Violence toward children in the United States. *Amer. J. Orthopsychiat.* 48(4):580-592.

19. Gil, D. 1975. Unraveling child abuse. *Amer. J. Orthopsychiat.* 45(4):346-356.

20. Gil, D. 1970. *Violence Against Children.* Harvard University Press, Cambridge, Mass.

21. Goldstein, J., Freud, A. and Solnit, A. 1973. *Beyond the Best Interests of the Child.* Free Press, New York.

22. Gusfield, J. 1967. Moral passage: the symbolic process in public designations of deviance. *Soc. Prob.* 15(2):175-188.

23. Hyde, J. 1974. Uses and abuses of information in protective services contexts. In Fifth National Symposium on Child Abuse and Neglect. American Humane Association, Denver.

24. Illich, I. 1976. *Medical Nemesis: The Expropriation of Health.* Random House, New York.

25. *Ingraham v. Wright*, 1977. 45 LW 4364 U.S. Supreme Court.

26. Isaccs, J. 1972. The role of the lawyer in child abuse cases. In *Helping the Battered Child and His Family*. R. Helfer and C. Kempe, eds. Lippincott, Philadelphia.

27. Joint Commission on the Mental Health of Children. 1970. *Crisis in Child Mental Health*. Harper and Row, New York.

28. Juvenile Justice Standards Project. 1977. *Standards Relating to Abuse and Neglect*. Ballinger, Cambridge, Mass.

29. Kempe, C. and Helfer, R., eds. 1972. *Helping the Battered Child and His Family*. Lippincott, Philadelphia.

30. Kempe, C. et al. 1962. The battered child syndrome. JAMA 181(1):17-24.

31. Kittrie, N. 1971. *The Right To Be Different*. Johns Hopkins University Press, Baltimore.

32. *Landeros v. Flood*. 1976. 131 Calif. Rptr. 69.

33. Martin, H., ed. 1976. *The Abused Child: A Multidisciplinary Approach to Developmental Issues and Treatment*. Ballinger, Cambridge, Mass.

34. Mercier, J. 1972. Who is normal? two perspectives on mild mental retardation. In *Patients, Physicians and Illness* (2nd ed.), E. Jaco, ed. Free Press, New York.

35. Newberger, E. 1975. The myth of the battered child syndrome. In *Annual Progress in Child Psychiatry and Child Development 1974*. S. Chess and A. Thomas, eds. Brunner Mazel, New York.

36. Newberger, E., Newberger, C. and Richmond, J. 1976. Child Health in America: toward a rational public policy. *Milbank Memorial Fund Quart. Hlth. and Society* 54(3):249-298.

37. Newberger, E. and Daniel, J. 1976. Knowledge and epidemiology of child abuse: a critical review of concepts. *Pediat. Annals* 5(3):15-26.

38. Newberger, E. et al. 1977. Pediatric social illness: toward an etiologic classification. *Pediatrics* 60(1):178-185.

39. Parsons, T. 1951. *The Social System*. Free Press, Glencoe, Ill.

40. Paulsen, M. 1966. Juvenile courts, family courts, and the poor man. *Calif. Law Rev.* 54(2):694-716.

41. Pfohl, S. 1977. The 'discovery' of child abuse. *Soc. Prob.* 24(3):310-323.

42. Piliavin, I. and Briar, S. 1964. Police encounters with juveniles. *Amer. J. Sociol.* 70(2):206-214.

43. Pitts, J. 1968. Social control: the concept. In *The International Encyclopedia of the Social Sciences* 14:391. Macmillan, New York.

44. Poitrast, F. 1976. The judicial dilemma in child abuse cases. *Psychiat. Opinion* 13(1):22-28.

45. Rheinstein, M. 1954. *Max Weber on Law in Economy and Society*. Harvard University Press, Cambridge, Mass.

46. Rosenblatt, S., Schaeffer, D. and Rosenthal, J. 1976. Effects of diphenylhydantoin on child abusing parents: a preliminary report. *Curr. Therapeut. Res.* 19(3):332-336.

47. Rosenfeld, A. and Newberger, E. 1977. Compassion versus control: conceptual and practical pitfalls in the broadened definition of child abuse. *J. Amer. Med. Assoc.* 237(19):2086-2088.

48. Rubington, E. and Weinberg, M. 1973. *Deviance: The Interactionist Perspective* (2nd ed.). Macmillan, New York.

49. Ryan, W. 1971. *Blaming the Victim.* Random House, New York.

50. Sanders, R. 1972. Resistance to dealing with parents of battered children. *Pediatrics* 50(6):853-857.

51. Scheff, T. 1966. *Being Mentally Ill: A Sociological Theory.* Aldine, Chicago.

52. Scheff, T. 1972. Decision rules, types of error, and their consequences in medical diagnosis. In *Medical Men and Their Work*, E. Freidson and J. Lorber, eds. Aldine, Chicago.

53. Schmitt, B. and Kempe, C. 1975. Neglect and abuse of children. In *Nelson Textbook of Pediatrics* (10th ed.), V. Vaughan and R. McKay, eds. W.B. Saunders, Philadelphia.

54. Schrag, P. 1975. *The Myth of the Hyperactive Child.* Random House, New York.

55. Schur, E. 1971. *Labeling Deviant Behavior.* Harper and Row, New York.

56. Stoll, C. 1968. Images of man and social control. *Soc. Forces* 47(2):119-127.

57. Tannenbaum, F. 1938. *Crime and the Community.* Ginn and Co., Boston.

58. Whiting, L. 1977. The central registry for child abuse cases: rethinking basic assumptions. *Child Welfare* 56(2):761-767.

Table 1
Dilemmas of Social Policy and Professional Response

RESPONSE	*FAMILY AUTONOMY*	*Versus COERCIVE INTERVENTION*
Compassion ("support")	1 Voluntary child development services 2 Guaranteed family supports: e.g. income, housing, health services	1 Case reporting of family crisis and mandated family intervention 2 Court-ordered delivery of services
Versus		
Control ("punishment")	1 "Laissez-faire": No assured services or supports 2 Retributive response to family crisis	1 Court action to separate child from family 2 Criminal prosecution of parents

12 Policy and Politics: the Child Abuse Prevention and Treatment Act

Ellen Hoffman

The line between policy and politics is a fine one. Frequently in analyzing a piece of legislation it is impossible—even through hindsight—to isolate the policy decisions from the political decisions. The Child Abuse Prevention and Treatment Act is a case squarely in point, for the answers to all of the policy questions raised during the drafting and passage of the act were to some degree influenced by consideration of whether they would help or hinder its passage.

Once Congress publicly identifies a problem, it can be predicted that a legislative solution will almost certainly be devised. It is not considered good politics to simply identify problems and leave them for others to solve. In this case, despite arguments that little short of social revolution would significantly address the problem of child abuse and neglect, a deliberate decision was made that "something is better than nothing." This paper examines the legislative history of the Child Abuse Prevention and Treatment Act, and focuses on the interaction of the policy and political decisions throughout that history. When the U.S. Senate Subcommittee on Children and Youth was created in February 1971 it was endowed with no legislative authority over existing programs, but with a mission potentially as broad as all of the problems of the nation's children and youth.

The Subcommittee, the first in Congress to offer a forum specifically devoted to the broad concerns of children and youth, was established at the request of Senator Walter F. Mondale as a subcommittee of the Labor and Public Welfare Committee, now called the Human Resources Committee. To Mondale the Subcommittee seemed a logical step in advancing the proposals made by the 1970 White House Conference on Children. Other Senate committees, however, had long ago staked out their legislative jurisdiction over such relevant issues as education, health, and child welfare. Hence it was understood from the beginning that the issues to be addressed by the new subcommittee would largely be those that had not yet been "discovered" by other committees, or those on which joint action with other committees could be pursued.

One such issue was the federal role in the identification, prevention, and treatment of the abuse and neglect of children. A rather nebulous federal role had for some time existed in the area of child abuse and neglect. Under Titles IV-A and IV-B of the Social Security Act, funds channeled to the states for a

Reprinted by permission of John Wiley & Sons, Inc. from *Public Policy* (Winter 1978).

157

variety of purposes could be used to care for abused children and to try to reunite their families. In 1963, experts assembled by the Children's Bureau in the Department of Health, Education, and Welfare produced a model state law for child abuse reporting. It is generally agreed that over the next decade this model law was a major factor in the movement that resulted in the enactment or updating of child abuse reporting laws in virtually all of the states. Still, the political atmosphere at the time the subcommittee undertook its work on child abuse was hardly conducive to major breakthroughs in children's legislation. In fact, the bill was enacted

> ...24 months after the Presidential veto of the comprehensive child care legislation; less than a year after a proposal for a drastic reduction in social services; at the same time that HEW was cutting back on staff for... the maternal and child health program....[a]

Nonetheless, the Subcommittee staff began research into the nature and extent of the federal role in child abuse, and attempted to identify successful programs that might serve as models for prospective federal legislation.

Those in the general public who were concerned with children's problems soon came to identify them as a possible focus of action, and the Subcommittee on Children and Youth began to receive letters from citizens concerned about child abuse. Some of the correspondents enclosed in their letters newspaper stories about child abuse cases. As is routine when a congressional committee receives inquiries on a particular subject, a request was made to the Library of Congress for background information on the problem of child abuse. The Library request yielded a packet of information, mainly journal articles on the medical and legal aspects of child abuse, most of them several years old. A compilation of these materials was published by the Subcommittee in a committee document, "Rights of Children, Part I," in December 1972. The publication of the document was the first public evidence of the Subcommittee's intention to consider legislation in the area of child abuse and neglect.

Drafting the Legislation

A basic assumption of the congressional committee system is that a subcommittee or committee may identify an issue deserving of attention and make most of the fundamental decisions about the nature and timing of action on it by the entire Congress. But although these decisions may be taken by a very few members of Congress and their staffs, these individuals of necessity reflect the views of their colleagues because they want their legislative proposals to be

---

[a]Walter F. Mondale, speech to Region Five Child Abuse Conference, Milwaukee, Wisc., May 3, 1976.

successful when acted on by the Senate and the House. In the case of the child abuse legislation, most of the basic decisions about the type of program to be created and the strategy leading to it were made in the Senate on the subcommittee level. Once the problem of child abuse had caught the attention of Congress, the fundamental question for the Subcommittee was whether action should be taken on it. Several factors entered into the decision to move ahead into hearings and legislation. One was the inability of HEW to document convincingly its contention that the federal role was already a full and effective one. Another was that it appeared that something could in fact be done to ameliorate the problem. In other words, there were working programs that were worthy, at the minimum, of further study, and possibly also worthy of replication and expansion. One such program that came to the early attention of the Subcommittee was that of the National Center for the Prevention and Treatment of Child Abuse and Neglect at the University of Colorado Medical School, and in fact a field hearing was eventually held in Denver. Discussions with the staff of the center were also important in shaping the legislation that was eventually introduced.

The next question facing the Subcommittee was what to do. A number of activities were considered particularly appropriate to the federal government, even though some people felt that actual service programs for child abusers and abused children should be left to the states. Support of research, development, and dissemination of training materials, collection and dissemination of research results and information on successful programs, and coordination and monitoring of existing federal activities all fell into this category. Even HEW, although it opposed the bill in the Senate, seemed to agree that these activities were appropriate for the federal government.

The most significant question concerning the federal role was whether direct services should be supported. It was clear to the Subcommittee that, for both economic and political reasons, any legislation that appeared to commit the federal government to a major new direct service program would face serious barriers to enactment. Yet, promising programs were in operation and could be used as models for others. The decision was made therefore to use the term "demonstration programs" for programs like those in Washington, Denver, and New York. This term suggested a more tentative, and less expensive, approach to the question of whether the federal government should have any role in providing direct services.

Another fundamental question in developing the legislation was who—which agency or agencies—should do what. The original Senate bill simply located the new National Center for Child Abuse and Neglect and its activities within HEW. One reason for this was genuine uncertainty about the most responsive locus for the program. Another was the fact that the Office of Child Development—a prime candidate for administering the program—has no statutory existence. Writing OCD into the law could have appeared to be a major, though back-door, endorsement by the Congress of the existence of OCD, and could have endangered enactment of the legislation. The original Senate bill reflected the uncertainty of the drafters about the best location for the program by not indicating which part of HEW should administer it. It was assumed that this question would be explored and resolved through the hearings and other phases of the legislative process. The ultimate decision to place the Center in OCD was carried out by an agreement between Congress and HEW, and was not written into law.

On March 13, 1972 Senator Mondale, joined by 13 cosponsors (including several key members of the Senate Labor and Public Welfare Committee), introduced S. 1191, then called the "Child Abuse Prevention Act." Because of the existence of the Denver Center, Mondale asked Rep. Pat Schroeder (D–Colo.) if she would like to introduce the same bill in the House. She readily agreed and did so. The legislation consisted of four parts:

1. A National Center on Child Abuse and Neglect was created within HEW. The Center was to compile a "listing of accidents involving children," publish a summary of research on child abuse and neglect, develop an information clearinghouse, and complete and publish training materials.

2. A program of grants and contracts was established for demonstration projects "designed to prevent, identify and treat child abuse and neglect." The amount of $10 million was to be authorized for fiscal year 1973, and $20 million for each of the succeeding four years.

3. A National Commission on Child Abuse and Neglect was created, consisting primarily of citizens outside the government, to study the effectiveness of existing child abuse and neglect reporting laws and "the proper role of the federal government" in assisting state and local public and private efforts in the field.

4. In order to continue to receive funds under certain parts of the Social Security Act, states were required to adopt procedures for the prevention, identification, and treatment of child abuse; to collect information and report to the Secretary of HEW on the adequacy of state laws; and to make cooperative arrangements with state health, education, and other appropriate agencies to assure coordination in dealing with child abuse and neglect cases.

Although S. 1191 was inevitably destined for changes in the course of the legislative process, several assumptions that underlay the original version of the bill were implicitly accepted by Congress throughout its deliberations on the legislation. These were as follows:

1. Although all 50 states had child abuse reporting statutes, these were not supported by adequate resources for investigation and provision of services in cases where families required them.

2. Certain key policy questions—including those concerning the adequacy of state laws and the appropriate federal-state-local relationship in this area—would require long, careful, and thorough study; Congress should therefore not make long-term definitive decisions on such matters in the pending legislation.

3. Child abusers are not all hopeless psychopaths; as many as 90 percent of them can be helped to the point where their previously abused children can live with them safely.

4. Child abuse is cyclical, appearing most often in families in which a parent has been abused as a child. It is therefore vital to attempt to identify abusers and break the cycle in order to protect future generations.

Going Public

The Subcommittee scheduled two open hearings in Washington in March 1973. The first was designed both to introduce the policy implications of child abuse and neglect to the Subcommittee and to offer members of the Subcommittee exposure to the "human" side of the problem. The policy implications were to be discussed in testimony by D. David Gil, Professor of Social Policy at Brandeis University and author of *Violence Against Children*, a nationwide study of child abuse. The principal witness on the human side of child abuse was Jolly K., a former child abuser (who still identifies herself by the shortened name) and founder of Parents Anonymous, a self-help organization.

Gil's testimony emphasized the broad social causes of child abuse and neglect. He suggested that any legislation as narrow as the proposed bill would be inadequate to the job of preventing, identifying, and treating the problem. In response, Mondale, who was chairing the hearing, made his position clear:

> What strikes me about your testimony is where you said there is no point in trying to ameliorate the problem; where you said that unless you can strike at the fundamental problem that causes deviant behavior, you are not doing any good ... you want a law against spanking ... you want a national program to bring up minimum family payments ... for which there isn't a dime in the national budget. I think if we are going to wait until that millenium arrives, there will be hundreds of thousands of abused children who are going to be untreated.[b]

This debate over whether it is possible or worthwhile to attempt to identify and treat child abuse instead of waiting for more fundamental social changes to occur is one that continues even today as the appropriateness and effectiveness of the federal legislation and programs are argued.

Perhaps the single most effective witness who testified in what became four days of Senate hearings on child abuse was Jolly K. An imposing, straight-talking woman, she told the Subcommittee that she abused her child "to the point of almost causing death several times. It was extreme serious physical abuse. . . . Once I threw a rather large kitchen knife at her [daughter] and another time I

---

b"Child Abuse Prevention Act, 1973," hearings before the Subcommittee on Children and Youth Committee on Labor and Public Welfare, U.S. Senate, 93rd Congress, 1st session.

strangled her because she lied to me. . . . This was up to when she was 6½ years old." With no hesitation in her voice, she stated that "in this society for so long the child abuser was the modern Salem witch. We were horrible, monsters who did these things to our children. Yes, the deeds are monstrous, but we are not monsters." Her description of attempts to seek help from ten different agencies underlined the assumption of the legislation that current programs were not sensitive or adequate to the problem. "I was having multiple problems in society that stuck out. These kinds of things stick out like neon lights," Jolly told the Subcommittee. Her appearance, which was reported on nationwide television, had a major impact in convincing the Subcommittee that child abusers are not necessarily hopelessly pathological monsters and that they could and should be helped.

The second hearing opened with statements by representatives of the Department of Health, Education, and Welfare. They testified that from fiscal 1971 to 1974, the federal government would be spending $233 million on child abuse or child abuse-related activities. Under questioning, the Department representatives conceded that because such activities are carried out under general programs of "protective services" it was not actually certain how much of the money was being spent on child abuse cases. The Department further testified that "it is the primary responsibility of the states and local governments to identify the abused child and its family. The federal role is one which provides assistance to the states in establishing mechanisms for identification of the abused child."

Although Departmental witnesses could provide only the most feeble answers to Mondale's questions about what was actually happening in the states, they concluded that

> [much] of what the bill proposes has already been done or is planned for the near future. . . . In the experience of the Department, the establishment of new categorical programs, rather than working toward solutions, in fact works against the development of successful means of dealing with our problems. The singling out of one part of a complex as a basis for dealing with the problem is not an approach which the Department favors.[c]

HEW's testimony was followed by a presentation, including slides of battered children, by the multi-disciplinary team from Children's Hospital in Washington, D.C. At subsequent hearings at the Denver Center and at Roosevelt Hospital in New York City, the Subcommittee heard testimony about the operations and effectiveness of these teams, which were made up of medical, social work, legal, and psychiatric personnel. Representatives of the American Academy of Pediatrics, the American Humane Association, and the state and city of New York also presented oral testimony. Vincent de Francis of the

[c]Ibid.

American Humane Association advocated, in addition to S. 1191, the strengthening and additional funding of existing child protective services under the Social Security Act. Most witnesses, however, endorsed most of the provisions of the bill and made suggestions for its improvement.

The hearings were widely reported in both the print and electronic media, and it became increasingly apparent that even a very veto-prone President would find it hard to veto a bill attempting to provide help to abused children and their families.

Between the end of the Senate hearings in April and the floor action on the bill in July, two events occurred that were to substantially alter the nature and fate of the proposed legislation. These two forces came together at the first National Conference on Child Abuse, held in Washington in June 1972.

At the conference, Stanley Thomas, Assistant Secretary for Human Development in HEW, announced unexpectedly that the Department had earmarked $4 million for "new activities focused on child abuse." The activities to be supported included revision of the model reporting statute, a survey of existing programs to identify program models and determine which could be replicated, a test of the feasibility of the creation of a national clearinghouse (which would have been created by the legislation), and the development of training materials (also provided for in S. 1191).

Shortly after the Thomas announcement, William Lunsford, a Washington representative of the Child Welfare League, circulated a statement calling on the administration "to do something about the vital issues of child abuse and neglect" by exempting protective services from matching requirements under the social services program, loosening social services eligibility requirements for protective services, and promoting an increased appropriation for support of protective services provided under Title IV-B of the Social Security Act. The statement asserted that HEW should pursue these goals "at the same time it is promoting the new initiatives within the Office of Child Development." Significantly, Lunsford said nothing about the pending bill, S. 1191, which was already a major topic of discussion among conference participants.

Lunsford's statement—of importance because it reflected the views of the Child Welfare League, the most important national organization in the child welfare area—did not come as a complete surprise. Earlier, he had visited the staff of the Senate subcommittee to offer his strong objections to the Child Abuse Prevention Act, and to protest that the League had been left out of discussions on the legislation. He was told that, before he joined the League, the organization had been contacted by the Subcommittee and advised that any contribution—including testimony and legislation recommendations—would be welcome. No response had been received until after the hearings, when Lunsford suddenly appeared and declared the organization's opposition to S. 1191. As a result of this confusion, the League developed a strong and clear position that was an important factor in determining the form of the bill reported by the House Committee on Education and Labor several months later.

Action in the Senate

The version of S. 1191 reported unanimously by the Senate Labor and Public Welfare Committee was very similar to the one introduced in March. Language was added to emphasize the Committee's belief that multi-disciplinary programs were particularly worthy of support, and to require HEW to distribute the demonstration program funds equitably among geographical areas and between urban and rural areas. In addition, the requirement that HEW compile a "listing of accidents" involving children (an attempt to move toward a national reporting system) was removed because of the civil liberties problems it might raise.

In an effort to respond to HEW's contention that adequate efforts to deal with child abuse were already underway, the Senate Committee stated in its report:[d]

> Federal support for programs dealing with child abuse—to the extent that it exists—has been available primarily through Title IV-B of the Social Security Act, which authorizes child welfare services including protective services. However, the child welfare program received only $46 million in 1973 and is budgeted for the same amount in 1974. And HEW told the committee that, of the $46 million available for IV-B activities in 1973, only $507,000 was spent on activities related to child abuse.
>
> Representatives of the Department of HEW testified that child abuse programs are a function of the individual states and should be implemented under the existing authority of Titles IV-A and IV-B of the Social Security Act. However, they also testified that they had no information about the effectiveness of these programs in preventing, identifying and treating child abuse, but were aware that they were not adequate. The hearing revealed further that not one employee of the Federal government works full time on the problem of child abuse.[d]

S. 1191 was reported out of the Labor and Public Welfare Committee on July 10. Four days later the bill suddenly was brought up for action on the Senate floor. With Mondale unavoidably out of town, Senator Randolph (D.–W. Va.), who had attended and actively participated in the hearings, became the floor manager. The debate was short and routine. Senator Jacob Javits (R.–N.Y.), the ranking minority member of the Committee, dutifully reported the administration's opposition to the measure. Javits, however, noted his belief that the bill did exactly what the administration said needed to be done. Senator Helms (R.–N.C.), who ultimately voted against the bill, indicated that he opposed it "because it is yet another step in the direction of centralizing further power and responsibility in Washington." The only amendment offered, which

---

dSenate Report 93-308, Child Abuse Prevention and Treatment Act, Committee on Labor and Public Welfare, July 10, 1973.

was readily accepted by Randolph and Javits, was a provision by Senator Matthias (R.–Md.) requiring the Secretary of HEW to prepare and submit to Congress and the public an annual report and evaluation of the programs funded under the legislation.

The strong bipartisan vote (57–7) in the Senate indicated that even if a child abuse bill were vetoed, the veto could probably be overridden.

Action in the House

The House Subcommittee on Select Education, chaired by Rep. John Brademas (D.–Ind.), opened its hearings on child abuse legislation on October 1, 1973. By that time more than 100 members of the House were already cosponsors of the Schroeder bill, as it was known in the House, and related measures. With the traditional Thanksgiving and Christmas recesses approaching and Senate action complete, the House Subcommittee conducted four days of hearings—three in Washington and one in New York—on the proposed legislation. Many of the Senate Committee witnesses also testified before the House Committee. By the time the bill reached the floor of the House, it had changed considerably from both the initial Schroeder bill and the Senate-passed version. The Committee included the following changes:

1. Addition of a definition of "child abuse and neglect," terms that were not defined in the Senate bill.

2. Creation of a program of funding, not less than 5 percent of the annual appropriation, for grants to states. This was to be separate from the demonstration program, for which public and private entities, including government agencies, organizations, and educational institutions, were eligible.

3. A requirement that in order to receive funds under the state program, states must meet ten criteria. These included having in effect procedures for reporting and investigating reports of child abuse, and having personnel and facilities available for treatment. The state funding program and criteria for it were developed primarily in response to the concerns of the Child Welfare League as discussed earlier.

4. A requirement that child abuse and neglect-related programs funded under the Social Security Act also meet the requirements of the state program.

5. Higher authorizations, $15 million for fiscal 1974, $20 million for fiscal 1975, and $25 million for 1976. The duration of the bill was three years, rather than the five years approved by the Senate.

Recognizing the inevitability of the passage of some type of child abuse legislation by Congress, the administration decided to try to have a role in shaping it. Thus, when Rep. Brademas brought the bill to the House floor he also brought to his colleagues the following statement from HEW Secretary Caspar Weinberger:

As the Department testified before your Subcommittee and before the parallel Senate Subcommittee, we are already deeply and firmly committed to substantial and enhanced efforts to cope with the problem of child abuse and neglect. Thus the administration is supportive of many of the objectives of this bill and is implementing them currently. Hence the administration does not oppose the measure in its present form.[e]

The changes made in the bill by the Committee reflected an attempt to make it more acceptable to the administration. It was understood that if certain changes were made, the administration would not encourage Republican House members to vote against it and Weinberger would not recommend a Presidential veto.

During the floor debate in the House, two members stated their opposition to the bill, one on grounds of economy and the other on the grounds that it would result in federal intrusion into the authority of state criminal laws. The vote for passage on December 3, 1972 was 354 to 36.

Reconciling the Senate and House Bills

After the December 3 House vote, Mondale and Brademas agreed to try to expedite enactment by working out the differences between the two bills by agreement, rather than by using the traditional conference committee procedure. This required a second House passage of an amended version of the bill, followed by Senate passage of that same measure. The legislative situation was complicated, however, when the respective Chairmen of the House Ways and Means and Senate Finance Committees, which have jurisdiction over the Social Security Act, expressed their concern that the legislation contained amendments to the Social Security Act that had not been considered by their committees. Thus the final version of the Act significantly reduced the criteria for compliance to provisions that the states could almost certainly meet immediately with no trouble (reporting procedures, requirement for investigation, confidentiality of reports, and cooperation with the courts).

Other compromise provisions reflected in the final version of the legislation were:

1. The Senate bill had no mechanism for funding through the states, whereas the House bill required that a minimum of 5 percent of each appropriation be funneled to states meeting the criteria. In the compromise, a ceiling of 20 percent of the annual appropriation was placed on the funding available through the state program.

2. The Senate bill authorized creation of a commission made up of public members, whereas the House bill created only an internal advisory board, made

[e]Congressional Record, Dec. 3, 1973.

up of government employees and having limited responsibilities. The "compromise" was acceptance of the House position, because the administration was adamant that it would not accept creation of a citizens' advisory council.

3. The Senate's 5-year, $90 million bill and the House's 3-year, $60 million bill were compromised to result in a 4-year, $85 million program.

4. The Senate bill creating the demonstration program "authorized and directed" (made mandatory) that the Secretary of HEW establish such a program. The House bill only "authorized" the Secretary to do so. In the compromise the Senate accepted the House language, but new language was added requiring that at least 50 percent of the annual appropriation be spent on the demonstration programs.

It was this version, approved by the Senate on December 20 and sent to the President, that became law on January 31, 1974.

Policy and Politics

The customary interactions of policy and politics produced the final version of the bill. Questions such as where the program should be administered, how the money should be distributed and spent, and who should receive services were resolved through a combination of Senate action, House action, and negotiation with the administration, followed by Senate-House-administration negotiations on the final shape of the program.

One issue that was resolved as much on political as on policy considerations was the question as to which subunit of HEW should administer the new program. As the child abuse legislation progressed through Congress, it became evident that the Democratic majority felt most comfortable entrusting its pet social programs to Stanley Thomas, the Assistant Secretary for Human Development. Members of Congress were clearly encouraged by the active personal role Thomas played in working out a compromise and staving off a veto. (In subsequent years, his office gained control of a number of other social programs as a result of his ability to convince the Congress that he was committed to trying to make social programs work.)

Governed by its intention to stimulate new and creative approaches to child abuse—rather than simply to add funds to the existing system—Congress did not want the Social and Rehabilitation Service (which administered the Social Security Act) to have responsibility for the new effort. If Congress had adhered to a policy of consolidating similar programs in a single agency, the child abuse program would probably have been housed in SRS. Members of Congress feared, however, that this agency would not make the effort to assure an adequate focus on child abuse within the massive and various welfare programs under its jurisdiction.

This same thinking influenced the decision to make a wide variety of public and private institutions, agencies, and organizations eligible for grants and contracts under the demonstration program, and to provide only token funding through the state program that was added to the legislation in the House. This attitude was reinforced by Jolly K.'s testimony about her attempts and failure to get help from public agencies, as well as by the existence of viable programs in the academic, medical, and voluntary sectors.

This approach of funding through two separate channels, the demonstration authority and the state program, employing different criteria was not quite as insulting to the states as it may have appeared. State agencies were and still are eligible to receive funds through the demonstration authority without meeting the state funding criteria, and a number of them have done so.

Several issues of great significance in implementing the program were the product of political compromise, rather than explicit policy debate. In some cases, the policy has only become evident in the implementation stage.

One critical policy question not directly addressed by the Congress was that priority to place on expenditure of funds for various purposes. The enacted law does present a sense of priorities by requiring that 50 percent of available funds be spent on demonstrations, that 5 to 20 percent of the funds be spent on state programs, and therefore that the National Center on Child Abuse and Neglect receive 30 to 45 percent of the funds for its activities, including research, information, training, and the clearinghouse. Congress gave no direction on the question of what percentage of the Center's funds should be spent on research, how much on the information system, and so on. The decision as to whether to offer the states 5 percent or 20 percent or something in between was left up to HEW.

These percentages, as has been documented here, were inserted in the legislation near the end of the process. They originated mainly because of the need to arrive at a compromise between the Senate, the House, and the administration positions on the bill. They were not the result of either a systematic or thorough consideration of available options.

It was only after the program had been in existence for at least two years that these built-in priorities and the nature of HEW's choices about priorities became a matter of serious consideration and debate. The debate, which still continues, seems to be most intense when the issue is "research vs. services." Some believe that information and research on the dynamics of child abuse and neglect are so inadequate that the government should support few or no services until more is known about how to make them effective. Others argue that providers are deluged with cases and suspected cases of child abuse, many as a result of the federal emphasis on reporting laws, which they cannot investigate and otherwise respond to because of lack of funds.

Another priority question revolved around whether the limited resources under the Act should be directed primarily at the children who are abused, children who are neglected, or both. The original Senate bill did not even define "abuse" and "neglect." It was felt to be unnecessary because the law was to be a program of services, research, and the like, not a punitive or regulatory measure. Moreover, an attempt at a federal definition might work unnecessary hardship on states and localities, which already had widely varying definitions in their own laws. The House, however, did insert a definition that included not only physical but also mental injury.

The authors of the bill had no illusions that it would serve all of the families implicated by reports of abuse or neglect so widely defined. This was a political judgment based on the recognition that funds available for the new program would not be adequate to provide services even to those children and families already identified as needing them.

Thus, although there is no statutory statement, the legislative history (testimony, committee reports, and floor statements) reflects the clear intent of Congress that priority be given to helping children who are the victims of physical abuse. Over and over again the supporters of the bill made reference to children who are "beaten," "tortured," "stabbed," and so on. Awareness of the lack of resources available also gave Congress the luxury of not plunging into the controversial area of a definition of "child neglect" or making a definitive statement on how the program should relate to it.

Other political decisions evident in the process were the decision to limit severely the authorization of funds to a level known to be insufficient for a major and comprehensive attack on the problem, and the replacement of the proposed citizen commission on child abuse with an internal government advisory board. Both decisions were taken in order to avoid a veto. The act's lack of emphasis on easily accessible funding for the traditional public child welfare agencies was also an intended signal from a Congress that had concluded that the clients of these agencies might be served better by the stimulation and competition of the development of other community resources than by a simple increase in funding through existing mechanisms.

Finally, the child abuse act reflects a policy as much by what it does *not* do or say as by what is in the act. An example of this is the absence of any provision for a national registry of child abuse reports. The need for such a registry was identified by a number of people in the field, who cited cases of child abusers fleeing to anonymity across state lines and committing the crime in different jurisdictions. Although Congress was aware of this problem, it shied away from such a provision in the law for two reasons. First, poor and minority families were considered more likely to be reported as abusers or suspected abusers because their lives are often under continuing scrutiny by the welfare system and other public agencies. Second, Congress believed that resources to deal with these reports were already inadequate and that names of alleged child abusers might languish indefinitely in computer memories, available for misuse and misinterpretation by anyone with access to them.

Perhaps because it was the only new children's program enacted on the federal level over a period of several years, the appropriateness and the success or failure of the National Center has become a subject of considerable controversy in child and family policy circles. One distinguished critic, Dr. Edward Zigler of Yale (who resigned as director of the Office of Child Development in 1972), has gone so far as to say that the federal effort was "doomed to failure." In a speech delivered at a 1976 child abuse conference, Zigler said:

> We must be willing to entertain the possibility that history will show that this particular bill actually proved to be counterproductive. My view here is that we do not legislate away major social problems like child abuse with a single bill. Social change is produced not by the stroke of a pen but by intensive and persistent efforts to change the human ecology within which the social target is embedded. Laws such as the Child Abuse Act do little more than give us the false sense of security that something meaningful has been done, thus interfering with our mounting truly effective measures.[f]

It is beyond the scope of this article to attempt to evaluate the effectiveness of the federal program or to judge whether the effort has been worth the cost. It should be pointed out that the program is a manifestation of the "incremental" approach to social change and social policy. It is a political approach, one that asserts that, in a time when economic and other forces militate against accomplishing major breakthroughs such as Social Security or Medicaid, it may be wise to take some modest first steps toward a broader, identified goal.

I therefore urge that programs such as the Child Abuse Act be judged at least in part by their intended goals, however limited they may be. In this case, some of the questions that should be asked are:

1. Can and did the federal government stimulate greater awareness of and response to the needs of abused and neglected children in this country?
2. Are more people with problems receiving help, or has the program only identified more people with problems and left them to cope with them on their own?
3. For the resources invested, did the taxpayer get an adequate return?

Only by posing and trying to answer such questions can policy makers learn from past experiences.

---

[f]Edward Zigler, "Controlling Child Abuse in America: An Effort Doomed to Failure," speech delivered to Meyer Children's Rehabilitation Institute, University of Nebraska Medical Center, Omaha, Neb., May 25, 1976.

13 Controlling Child Abuse in America: An Effort Doomed to Failure?

Edward Zigler

Child abuse is an area of concern that one has great difficulty approaching objectively and analytically. It is a phenomenon that arouses moral outrage and other intense emotions associated with a number of poorly understood prejudices and anxieties. Allow me to give an example from my own experience of the common revulsion toward child abuse. As a pedagogic exercise used to highlight the cultural relativism of most moral strictures or values, I have asked my classes of Yale undergraduates what behavior they can think of that is inherently evil as assessed by any and all value systems. A behavior regularly nominated by my students as the ultimate of evil is the striking or killing of a defenseless child. I am far from sure why child abuse is singled out by this group of educated laymen who characteristically are willing to find so many reasons for socially unacceptable behavior as to excuse the perpetrators. It is interesting to me that the enlightened Yale undergraduate does not seem to view the child abuser as yet another victim of social forces beyond his or her control.

I would offer three hypotheses as to why child abuse meets with such great revulsion. First, the phenomenon of child abuse probably touches on everyone's primitive and deep-seated dependency needs. There is something very threatening about the thought of being small and helpless and not being given proper care and concern. Secondly, child abuse must appear as a monstrous perversion to so many adults whose greatest satisfaction and joy in life come through having loving relationships with their children. Finally the revulsion concerning child abuse may stem from the belief that such behavior is contrary to our species' basic instincts. In this regard, many laymen as well as a few professionals seem willing to resurrect an outmoded and bankrupt instinct approach to human behavior and assert that the basic problem of the abusing mother is that she is lacking the maternal instinct.

Is There A Child Abuse Problem?

Concern with child abuse as a delimited social problem is of relatively recent vintage, and a controversy has arisen over whether or not child abuse in our

Reprinted by permission from D. Adamovicz, ed., *Proceedings of the First National Conference on Child Abuse and Neglect*, Department of Health, Education, and Welfare, 1976.

country actually constitutes a major problem. Perhaps for the reasons mentioned above, many people react toward child abuse with the psychological mechanism of denial, that is, either disbelieving that it takes place or that it takes place too rarely to be considered a national problem.[1] We get some idea of the reluctance to recognize child abuse by noting that this phenomenon was not initially reported by mental health or social service workers, but rather by radiologists who noticed a great number of unexplained fractures appearing on their child patients' x-rays.[2] Even leading workers in the area of child abuse have called into question the view that child abuse is a major problem. For example, Gil wrote, "The classical 'battered child syndrome' is a relatively infrequent occurrence. Even if allowance is made for the gross underreporting of fatalities, physical abuse cannot be considered a major killer and maimer of children."[3] Gil makes this assertion despite the fact that his own data suggests that an upper limit of between 2.5 million and 4 million American adults polled in a single year had personal knowledge of a case of child abuse.[4] Gil says his method is indirect, of unknown reliability, and intrinsically susceptible to overestimate.[5]

The argument about whether child abuse is an extensive problem has been made murky by the failure to state whether one is making judgments on the basis of absolute or relative numbers. In Gil's survey (cited above), only about 3 percent of the adult population knew families involved in child abuse, although this amounted to up to 4 million people. Certainly one can point to other negative events experienced by children that occur more frequently than does child abuse. For example, it has been estimated that over 1,750,000 infants suffer a damaging fall during their first year of life;[6] and falls are only one type of accident experienced by children. Thus speaking relatively, one can rationally make the point that child abuse is not as large a problem as are childhood accidents.

It is my view that such a relative approach to the designation of social problems suffers from the same inadequacies as does the relative approach to moral decisions. The dangers of the comparative numbers approach were brought home to me recently when I attempted to induce decision makers to provide continuing help for the two thousand Vietnamese children brought to our country during the babylift operation. A response I frequently encountered was "how can we give special help to these two thousand children when there are hundreds of thousands of native-born children who are also in need of the same type of help." Taken to its extreme, the comparative approach would lead to total inaction in most of those problem areas in which child advocates are currently working to improve the status of America's children. This line of thought leads me to support the absolute approach to the problem of child abuse and to argue that whether there are one thousand or one million abused children, child abuse constitutes a real social problem that merits our society's concern and intervention.

The Incidence of Child Abuse

How many children actually do suffer from child abuse? We should state openly and frankly that we do not have a very reliable estimate. Factors that make difficult the accurate measurement of incidence include: (1) There is still no widely accepted definition of child abuse; and (2) Current incidence data are based primarily on information contained in case reports of child abuse. However, such reports are at best a very rough index of the actual incidence of child abuse, since many child abuse cases are never reported and are thus unknown to the authorities. Undetected cases of child abuse are especially numerous in the more affluent segments of the population. The pediatrician in private practice continues to be reluctant to report an injured child coming from a "good" home as a victim of child abuse.[7] Given the suspicion of the authorities on the part of the poor, and the fact that it is probably easier for the economically disadvantaged to identify with and feel sympathy for their neighbor than it is to cooperate with the authorities, many instances of child abuse among the poor also go unreported. The nonreporting of child abuse has been referred to as "a conspiracy of silence," with perhaps 3 million adults participating in this conspiracy.[8]

What then is our best albeit imperfect estimate of the incidence of child abuse in our country? Gil projected an upper estimate of between 2.5 and 4 million cases each year.[9] Another estimate has put this figure as low as 200,000 cases per year.[10] Given the wide range of estimates, we can probably do no better than accept the estimate of the National Center on Child Abuse and Neglect that there are approximately 1 million cases reported annually.

Incidence Trends

The lack of reliable incidence data makes it difficult to ascertain whether child abuse is increasing or declining in our nation. Since we have only recently turned our attention to the phenomenon of child abuse, the myth has grown that child abuse has but recently appeared on the human scene. A corollary of this myth is that the condition of children has become progressively worse over ages. The fact of the matter is that the physical abuse of children has been commonplace over a period of many centuries, and that it is less common today than it was during any earlier century.[11] Thus, if we are employing a time frame of several centuries as our reference point, child abuse is clearly on the wane. However, one must consider the significance of the fact that the beating, maiming, and even killing of children has a history of several hundred years. I consider the implications of this fact to be ominous in regard to our current efforts to reduce child abuse in America. I agree with those who have argued that this long history of child abuse has left an historical residue which makes the physical punishment of children an acceptable social form.[12]

Of course our immediate concern is whether child abuse is currently on the increase or on the wane. If reported cases of child abuse can be utilized as a rough indication of the actual incidence of child abuse, it would appear that child abuse has been increasing at a rapid rate over recent years.[13] For example, in 1974 the state of Massachusetts was averaging 58 reported cases of child abuse per month; by the middle of 1975 this figure had nearly tripled to 154.[14] However, while there is a strong supposition that child abuse has been increasing, the problems of definition and unreported cases again make it difficult to determine whether we are becoming more or less a nation of child abusers.

Workers in the field of child abuse are thus attacking a problem whose overall magnitude is not very well specified. The area would greatly benefit from an effort to discover the true incidence of child abuse in America. The Center on Child Abuse and Neglect would be performing a real service to our society if it would continuously collect reliable data on the incidence of child abuse. There has been much discussion in the social science area concerning social indicators. I would propose the incidence of child abuse in our society as one such important social indicator.

The Problem of Definition

There is today no widely accepted definition of child abuse, a dilemma which has been noted by many workers.[15] This lack of definition is the most telling single indicator that the child abuse area is at an extremely primitive level of theory construction, a fact which has hampered both practical and scholarly efforts in the field. How does one investigate a phenomenon that has no commonly accepted definition? I am more interested here in the pragmatics of definition than with its conceptual niceties. We should remember that definitions are not so much right or wrong as they are useful or nonuseful,[16] and that definitions can have very practical consequences since they often serve as guides to action. For instance, Newberger pointed out how our definition of child abuse can determine what families will and what families will not receive services that they badly need.[17]

Resolution of this definitional dilemma must become the first item of business among workers in the child abuse area. To avoid the fate of other areas in the behavioral sciences that have floundered on the problem of definition, we should look to those interested in the philosophy of science for help in this effort. The critical factor in defining any construct is how that construct fits into the nomological network constructed to explain some limited number of phenomena of interest. In this regard I recommend Haim's remarks concerning the definition of suicide which appear to have considerable applicability to the problem of child abuse. Haim stated:

I have demonstrated, I think, how uncertain the delimitation of the suicide field can be ... the choice of a definition of suicide is very difficult and demands the utmost care ... the definition that we finally adopt must be sufficiently flexible, and must go beyond the bounds of excessive objectivity ... but it must not include innumerable modes of human behavior that would dilute the concept.[18]

The definitional problem is of such great magnitude that there may be some value in noting certain interrelated subproblems that must be solved if we are to develop a sound and useful definition of child abuse. One finds in the literature a vacillation between a narrow definition emphasizing serious physical abuse,[19] a somewhat broader definition emphasizing maltreatment,[20] and a broad definition focusing on the fulfillment of the child's developmental needs.[21] Alvy's comprehensive definition has considerable appeal for me since it not only flows unerringly from a sense of what children are and what they need, but also readily leads to a plan of action for improving the lives of many vulnerable children who are at risk not only from child abuse but from a myriad of socially sanctioned practices that interfere with the fulfillment of their developmental needs. I am aware of how threatening Alvy's definition of child abuse could be to our society since it leads to the inference that to the extent we silently allow ills to befall our nation's children, we are all guilty of child abuse. (I made this point concerning common guilt in testimony delivered before Senator Mondale's Subcommittee on Children and Youth.)[22]

Another major subproblem in the definitional dilemma is the determination of at exactly what point on the punishment continuum does discipline end and child abuse begin. This perplexing problem has been noted by several workers,[23] and has been stated succinctly by Gil:

Excessive use of physical force against children is considered abusive and is usually rejected in American tradition, practice and law. (However, there are) no clear cut criteria concerning the specific point beyond which the quantity and quality of physical force used against children is to be considered excessive.[24]

I find myself in essential agreement with others that so long as corporal punishment is a socially sanctioned method of disciplining children, we must invariably have child abuse.[25] I see little diminuation over recent years in our society's willingness to accept the corporal punishment of children providing this punishment is labeled "discipline" or "setting limits." Indeed, given the current attacks on permissiveness in child rearing, I would think that the physical discipline of children is becoming more rather than less popular. This brief analysis of the discipline-child abuse issue is one indicator of why I am pessimistic concerning our society's ability to control child abuse.

Classification Systems

A final subproblem in the definitional dilemma is the need for a reliable and theoretically useful classification system for child abuse. (See Farber and Zigler and Phillips for discussions of how classification systems are constructed and their value to theory formation.)[26] I believe we have gotten about all the mileage we can out of the simple two-category system we have been employing in which we essentially discriminate between those children who suffer child abuse and those who do not. An interesting effort to reconceptualize child abuse and include it in a broader classificatory system involving pediatric social illness was reported by Newberger and his colleagues.[27]

The nature of child abuse is also in need of a more differentiated and conceptually based classificatory system. Child abuse is a phenotypic event having a variety of expressions and causes, and we will make little headway so long as we insist on viewing every act of child abuse as the equivalent of every other. Perhaps there would be some profit in searching for the correlates of circumscribed child abuse. A number of subcategories immediately come to mind, for example, punishing a child to the point that he is physically damaged, torturing a child, sexually abusing a child, or starving a child. At a somewhat higher level of conceptualization we might think of a classificatory system that differentiates between acts of commission, which currently are used in the narrow definition of child abuse, and acts of omission, which are currently employed to define child neglect as distinguished from child abuse.

Both the existing and suggested new classificatory systems for child abuse seem to place total emphasis on behavioral acts emitted by the adult caretaker and experienced by the child. Although this has certain value for the tight formation of operational definitions, I believe this value is purchased at too high a conceptual price. What appears to be missing in the classificatory systems that emphasize observable behavior is any concern with the actor's intention. I am indebted to Piaget whose writings on moral development have shown that over the course of development, the child's moral judgments shift from an orientation around the consequences of an actor's behavior to a concern with the actor's intentions. It is clear that as a field, child abuse is at a relatively early stage of development since we concern ourselves much more with the consequences of the acts of abusing parents rather than with their intentions.

There is thus something inherently erroneous in a classification system based on overt behavior that would essentially divide parents into two groups, those who abuse their children and those who do not. Such a typology does not reflect the underlying nature of child abuse. In regard to a theoretically useful child abuse classification system, it would make better sense to conceptualize child abuse as a continuum on which everyone can be placed. At one end would be the parent who never abuses the child under any circumstances. At the other end might be the parent who actually kills his or her child. In the center of this continuum we would place common occurrences that are not currently viewed as forms of child abuse, such as excessive shouting at children. (It is interesting to note that if a parent shouted at a strange adult in the same manner that a parent often shouts at a child, such a verbal assault would make the parent vulnerable to criminal prosecution. Although I am not in sympathy with what I consider to be the excesses of the children's rights movement,[28] I do feel that it would be to everyone's advantage if we would treat children more thoughtfully and with more respect for their psychological integrity.)

It is easy to see why most people would prefer the two-class typology, abusing parent vs. nonabusing parent, over the continuum approach recommended here. Child abuse is currently considered deviant behavior, and we all try to put as much distance as we can between ourselves and those whom we perceive as deviants.[29] It is somehow reassuring to a parent to view the child abuser as some strange breed of human altogether unlike the rest of us. The continuum approach is threatening because within it the child abuser is viewed as very much like the majority of parents who have never been reported for child abuse. Furthermore, this approach suggests that we are all capable of some sort of child abuse if the environmental conditions are just so. I can see many readers denying that they would ever be able to hurt their children. I ask these naysayers if they can remember some particularly frustrating days with their child in which they toyed with the fantasy of how serene life would be if the child were gone, or a time when in anger they gave the child a wallop across the buttocks "for the child's own good." I am sure there are many who may even remember a time that they became so angry at their child that they shouted, "If you don't quit, I'll kill you." Of course they didn't mean it. As we will see below, neither do many parents who actually do kill their children. I can only conclude that as human beings we are all potential child abusers, and that parents only differ in degree rather than in kind in the sort of abusive behavior that they emit.

The continuum approach advanced here has some real implications for our society's willingness to provide help for those charged with child abuse. As a society we are much more ready to help individuals viewed as being much like ourselves than we are to help those who are viewed as rare deviants sharing no psychological features with us. When confronted with rule-breaking deviants, our society appears more motivated to separate them from the rest of society and punish them than it is to provide help. If the continuum approach were adopted, our society's efforts to control child abuse would more likely be directed toward primary rather than secondary treatment or prevention. (See Alvy for a cogent discussion of the primary vs. secondary prevention issue.)[30] Primary prevention refers to the prevention of physical abuse before it occurs. Secondary prevention is after-the-fact or postincidence intervention. My reading of the current social scene is that our society is willing to engage in secondary prevention but is almost totally uninterested in primary prevention. This state of affairs once again leads me to be pessimistic about our country's ability to solve the child abuse problem.

The primary vs. secondary prevention of child abuse is related to the issue of treating symptoms vs. causes. I am indebted to my colleague Sally Provence, who pointed out to me how much work in the child abuse area is a matter of treating symptoms rather than causes, a phenomenon that has been noted by other workers as well.[31] The issue of treating symptoms vs. treating causes is of course related to the broad vs. narrow definitional issue. This brings me back to my original theme that the definitional dilemma is in urgent need of resolution in order for workers to make any progress in their efforts to control child abuse.

Quality of Current Thinking Concerning Child Abuse

There is general agreement that theoretical and empirical research efforts in the child abuse arena remain primitive and rudimentary.[32] The definitional dilemma of course represents a major theoretical shortcoming affecting empirical study. In addition, the work done has been relatively recent, relatively limited in quantity, and poor in quality. Concerning the quality of the work, Gelles has pointed out and criticized the circularity inherent in those explanatory efforts that commonly imply that abusive parents have poor emotional control so they react to their children with poorly controlled aggression.[33]

A particularly telling indicator of the poor quality of scholarly efforts in the child abuse area is their circumscribed, isolated, and fractionated character. There has been next to no cross-fertilization of thinking concerning child abuse with related areas in the behavioral sciences such as child rearing, attachment, and human aggression. A task of high priority for workers in the child abuse area should be to examine the literature from these well-established, relevant fields of investigation. Not only would such cross-fertilization enhance the sophistication of thinking in the child abuse area, but the methodological rigor of empirical efforts could quickly be improved by incorporating procedures, approaches, and measures that have been developed in related areas that have been much more intensively researched.

I have a parallel plea to make to workers in more established research areas in the behavioral sciences. I would ask them to concern themselves and deal explicitly with the problem of child abuse. It is amazing how so little direct attention has been given to child abuse by those hundreds of workers interested in socialization. Even the more narrow literature on child-rearing practices is strangely silent on the phenomenon of child abuse. (See Zigler and Child for a review of the socialization literature including the research on child rearing.)[34]

I am not sure why there has been such isolation of the child abuse literature from the general socialization literature. I suspect that this isolation has something to do with the basic-applied distinction in research. Workers in the general area of socialization view themselves as basic researchers who may feel that they will somehow be sullied if they turn their attention to such a practical and applied problem as child abuse. On the other hand, workers directly in the area of child abuse view the problem as immediate and pressing, and they may feel that the general socialization literature is too esoteric and ephemeral to be of much value. I add my voice to those of my esteemed colleagues Bronfenbrenner, Garner, and Sarason, who have convincingly argued that both basic and applied research are enriched by cross-fertilization between these two realms.

Improving Research in the Child Abuse Area

Certain subareas of investigation in the behavioral and social sciences would have particular relevance to the study of child abuse. Light suggested that thinking in the child abuse area would be enhanced if child abuse were approached from the vantage point of those many general studies on child rearing.[35] A closely related area that would have value for work in child abuse is that well-developed field dealing with attachment behavior and the nature of the bond between parent and child. It would appear almost circular to state that there is something markedly unusual in the parent-child bond in those families where the parent abuses the child. Yet to the best of my knowledge no studies have employed the methodology found in the attachment literature to investigate the nature of the parent-child bond in those families where child abuse occurs. That the quality of the bond between parent and child is an important determinant of child abuse is suggested by the often overlooked finding that younger children are more likely to suffer abuse than are older children.[36] To explain this I would propose that the older the child, the more likely that an attachment bond has developed between parent and child, a bond that must be breached before the parent can bring himself to mutilate the child. This proposal is only one example of the conceptual avenues that could be opened if workers in the field would attend to the attachment literature. Another example comes from as fine a thinker as Konrad Lorenz, who pointed to the inadequacy of parent-child attachment during early babyhood as a major cause of aggression in general.[37]

Another area of obvious relevance to the phenomenon of child abuse is the widely explored area of human aggression. After all, child abuse is but one form of the aggression of one human being toward another; thus it would be interesting to discover what aspects of child abuse have in common with other forms of human aggression. Certainly some manifestations of child abuse appear to be consistent with the frustration-aggression formulation, that is, aggression is more likely to occur following frustration.[38] Disinhibition theory in the general field of aggression would appear to be another promising area in which to explore causes of child abuse.[39] Given man's capacity for violence and aggression, the surprising phenomenon is not that humans aggress against each other, but rather that they engage in overt aggression so rarely. There can be little question that over the long course of socialization individuals develop a strong inhibition against overt and naked violence toward other human beings. It is intriguing to speculate about what social stimuli cause this strongly entrenched inhibitory system to break down. Work done to date strongly suggests that whenever we observe aggressive behavior, this observation reduces our inhibition for aggression and thus raises the likelihood that we will also engage in overt aggressive behavior.

This formulation has great potential significance for our understanding of child abuse. The greater the number of aggressive acts tolerated by a society, the greater is the likelihood that a member of that society will disinhibit his taboos against aggression and engage in aggressive acts including child abuse. If child abuse is so correlated with the number of aggressive acts tolerated by our society, then our hopes of controlling child abuse are small indeed. The fact of the matter is that aggression pervades almost every feature of American life. This sort of pervasive aggression must be overcome if we are to make any headway with the child abuse problem.

A final area that is particularly relevant to the study of child abuse is the field of comparative psychology. There would be much value in examining the comparative psychology literature for instances in which infrahuman species engage in behaviors that have some parallels to the child abuse behavior encountered in the human species. For example, Morris, in *The Naked Ape*, suggests that the paddling of the anal area is a cryptosexual relic of primate behavior. Morris highlights the vestigial sexual aspects of paddling in his statement, "The female rump presentation posture as an appeasement gesture . . . with rhythmic whipping replacing the rhythmic pelvic thrusts of the dominant male."[40]

Interestingly, some experimental evidence from the comparative psychology literature has been employed to support the thesis that an individual who experiences abuse as a child grows up to become an abusing parent. This represents one of the rare instances where workers in the child abuse area have attended selectively to other work in the behavioral sciences. The work noted has been Harlow's classic effort in which he discovered the monkeys experiencing an atypical childhood grew up to be pathological adult monkeys whose pathology, at least in the case of females, included abusing their young.[41] Unfortunately, workers in the child abuse area have not been sufficiently sensitive to the dangers involved in generalizing from one species examined in an artificial laboratory setting to another species functioning in their natural habitat. I do believe that the comparative psychology literature is a rich source of hypotheses for workers in the child abuse area, but they will have to attend to this literature much more completely than they have done to date. For instance, an intriguing aspect of Harlow's work is the ameliorative effect of peer relations on the behavior of monkeys experiencing atypical child histories. One searches the child abuse literature in vain for any discussion of the abused child's relations with siblings and peers.

Implications of Theoretical and Empirical Shortcomings

The poor current status of theory and research in the child abuse area has some dire implications for how well-informed our efforts to control child abuse can be. Given the embryonic and limited state of knowledge we now possess, it is not surprising to discover the child abuse area more replete with myths than with well-validated facts. The dangers of this situation can perhaps best be illustrated if you will allow me to digress for a moment. The child abuse area today reminds me a great deal of the mental retardation area when I came to it some twenty years ago. The knowledge base was thin, and myths abounded including the well-accepted myth that retarded children were inherently cognitively rigid. The fact that this assertion was no more than a myth did not stand in the way of workers in the field employing it to design care and treatment practices for the retarded.[42] Thus the retarded were trained in repetitive tasks to take advantage of this assumed inherent structure. By the same token therapeutic interventions were denied the retarded since it was believed that they were too inflexible to profit from such experiences.

The child abuse area appears to have its own mythology, with the myths' only claim to validity resting on the fact that they are so frequently repeated. (Remember if you will that the centuries of repeating the assertion that the sun revolved around the earth did not make it so.) We have already examined the myth that child abuse is of recent origin, a myth that would lead us to ignore any lessons from history. A second myth having wide currency is that the individual who experiences abuse as a child develops into an abusing parent. This assertion is so well-accepted that it is now noted as fact in some introductory psychology textbooks.[43] As is true of so many stereotypes, this assertion contains a modicum of truth. However, placing too much value on such a weakly based finding could impede further study into the characteristics of those prone to abuse children. Perhaps the biggest danger of these and other myths is that when the emphasis is on social action, as it currently is in the child abuse area, the myths become the guides to action. Since we lack adequate knowledge concerning child abuse, such myths are all that are available to inform social policy and intervention efforts.

It is the poor state of knowledge, theory, and research in the child abuse area that partially led me to the pessimistic and apocalyptic title for this chapter. I believe that there is a logical relation between the knowledge base in an area and the ability of workers in that area to mount effective interventions. Stated most baldly, I feel that the knowledge base in the child abuse area is much too simplistic and limited to direct us to any socially acceptable and realistic interventions of far-reaching effectiveness.

I am thus greatly troubled by the restrictions placed on research funding in the Child Abuse Prevention and Treatment Act of 1974. I am afraid these restrictions reflect the negative attitude concerning behavioral science research currently in vogue in Congress. When will decision makers learn that our ability to help individuals cannot outdistance the relevant and valid information we have about them? The emphasis on services contained in the bill partakes of the Washington dictum, "Don't do anything, just stand there." If there is anything that must be done first and done quickly in the child abuse area, it would be the development of a sound knowledge base upon which to build social practices to reduce child abuse. The research money contained in the Child Abuse Act is unquestionably too small to fund such a task, so we must look elsewhere for the necessary research funds. I therefore call upon the National Center of Child Abuse and Neglect to use its pivotal position in HEW to lead a coordinated research effort in which the funds of several HEW agencies (for example, NICHD, NIMH, and OE) are used to support research in the area of child abuse. OCD has placed such a successful coordinating role around the issue of early childhood education. It could and should do the same for the area of child abuse.

Although we must await the development of the type of knowledge base that would be a prerequisite for cost-effective interventions capable of significantly reducing the incidence of child abuse, a warning on this point is in order. As I have noted in another context, I consider research to be the servant of social action. The absurdity of delaying action until the last bit of scientific evidence is in was recently pointed out by Farber,[44] and I implore you not to use the relatively poor quality of scholarship in the child abuse area as an excuse for inaction. Poor though our knowledge base might be, we already know more about effective intervention than we are implementing in our social action efforts. At this level the problem is less one of inadequate knowledge than of our society's lack of resolve and commitment of resources to services known to be effective in at least reducing the incidence of child abuse.

Characteristics of the Abused Child

Primitive though the work in the child abuse area may be, some tentative information does emerge. A small but still substantial amount of work has been done in an effort to discover the characteristics of the child who is prone to being abused.[45] The characteristics of abused children that have been investigated include age, gender, birth order, temperament, physical development, and congenital features. These characteristics are often highly interrelated, which makes interpretation of findings somewhat speculative. For example, there is a suggestion that children small for their age are more likely to be abused. Body size is sometimes related to prematurity, a characteristic known to be associated with child abuse. Another suggestive finding is that children with deviant congenital characteristics are more likely to be abused than are children without such defects.[46] Congenital defects may be related not only to body size and prematurity, but also to mental retardation, another child characteristic found to be associated with child abuse.[47]

The discovered relation between child abuse and the child experiencing the abuse being mentally retarded poses other problems of interpretation. Do parents physically assault a child because he is retarded, or does the child become retarded as a result of the abuse he experiences? Workers both in the areas of child abuse and mental retardation (MR) would have much to gain by pursuing the nature of the relation between MR and child abuse. To illustrate such mutual benefit, I would note that as is true in the child abuse area, workers in the MR field are also burdened by questionable stereotypes. One common stereotype is that the parent (particularly the mother) of the retarded child is overprotective toward the child rather than abusive. The child abuse literature instructs us that more work is needed on the range of reactions that parents display toward their retarded children. Furthermore, if it is substantiated that a sizeable number of retarded children are abused, this would help explain the finding in the child abuse literature that abusing parents have unrealistic expectations of their children.

As a reader of the MR literature for the past two decades, I am truly amazed at how infrequently the phenomenon of child abuse has been noted. That I am as guilty of tunnel vision as are other workers in the area was brought home to me when I reread my dissertation, conducted almost twenty years ago. At that time I reported that 45 percent of the mildly retarded children I examined had histories of extensive physical abuse or neglect. In the many studies that I conducted following my dissertation, I routinely read the retarded children's preinstitutional social deprivation but never noted clearly that the social deprivation experienced by many of these children was so severe as to constitute child abuse. The problem here is that my theorizing had a great deal to do with social deprivation and very little to do with that phenomenon which other workers are calling child abuse. This highlights once again the need for cross-fertilization of thinking in related fields, in this case between the unexplored area of child abuse and an area that has been intellectually mined for decades, social deprivation.

Perhaps related to the MR and child abuse phenomenon is the repeated report that premature children experience a heightened incidence of child abuse.[48] Again we have no very satisfactory interpretation of this relation. At least three possibilities come to mind: (1) From the comparative psychology literature we learn that other species may destroy their young shortly after birth if the young are perceived as physically inadequate, in some way. Could there be some such primitive instinct in Homo sapiens? I doubt it, but it should at least be considered. (2) The very nature of premature birth produces considerable general stress in a family's life,[49] and it may be this general stress phenomenon that mediates the relation between prematurity and child abuse. (3) Premature infants probably do emit a higher incidence of noxious behaviors (for example, crying), and such unpleasant behaviors may precipitate the parents' abuse.

But again we need await no lengthy program of research to assert that we could reduce the incidence of child abuse in America if we were willing to mount a national effort to reduce the incidence of premature births. One would want to do this for many reasons in addition to its impact on the incidence of child abuse. Furthermore, we already know how to markedly reduce the incidence of prematurity. If we mounted a war against prematurity analogous to the one mounted against cancer, it is likely that we could successfully defeat the prematurity problem. Unfortunately, any massive intervention effort to combat prematurity is far from becoming a reality. Although we have the medical know-how, what is lacking is the resolve and the commitment of required resources. The battle against prematurity will not happen until the nation becomes more concerned with the problem or until decision makers reorder their priorities so that the life of the newborn has as much importance as the thousand-and-one other matters to which these decision makers attend.

Another child characteristic that has been found to be associated with child abuse is age, that is, younger children more often suffer abuse than do older children.[50] (It should be noted that Gil attributes this common finding to sampling biases.)[51] This phenomenon might best be understood by drawing upon the knowledge provided by the study of attachment between parents and young children. There are several ways in which child abuse might be conceptually linked to a parent-child attachment bond that is in some way deviant. I am grateful to the distinguished pediatrician, Dr. T. Berry Brazelton, who suggested to me that an abnormally strong attachment on the part of a parent might make it difficult for her or him to accept a young child's first moves toward independence. That is, a parent who has nurtured dependency might feel resentment or rejection when a child begins to do things for himself, thus increasing the likelihood that the parent will strike out and abuse the child.

Of course a parent-child attachment bond that is too weak could also be a direct cause of child abuse. It is undoubtedly easier to strike out at someone separated from you by a considerable psychological distance than it is to strike out against someone you know well and to whom you are attached. The nature of human development is such that the very young child has little of consequence to contribute to an interpersonal relationship with the parent. The infant is an inarticulate, dependent individual who needs a great deal of attention and care but has very little in his behavioral repertoire with which to establish a meaningful relationship with his adult caretakers. By the time a child is a few years old he is no longer an odd and mysterious stranger utilizing more than his fair share of the family's resources. Rather he is a person who has developed both an identity and a relationship with the parent, and it is this new closeness and sense of the child that reduces the likelihood that the parent will strike out against the child.

Here again we see some avenues to pursue if we genuinely would like to reduce child abuse. The problems posed by an attachment bond that is too

strong could be alleviated by educating parents in the nature of child development. That is, parents who understand the child's natural course of development
from dependency to independence should be better able to cope when this
separation occurs. Unfortunately, the more common case of the too-weak
attachment bond has antecedents which would be much more difficult to alter.

We might ask what has been happening in our society in regard to the
strength of the bond between parents and their children. One of America's
wisest social critics, Urie Bronfenbrenner, has pointed out that as a result of a
variety of social practices, the bond between parents and children has been
greatly weakened in recent years. Children in our society are no longer as much a
part of adults' lives as they once were. In too many homes, the children's hour
has become the cocktail hour, and the children socialize each other rather than
receive the parental attention and guidance that optimal development requires.
The end product of all this can be seen in a recent survey of children between
the ages of four and six; 44 percent of these children preferred the TV set over
their father. (The bond between father and child appears to be suffering more
than that between mother and child since the large majority of children in this
age group preferred their mother to the TV set.) I can only conclude that
today's parents just do not invest the time and effort that is needed to develop
the strong and healthy bond that is the child's first line of defense against
parental abuse.

Characteristics of Abusing Parents

A considerable amount of work in the child abuse area has focused on the
psychodynamic and socio-cultural characteristics of abusing parents.[52] This line
of investigation can be traced back to Tardieu who, writing in France in the
1860s, described some of the behavioral characteristics of the abusing parent and
also identified socio-cultural conditions associated with child abuse including
unemployment and social isolation. As Hurt notes, much of what Tardieu
reported is consistent with modern research findings.[53] This should not be
interpreted to mean that by today we have a large and solid body of evidence on
the abusing parent. On the contrary, the literature in this area is often sketchy,
indefinite, and in need of much added work.

At a psychodynamic and somewhat tentative level, it has been reported that
abusing and neglectful parents have poor self-concepts or poor self-esteem.[54]
Alcoholism and drug usage have also been found to be associated with being an
abusing parent.[55] The myth alluded to earlier that the abusing parent experienced abuse as a child has been given only minor support. In one review, Gelles
notes Gil's finding that 11 percent of abusing parents were abused as children. In
Gil's survey data, this amounted to 14 percent of abusing mothers and 7 percent
of abusing fathers having been abused during their childhoods.[56]

Although the correlation between experiencing abuse as a child and becoming an abusing parent is greater than zero, the literature is either silent or misleading on how such a relation should be interpreted. It is not surprising to discover the common problem here of confusing correlation with causation. DeMause has wisely advanced an alternative to the causation interpretation by noting that it is very likely that parents and their children share the same social norms, and that these common norms may be what mediate the relation between being an abused child and becoming an abusing parent.[57] The literature taken in toto strongly suggests that abusing a child produces a pathology in that child which may spell itself out in part in the child becoming an abusing parent.

Turning to other parental characteristics, there is considerable converging evidence indicating that child abuse is more frequently found in a single (female) parent home in which the mother is working.[58] Further, the abusing mother in such homes experiences considerable stress which is exacerbated by her sense of isolation and separation from any effective social support system. Additional study is needed to determine the effects of father absence on maternal child abuse.

Also deserving of further investigation is the gender of the abusing parent in the intact home. In the child abuse area much more attention has been given to mothers than to fathers.[59] I am indebted to my colleague Michael Lamb for pointing out to me that the underinvestigation of the father is a general characteristic in the psychological and sociological literature. Our knowledge concerning the gender issue is so cursory that the literature is inconsistent on the basic point of whether the mother or the father is more likely to abuse the child. Gelles' review indicates that the child abuser is more often a female. However, Gil reports that if one controls for the varying rates of involvement that mothers and fathers have with their children, there is a higher incidence of child abuse among fathers.[60]

Other aspects of family constellation have been suggested as being related to child abuse. For example, families with larger numbers of children were found to be more likely to engage in child abuse,[61] and the youngest child was more likely to be the target of such abuse.[62] Clearly, more work must be done in this area, since family constellation factors are so correlated with one another that their individual effects must be teased apart before they can be understood.

Socioeconomic Variables

There is some evidence that the working and lower socioeconomic status (SES) groups are overrepresented among child abusers, even after correction is made for the well-known SES bias in the reporting of child abuse.[63] At this point all we can say with some certainty is that a negative correlation exists between a family's socioeconomic status and the incidence of child abuse. The field is far from reaching a consensus on just how this statistical relation is to be interpreted. The literature in the social class and child-rearing area indicates that the SES-child abuse relation cannot be explained simply in terms of differing child-rearing practices in differing SES groupings.[64] Given the ambiguity of this literature, workers in the child abuse area would do well to design new studies investigating the relation between SES membership and child-rearing practices. Another promising line of research here would be to investigate further the willingness of different SES groups to engage in unmodulated physical acting-out behaviors.[65] A quite different approach which is gaining considerable currency is to study families of differing SES for variations in amount of stress experienced. The hypothesis here would be that it is the amount of stress a family experiences rather than its preferred childrearing practices that mediates the relation between SES and incidence of child abuse.

Although not as well documented as the SES-child abuse relation, some evidence has been presented that child abuse is more prevalent in black than in white families.[66] Again we have no very satisfactory interpretation of this relation. Immediately needed is a study to determine whether ethnicity does contribute to the incidence of child abuse when SES and other demographic characteristics are held constant. To begin to understand such a relation, I can do no better than to recommend some autobiographical accounts such as Claude Brown's *Manchild in the Promised Land* and James P. Comer's *Beyond Black and White*, which give some inkling of the role of physical aggression in black families and communities. A particularly rich source that could be employed to generate hypotheses concerning the ethnicity-child abuse relation is the thoughtful book by Silverstein and Krate, *Children of the Dark Ghetto: A Developmental Psychology*.

Certainly a warning is in order that the correlations of modest magnitude that have been found between child abuse and SES or ethnicity should not be used to further disparage the poor or minority members of our population. The best individual prediction for any child growing up in an economically disadvantaged or minority group home is that the child will not experience abuse. Stated somewhat differently, the fact is that the overriding majority of nonwhite or economically disadvantaged parents do not abuse their children, whatever definition of abuse is used.

Parental Expectations

In terms of implications for effective intervention, the literature on the characteristics of abusing parents provides us with the important finding that abusing parents often have unrealistic expectations about what behaviors their children are capable of or a general lack of knowledge concerning the development of children or both.[67] Several investigators have further described a common characteristic of abusive or neglectful parents to be the lack of "mothering skills."[6][8]

It thus appears that anything we can do to teach the general population about child care and the normal cause of the development of children would be helpful in reducing the incidence of child abuse. I therefore endorse the suggestion of many workers that our nation commit itself to teaching parents how to be parents, with courses in parenthood becoming part of the curriculum of every high school in America. A model for such an effort is the Education for Parenthood program mounted jointly by the Office of Child Development and the Office of Education.

Whether the national implementation of courses in parenthood would reduce child abuse is an empirical issue. Although demonstrated effectiveness should be the primary requirement of any social action program, two other considerations that go into the selection of social action efforts are cost and social acceptability. I endorse the national implementation of courses in parenting not only because I think they will be effective in reducing child abuse, but I also know that the cost of such a program is relatively small. Furthermore, thanks to the work of George Hecht and others who have championed parent education for many years, I believe our society is prepared to support an effort directed at educating all our young people to become better parents. Young people themselves appear to react positively to such courses.

This does not mean that I would not expect some rumblings on the right concerning government-subsidized education for parenthood programs. We can anticipate the charge that government is intruding itself into the nation's rearing of children. The credence given to such a charge will depend on how successful we are in constructing courses for parenthood that eschew the inculcation of values and emphasize instead hard information concerning the development of children (for example, the benchmarks of human development, what realistic behavioral expectations can be made of a two-year-old, and what experiences can interfere with optimal development).

I must emphasize that I am not recommending courses in parenthood for the economically disadvantaged alone. Training in parenthood is needed by all of our young people regardless of their economic circumstances. In this regard we must return to our concern with the definitional dilemma and assert that our society is not divided between abusing parents who have one set of problems and nonabusing parents who have a quite different set of problems. There is much more commonality between abusing and nonabusing parents than most of us would like to believe. For instance, we know that abusing parents tend to have unrealistic expectations of their children and have difficulty in accepting their children's limitations. A parallel phenomenon can often be found in the middle SES. I refer here to those thousands of middle-SES parents who buy books with such titles as *Teaching Your Child to Read at Two* or *Give Your Child a Superior Mind*, and those parents who read and reread the *Reader's Digest* article entitled,

"How to Raise Your Child's IQ 20 Points." I consider much of this popular phenomenon of the past ten years a form of child abuse, since it is characterized by a lack of knowledge about children and unrealistic expectations of them. Furthermore, the child who cannot fulfill these expectations must encounter a lesser degree of acceptance on the part of his parents.[69]

Another area where parents in the middle rather than the lower SES are more likely to make unrealistic demands on children is in the realm of organized children's sports activities. In these activities children are treated as miniature adults and are expected to be capable of mature behaviors which are not in keeping with the physical and cognitive limitations of children. The abusive nature to children of organized competitive sports such as Little League has been pointed out by no less a sports hero than Robin Roberts.[70] For instance, elbow and shoulder injuries are now quite common in eight- to twelve-year-old boys who play Little League baseball.[71] These injuries are encountered much less frequently when children play for recreation rather than for the adult-organized competition so dear to suburban America.

Rather than correcting the ills caused by such unrealistic expectations on the part of parents, our society appears ready to extend the resulting abuse to another segment of the child population, that is, to girls. As the courts force more organized competitive sports to open their doors to girls, we can expect girls to become the target of the same physical and psychological abuse to which their brothers have long been subjected.

Within this formulation, I consider any unrealistic expectation of a child a form of child abuse. We have to look no further than our TV sets to find another flagrant example of children being dealt with unrealistically. I am thinking here of the tendency of the advertising and TV industries to approach the child as though he were nothing more than a consumer to be manipulated into buying this or that product. Indeed countless hours are spent in the subtle and not-so-subtle cajoling of our children to buy this or that product. We are all familiar with the dictum "buyer beware." What advertisers do not care to realize is that such a dictum is relatively meaningless when dealing with children who simply do not have the cognitive wherewithal necessary to assume the skeptical and questioning attitudes that makes the struggle between advertiser and consumer an equitable one.

Not only do I consider these practices a manifestation of socially acceptable child abuse, but I also feel that they result in consequences that can exacerbate typical interests of child abuse in America's homes. Children exposed to continuous exortations to buy, buy, buy, develop some protective mechanisms at surprisingly early ages. They learn relatively quickly that advertised products are not all that the advertisers say they are. What results from this is a disbelief in advertising as well as a general distrust of the truth in what adults say. I would suggest that this distrust of adults on the part of children interferes with the development of open and warm relations between children and their parents and can thus become one further determinant of child abuse.

Individual vs. Social Approach

We come now to what appears to be the most salient conceptual issue in the child abuse area, namely whether child abuse is best conceptualized as a pathological phenomenon most appropriately understood in terms of the character traits or psychodynamics of individual abusing parents, or whether it is most appropriately viewed as a socio-cultural, ecological phenomenon in which the causes of child abuse are thought to reside in the extremely stressful nature of the abusing parent's ecological niche.[72] Within this latter emphasis, special attention is given to the effects of poverty, alienation, and the lack of an effective social support system for the parenting function. An echo of this controversy may be found in general psychological literature on the issue of whether traits or situations are the primary determinant of behavior.[73]

Individual Pathology

The psychodynamic-individual approach to the problem of child abuse has long and honorable roots and can be traced back to Freud's essay, "A Child is Being Beaten," in which Freud's theoretical formulations were employed to describe the dynamics of the child abuser. Yet the individual pathological point of view remains badly in need of further exegesis. Workers in the area would be wise to note Becker's work which makes the distinction between a deviant behavior which itself indicates an underlying pathology vs. a deviant behavior such as child abuse as the product of some recognized psychiatric entity, for example, psychopathy.[74] Some supporters of the individual approach treat the abuse itself as indicative of an underlying disease or abnormal process. Other supporters of the individual approach view the abusing individual as deranged by criteria other than the child abuse itself, and view the child abuse as emanating from the derangement.

It should be noted that in the child abuse area there are currently more supporters of the social than of the individual approach. Nevertheless, there can be little question that a small percentage of abusing parents are pathological in terms of our current psychiatric definition. In this regard it is interesting that Gil, who is one of our nation's most articulate supporters of the social approach, provides evidence in support of the individual psychopathological approach in reporting that, "in over 46% (of child abuse incidents) the perpetrator was viewed by others as suffering marked emotional deviations."[75] Furthermore, it is very likely that individuals with certain personality characteristics are more likely to engage in child abuse independent of the ecological situation in which they find themselves. By the same token, the individual approach receives some support in the fact that other individuals never engage in child abuse no matter what degree of social stress to which they are subjected.

How this individual vs. social conceptual issue is resolved has real implications for the social efforts we choose to mount to reduce the incidence of
child abuse. If we commit ourselves to the individual psychopathological
approach and select psychiatric intervention as the treatment of choice, I can
inform you that there is not enough money nor numbers of mental health
workers to treat all the adults guilty of even gross and severe child abuse. (In
other words, employing the individual pathological framework as our map, we
simply cannot get there from here.)

Another intervention implication within the individual approach is that
child abuse is something of a trait with which the abuser needs help in dealing.
Within this framework the abusing parent may be seen as addicted to child abuse
in much the same way that the alcoholic is addicted to alcohol and the gambler
to gambling. It is a short step from this notion to the implementation of
parents-anonymous groups and the establishment of hot lines, interventions
which have proven effective with other types of addiction. Yet I feel that
workers in the child abuse area have been too impressed with the phenomenon
of abusing parents sometimes coming foreward to ask for help for themselves.
Furthermore, I believe that such interventions will prove ineffective because
they are based on an inadequate conceptualization of the causes of child abuse.
My colleagues Urie Bronfenbrenner and Julius Richmond have convinced me
that efforts such as these which do nothing to improve the ecological system
impacting on the child abuser will be ineffective.[76]

In my opinion it is already too late in the day to view child abuse totally
from the individual perspective. We must concern ourselves with the social
factors that contribute to the incidence of child abuse. In this regard I am
troubled by the disputations nature of the literature concerning the individual
vs. social approaches. Workers do not appear sufficiently aware that the
individual vs. ecological alternatives are not mutually exclusive. This is to say
little more than to repeat that child abuse is a complex phenomenon determined
by a broad array of causative factors. There is still so much to be explained that
it would be a mistake to allow our theoretical prejudices (often tied to nothing
more substantial than the professional discipline with which we identify) to lead
us to discount any of the current possibilities. I would therefore recommend
that we maintain both the individual and social alternatives as working
hypotheses.

The Ecological Approach

I personally believe that the ultimate model to be developed for explaining child
abuse will be an interactive one in which the child abuser will be conceptualized
as a part of a family that is itself embedded in the social, economic, and political
realities of the family's ecology. We have but to turn to the classic work of

Whiting and Child to discover the relation between a culture's child-rearing practices and its social norms. But if child abuse is in *large* part caused by general ecological factors, I again have no choice but to be pessimistic about our society's determination to control child abuse. Our society has taken some tentative steps to correct environmental pollution. It has done precious little to correct the social pollution of many Americans' ecologies. It is exactly this polluted ecology that drives many parents to child abuse.

My pessimism here leads me to join Gil, Gelles, and Newberger and Hyde in asserting that our society may be in need of the phenomenon of child abuse. So long as we attend only to the symptom of child abuse and engage in the tokenistic efforts flowing from this narrow concern, so long can we avoid dealing with its underlying social determinants which would be much more costly to correct. In this regard, Newberger and Hyde stated:

> Simply summarized, the question is whether the sensational nature of the problem conveniently obscures its true social determinants . . . both because of society's need to obscure its neglect of so many of its young by depriving them of the resources necessary for them to grow in families whose basic needs for goods and services are met, and because of individual families' needs to make acceptable their own violent parenting practices.[77]

At first the social factors that might be considered as causes of child abuse would seem almost overwhelmingly difficult to correct. These factors are woven into the very fabric of our society and therefore could not be tackled in isolation from the broader social entity. For one, our society is currently characterized by a complete lack of a social support system such that we are truly a nation of strangers. Our increased alienation is undoubtedly related to the incidence of child abuse. Otherwise how do we explain such heart-rending phenomena as the increase in child abuse incidents in the week before Christmas?[78] In explaining this phenomenon, Newberger and Hyde indict the social support system in their statement:

> This implies that child abuse, like such other human troubles as suicides, disturbances in prisons and mental hospitals, and violent crimes, gets worse at times of year when people long for missing family supports and, in their desperation, may turn on their children when they make unacceptable nurturing demands.[79]

The lack of community support for families also contributes to the incidence of child abuse by making child rearing more difficult today than it once was. Workers in the area of child-rearing practices have noted the diminuation over the years in the community's involvement in helping parents in the difficult job of raising and socializing their children.[80] Indeed the very sense of community seems to be a remembrance of the past. This loss has had profound effects, described by James Comer:

> Our soaring crime rate is not due to spared rods and spoiled children. It is attributable to a breakdown in 'community' and increased stress on parents and families due to the effects of modern technology and to social policy that has not permitted communities and families to remain strong and supportive in spite of it.[81]

This loss of a sense of community and the support system for child rearing that such a community can provide has taken place over several decades and is due to a variety of historical factors. Some probably merit special attention, including the decline in the extended family, the rise in commuting and suburban housing patterns, the demarcation of America's social activities along age lines, and of course the greatly enhanced mobility of many Americans,[82] a factor which has been found to be related to child abuse.[83] How does one develop a sense of community if he knows he will pull up stakes and move shortly? Under such circumstances we tend to keep our social ties to a minimum. The new morality then works against our getting involved with our neighbors and motivates us instead to appreciate our own privacy and not to interfere in the lives of others. This has a certain appeal until a family is in the middle of a crisis, as so many families are who engage in child abuse. To whom is such a family to turn for help? Who will even listen, to say nothing of expending some energy on behalf of a family-in-crisis? The answer here too often is no one. It should therefore not be surprising to discover that a common theme that runs through many case studies of child abuse is a parent's sense of loneliness, isolation, and alienation from the surrounding community. This situation generates one of the general conclusions of my analysis, namely that the control of child abuse is much more likely to come from efforts to beef up our nation's general social service programs than it will from efforts specifically directed against child abuse.

Improving the Social System

The ecological approach does direct us to certain aspects or institutions in the family's ecology where some effort might have particularly high payoff in terms of reducing the incidence of child abuse. For example, in view of the finding that abused children are often the product of an unwanted pregnancy, programs directed towards family planning should be effective in lowering the child abuse incidence. Another program that would be an integral feature of a social support system to aid families who are experiencing difficulties is homemaker services. Not only would homemaker services have a direct and immediate effect on the reduction of child abuse, but they would also help keep families intact and children out of a foster care system that frequently involves the child being moved from impermanent home to impermanent home until the child reaches maturity. Within the broader definition of child abuse recommended above, it should be noted such treatment of children in the foster care system itself constitutes a form of legalized child abuse.

Another feature of the ecology important in determining the incidence of abuse is the availability of child care. A logical consensus has developed that the incidence of child abuse would be reduced if parents could more readily avail themselves of child care of various kinds.[84] This would be particularly helpful to single-parent families headed by a working mother. As appealing as such a view is, I must nevertheless insert a note of caution. To the extent that the availability of child care reduces the stress in a family, it should reduce the incidence of child abuse. On the other hand, placing the child (particularly an infant) in a child care setting may interfere with the development of an attachment bond between parent and child, which could result in an enhanced possibility of child abuse.[85] It would be interesting to discover the incidence of child abuse in comparable families that did and did not avail themselves of infant day care.

In view of the general unavailability of homemaker services and child care, these entire points must be considered somewhat academic. What good would it do if we all agreed today that the availability of homemaker and child care services to a family results in a reduced incidence of child abuse? Our society appears to be extremely reluctant to provide such programs which so many American families need desperately. To support this point, I would note that in the Netherlands, homemaker services are provided at a level approximately twenty times as great as that in the United States.[86] In regard to child care, the 1970 White House Conference on Children named the need for quality day care as the greatest child care need in the nation.[87] Some six years later the situation remains little improved. I must ask why a society which says it wants to control child abuse does so little to provide families with the services which would ease their burdens.

Another ecological phenomenon related to the incidence of child abuse is unemployment. Evidence is already in that an unemployed father in the home is associated with a higher incidence of child abuse.[88] I therefore need to await no further research to assert that if our nation really would like to decrease the incidence of child abuse, it should pursue a policy that would provide employment for those who want it. Here again you must see my pessimism concerning our nation's commitment to reducing child abuse. How can I be sanguine when I see a calculated government policy which allows a national unemployment rate of over 8 percent? I wish to be fair. Those governmental decision makers who argue that our high unemployment rate is the cost we must pay to reduce inflation are not evil people consciously bent on the abuse of America's children. They may feel that inflation is also detrimental to family

life, and that this concern must have priority over the concern of unemployment. Such an opinion may or may not be substantiated. Although we already
know that unemployment is related to child abuse, what is needed is data on the
empirical relation between inflation and child abuse.

Asking for further empirical study is both easy and safe. I would like to
make another request which is neither easy nor safe. The issues discussed in this
section, particularly the unemployment-inflation and child abuse issue, lead me
to urge decision makers to consider the health of families as a variable in their
cost-benefit equations that lead our government to pursue one course of action
rather than another. As I have pointed out before, we have no explicit family
policy in America, and we have yet to begin the critical task of determining the
impact on families of the policies implemented by our political leaders. My
reading of the child abuse literature is that the single overriding factor in
determining whether a child will experience abuse is the viability and strength of
that child's family. How can our nation hope to control child abuse if it
currently is not even taking into consideration the strength of America's families
and how a variety of social policies influence this strength?

Changing Role of Women

Worthy of special mention is another social phenomenon that has far-reaching
and ominous implications for controlling child abuse in America, namely the
changing role of women that we have witnessed in recent years. My purpose here
is not to pass judgment on these changes, but only to examine their implications
for the incidence of child abuse. By theoretical predilection I am committed to
the importance of our affairs of evolution, of both the biological and social
variety. My reading of our species' evolutionary history is that adaptive
specialization has taken place in which both biological and social evolution have
been responsible for the development of social forms that contribute to the
adaptation and therefore to the survival of our species. For example, as we look
at life, as we look at behavior among the other species and among primitive
people who still inhabit our globe, we see the development of specialized and
discriminable different roles for males and females. Although certain differences
in current sex roles are the result of little more than historical and social
happenstance, these sex roles generally represent the end point of a slow
accretion due to biological and social factors. I join with Professor Campbell
who, in his presidential address to the American Psychological Association,
pointed out the intrinsic value of many developed social forms as well as the
danger to society in the disparagement or abrupt change in these slowly evolved
adaptive social phenomena.[89]

From wherever the difference between men and women might come—the
biological and inherent vs. the social and learned—over our long evolutionary

history there has been value in women pursuing one set of functions, often related to the production and rearing of children, while men pursued other functions, for example, providing food and shelter and fighting off predators. I do not know what combination of biology and social history produced it, but there can be little question that over the past couple of millenia women compared to men have been less aggressive, and more gentle, warm, and sympathetic towards the dependent young of our species.[90] With the strong impetus from the women's liberation movement, women are being asked to repudiate such an historically evolved sex role. Indeed when placed within the rubric of the most militant form of women's liberation, even speaking of the adaptive significance of women's role vs. men's role is seen as little more than a naked effort to chain women to hearth and home and thus interfere with their self-actualization—which some feel could be better obtained if one androgenous sex role was brought to characterize both sexes. It would take us too far afield to discuss all that might be good and bad in men's and women's roles becoming more alike, but to ensure that children continue to receive adequate care, such a change probably would not be brought about overnight.

In recent years how successful have women been in becoming more like men? At least in regard to the overt expression of aggression, more successful than many realize. Some years ago I found that the symptoms of female mental patients were more self-pejorative and self-punishing than were those of male patients, whose symptoms were more indicative of self-indulgence and striking out against others.[91] Considerable recent clinical evidence indicates that the symptoms of females have become more like those of males, that is, more characterized by aggressiveness. If women are becomg increasingly aggressive, are they actually engaging in more violence and therefore becoming more prone to abuse their children? The evidence leads me to reply yes. How many of us would have believed a short decade ago that we would witness two assassination attempts on the president of the United States, made in the same year, both by women. In the state of Connecticut we were treated to the spectacle of a highly promoted prize fight between two women. This of course is just the logical end point of the movement to allow women to participate in sports thought to be the province of men alone.

If this evidence appears too anecdotal to support a concern that the changing sex role of women may result in their engaging in more violent acts, which could include child abuse, I refer you to the well-documented shift in the statistics concerning female criminality. We have already witnessed a marked shift in women's involvement in crimes that have heretofore been thought to be almost totally male dominated, for example, murder, robbery, and assault. From an evolutionary viewpoint such behavior impresses me as a long step backward by women into the primitive and animal past. What I find particularly ominous is the fact that such instances of naked aggression are not only tolerated by some figures in the women's liberation movement but are applauded as indicative of women's progress toward the equality that is every women's right.

Who are the current heroines of the women's liberation movement? They include the young black women in North Carolina who protected her sexual integrity by stabbing a jailer to death. Another heroine is a Chicano woman in California who said she shot a man who held her down while another man raped her. Certainly not a heroine is that woman who receives great fulfillment in being a homemaker and from the warm attentive upbringing of her children. All too often the rhetoric of the women's liberation movement would have us believe that such women are second-class women who have succumbed to the social brainwashing of a society that wishes to subjugate them. Cottle too has noted how many liberationists would have women believe that mothering is a dirty second-rate occupation.[92] Whatever the overall value of women's liberation might prove to be, I have little hesitancy in predicting that child abuse will be more prevalent among women who view childrearing as a demeaning activity than among women who view child rearing as an important and valuable function.

It would be a mistake to view the women's liberation movement as though it represented a single voice reflecting a single consensual point of view. In fact, certain views that can be found in the women's movement would be conducive to less rather than more child abuse. Certainly a distinction should be made between the liberationists who feel women should become like men vs. those who feel that women should be respected as worthwhile human beings whatever behavioral path they might pursue. This second point of view was articulated by Juliet Mitchell, who stated, "It is not differences but oppression that is oppressive," and "If the roles were of equal weight it would not matter which sex performed them."[93] This is a sound point of view, and I endorse not only the rhetoric but the implications these words have for our society. Why should a mother work at being a good mother if the society places little value on the maternal function? I look in vain for the social message that mothering (and parenting in general) is a difficult and demanding task, and those who carry it off successfully have much to be proud of. Our society must find meaningful ways of transmitting this message to parents (we have probably gotten about as much mileage out of Mothers' Day and Fathers' Day as we can), or we will probably continue to witness increasing child abuse incidence figures.

Pervasiveness of Social Support for Child Abuse

Just as child abuse, narrowly considered, will never be completely understood without a consideration of the social exology in which families function, so too the ecology must be examined for the part it plays in socializing adults in their parental function. The facts here are that parents too often receive subtle, and sometimes not so subtle messages that it is all right and perhaps praiseworthy to behave aggressively as well as to physically punish children. I must sadly conclude that while our society provides little outside support for what is good and right about so many of America's families, it provides plenty of support for many families' behavioral styles that are conducive to a high incidence of child abuse.

Undoubtedly the single most important determinant of child abuse is the willingness of adults to inflict corporal punishment upon children in the name of discipline. Well over half of all instances of child abuse appear to have developed out of disciplinary action taken by the parent.[94] All too often an adult begins an effort to discipline a child and ends up damaging the child much more than was intended. This train of events is exacerbated by the parents' lack of knowledge about the physical vulnerability of the child. Most parents are not aware that even giving a young child a severe shaking can result in brain damage. It is sad indeed to describe the typical case of child abuse in a social history. The social worker usually encounters a sad and contrite parent who is shocked that such a tragic outcome could have resulted from their well-intentioned desire to supply the discipline that growing children need.

We might ask ourselves who is the real villain in this common scenario. Certainly not the child, unless we wish to take the atavistic stance that the young child is inherently morally perverse. It is not the parent, who often feels that he is doing what society expects of him in providing discipline for his child. No, the real villain is those child-rearing practices that permit the corporal punishment of children and a society that approves such a method of child discipline. I add my voice to those of many others such as Alvy, Garbarino, Gelles, Gil, Maurer, and Newberger and Hyde, and assert that so long as corporal punishment is accepted as a method of disciplining children, we will have child abuse in our country.

Our society not only expects but engages in the physical abuse of children. Our highest repository of society's values, namely government, sets a very poor example in its treatment of children who reside in settings funded with taxpayers' dollars. What message do we give parents when they see the socially sanctioned abuse and neglect of children which takes place in institutions run by governments at the federal, state, county, and city levels? Instances of the legalized abuse of institutionalized retarded children have been amply documented by Burton Blatt.[95] The fine television program, "This Child is Rated X," presented evidence on the physical abuse of children in training schools for delinquent children as well as in hospital settings for emotionally disturbed children. Instances of child abuse in our nation's day care system were reported in the National Council of Jewish Women's study, *Windows on Day Care*. Again, as I pointed out in my testimony before a committee of Congress in 1973, this abuse of children is being purchased with your tax dollars and mine, making us all guilty of child abuse.

Where else in our society do we find the legally and socially sanctioned abuse of children? I point to that social institution that, after the family, is the most important socializing agent in America: the school. Most Americans are now aware of how commonplace corporal punishment in the schools has become. For example, in Dallas, Texas, 24,035 instances of corporal punishment were recorded for the 1971-1972 school year, some so severe as to need medical attention and in some cases, hospitalization. Nat Hentoff researched corporal punishment for the American Civil Liberties Union, and in November 1971, he reported that corporal punishment in the schools was so widespread as to indicate that "the brutalization of children appears to be a part of the core curriculum."[96] It should be noted that only three states, Maryland, Massachusetts and New Jersey, forbid corporal punishment in public schools, and seventeen states have laws that expressly allow the physical punishment of students.[97]

A family's ecology is best conceptualized as a rubric of interacting social institutions. The school is an important institution embedded in this rubric, and its practices not only reflect the values of America's families but also influence the development of familial attitudes and practices. If you wish to decrease the incidence of child abuse in America, make it illegal for school personnel to apply corporal punishment against school children under any circumstances. In this regard, I am troubled by the Supreme Court's recent decision upholding the right of school personnel to physically punish children. This ruling not only sanctions the abuse of children in school buildings; probably more importantly, as a result of the example it sets, it makes much more likely the abuse of children in the home, where the more severe forms of child abuse currently take place. I can only wonder at the further impact of this decision, made by the highest judicial body in the land, which in effect asserts that corporal punishment may be in the best interest of the child and of the society.

The violence occurring in the schools not only interferes with but influences the students' learning. On this point how can I be sanguine about the good effects that would accrue if schools instituted courses in parenting when I know that schools themselves engage in the physical abuse of children. We would have here a case of the schools preaching one thing while doing another, a phenomenon that Escalona has pointed to as having particular pernicious effects.[98] The immediate and future effects of this training in violence in the schools are readily predictable. In a school in England, for example, three hundred teenage girls rioted after the principal threatened to eliminate the school's policy of sex discrimination in punishment, and to subject girls to the same punishment as boys, that is, a leather strap.[99] The girls' riotous behavior suggests to me that violence breeds violence. Further, such a form of punishment in the schools teaches girls to be more aggressive, a trait that could carry into their behavior as mothers.

Allow me to press home the point that the school and the family do not function in isolation but rather operate in interaction and mutually influence one another. The superintendent of the West Haven, Connecticut schools was quoted as follows:

I give fair warning, unless parents—all parents—once again take control
of and responsibility for their children's behavior, expect the problems
of discipline in the schools and unrest in society to grow ... the
greatest single need is for parents to reinstill in their children a basic
respect for authority and a realization that laxity in parental discipline,
as is presently the case, can only have one result—chaos in society ... The seed doesn't fall far from the tree. Show me a kid in
trouble in school and I will show you a home where discipline is
lacking.[100]

How can a parent of any social status react to this except with a greater use
of corporal punishment in the home? The superintendent is certainly right on
the point that what happens in the home influences what happens in the school.
I would only add that the opposite is true as well.

I do not believe that era of violence in the schools should be attributed to
an underuse of disciplinary measures in the home. It appears rather to reflect a
growing acceptance of violence in our general society. One finds violence,
hostility, and aggression everywhere, including TV, the movies, and many of our
everyday social relations. What is worse, such behaviors are not only permitted
but are often held up for approbation. What is the significance for child abuse in
the findings of a recent survey that showed that 50 percent of the individuals
polled felt that it is good to be aggressive? It is clear that aggression is associated
in many people's minds with the motivation to achieve.

Given my reading of the human aggression literature, the evidence is
overwhelming that we are conditioned from the cradle onward to strike out and
injure those who frustrate and trouble us. The relation between the pervasiveness
of our willingness to injure others and child abuse has been pointed out by
several workers, among them Besharov and Durea, Bronfenbrenner, Cohen and
Sussman, Gil, and Newberger and Hyde. In Gil's national survey, the question
was asked, "Could you injure a child in your care?" Six of the ten respondents
replied yes.[101] This must be considered most ominous by those interested in
reducing the incidence of child abuse. This message of injuring others is even
presented by those who are society's first line of defense against naked violence,
the police. The police chief of Kansas City, Missouri, stated:

We must send this very, very definite message to people who might
commit violence. That we as a society will deal with it very harshly.
Because by dealing with it harshly, we are reinforcing the belief that
this kind of conduct is wrong.[102]

This plea for harshness can do nothing but produce even greater violence. The
human aggression literature is clear in informing us that the one unavoidable
consequence of harshness and violence for whatever reason is an escalated level
of violence.

Behavior Modification

In discussing the pervasiveness of the socially sanctioned support for the corporal punishment of children, some special attention should be given to the behavior modification movement in America.[103] The behavior modification approach and the specific techniques emanating from it are currently being widely employed in our society in homes, schools, children's camps and other institutional settings for children, therapists' offices, and psychologists' research laboratories. I am convinced that the behavior modification movement has contributed to the acceptability of inflicting physical pain upon children. Let me be clear on this point. I know of no responsible element of behavior modification who would baldly counsel parents to use physical punishment in disciplining their children. In point of fact, most behavior modification adherents point out the possible negative consequences of aversive or negative reinforcement, and typically adopt the position that positive reinforcement is more efficacious in the shaping of behavior.

If this is so, why then point to behavior modification as a pervasive force contributing to the acceptability of the physical punishment of children? First of all, behavior modification theorists have not been altogether consistent or unanimous in their disavowal of the efficacy of physical punishment as a shaper of behavior. Indeed, the basic thrust of the behavior modification formulation is that physical punishment (certainly an aversive consequent) should be effective in reducing proscribed behaviors emitted by children. One has to be an expert and read both the fine print and the footnotes to come away from the behavior modification literature with a sense that physical punishment does not benefit children. Most parents are not sophisticated theorists with the training to interpret the many studies done on the relative efficacy of positive vs. negative reinforcement. My own view is that whether behavior modifiers endorse the physical punishment of children or not, many parents who encounter simplified versions of the behavior modification formulation come away with the view that physical punishment is an acceptable and effective method for shaping children's behavior. I am saying no more than that the behavior modification position is highly susceptible to this interpretation (although behavior modifiers would call it a misinterpretation).

This point is debatable and could use some supporting evidence. Consider the advertisement for the book, *Parents and Children, Love and Discipline*, written by two established authorities in the behavior modification field, Clifford K. Madsen and Charles H. Madsen, Jr. This book, directed at advising parents in their parental function, does make the point that positive reinforcers are preferable to negative reinforcers. Thus the advertisement for the book reads:

Parents and Children, Love and Discipline contains advice on how to express approval in ways children appreciate, and includes especially helpful lists of words, sentences, facial and body expressions, activities, and tangible things to use to advantage as well as similar lists of negative responses, most of which the authors believe should *never* be used.[104]

I am afraid that most parents reading this book will find this depreciation of the value of negative reinforcement to be illogical and inconsistent. In this regard, we find in the same advertisement the statement:

Parents should take fast, positive action when children misbehave. The authors . . . explain why long, involved analysis of a child's personality is unnecessary, and probably counterproductive. This easy-to-understand, easy-to-use book tells how to teach children essential behavioral guidelines such as, "If you do good things, good things happen to you."[105]

I believe that the not-so-hidden message here is that the behavior modifiers would also have children learn that "If you do bad things, bad things will happen to you." Further, it is exactly the "fast, positive action" that Madsen and Madsen recommend that is a primary cause of injury and even death to many children. I for one would prefer that before hitting a child, parents engage in exactly the long, involved analysis that these authors denounce.

There is no dearth of examples that can be given indicating how children have been brutalized under the banner of behavior modification. Given what I have said about the schools, it is not surprising to learn that the American school has been particularly ready to employ aversive behavior modification techniques to discipline unruly students. Thus it became necessary for the Butte, Montana school board of trustees to order an immediate halt to the practice of locking retarded children in a coffin-sized box as a form of punishment. (This practice would be cosmetized among behavior modifiers by referring to it as a "time out" procedure.) If spending a few minutes in an enclosed box seems harmless, read what the mother of a child experiencing this punishment had to say:

He tears his clothes in the box. He wakes up in the middle of the night and wanders around the house and is terrified of the thing. He's been going out a great deal after school. Usually he stays in and talks to me a while, but he has been going out and staying out. Maybe he feels he has to have air.[106]

Retarded, emotionally disturbed, and autistic children appear to be particularly vulnerable to the recipients of behavior modification techniques. The TV program, "This Child is Labelled X," told of an emotionally disturbed girl who had been tied to a bed for twenty-four hours; the rationale for this treatment was that behavior modification was being tried in an effort to help the patient. A program for autistic children in Denton, Texas, includes slapping children, placing them in a dark closet, and using cattle prods, which deliver a painful electric jolt, to shape the children's behavior. The professionals directing this program were quoted as stating: "We punish them to reduce the rate of response we're trying to eliminate. Then we go in and teach them something else, an alternative."[107]

It might be argued that these examples represent no more than the overenthusiasm and misinterpretation of the behavior modification formulation on the part of school personnel and therapists, who are themselves not particularly expert in regard to the fine points of behavior modification. Unfortunately, some leaders in this field have provided approbation for the use of extremely punishing events in the training of children. I am thinking here of O. Ivar Lovaas, whose well-known program at UCLA for modifying the behavior of autistic children was reported in as prestigious and popular a magazine as *Life*. Lovaas also uses electric shocks to shape children's behavior, that is, an electric grid to promote approach behavior and electric shocks to prevent self-mutilation.[108] When parents read that psychologists, individuals supposedly knowledgeable about human behavior, employ electric shocks to shape children's behavior, why should parents not employ even less aversive stimuli to discipline children?

Unfortunately, there is no unanimity among American psychologists on this issue of whether physical punishment should ever be employed in disciplining a child. I find myself in essential agreement with the position of Maurer which is "no, never, not under any circumstances." This does not mean that children should never be subjected to any form of discipline. Maurer's plea is that we forego corporal punishment and utilize less brutalizing forms of discipline.[109] It is interesting that one of America's finest psychologists, Lloyd Humphreys, has taken issue with Maurer, finding his position simplistic and incorrect.[110] The controversy here appears to center around those instances in which corporal punishment is employed to deter the child from emitting a behavior that could be more damaging to the child's physical being than the damage produced by the aversive punishment. One thinks here of the child who bangs his head on the floor so vigorously that his life might be in danger, or the child who mutilates himself by biting his body. The question of whether some electric shocks would be more preferable is a legitimate one and should be thought through and discussed.

In his rebuttal to Maurer, Humphreys displayed the thoughtfulness he is known for and advanced three resolutions that could be employed when dealing with this complex problem: (1) "In the case of conflict, ends are weighted more heavily than are means." (2) "In the case of conflict, long-range effects are weighted more heavily than are short-range effects." (3) When conflict occurs, the general good is weighted more heavily than is the welfare of the individual."[111] Humphreys general position is clear in his statement, "Sufficient data are available as of now, however, to support the sparing, discriminating, and appropriate use of aversive consequences for certain behaviors."[112]

I am afraid I must reject Humphreys' three resolutions and his general position as well. When an individual child's well-being is at stake, statements concerning means vs. ends, long-range vs. short-range effects, and the general good vs. the individual good, seem to me little more than an exercise in sophistry. Let me begin with a concrete case and examine it within the rubric of Humphrey's three resolutions. Our hypothetical case is that of an autistic child who routinely bangs his head against the wall hard enough to crack his skull. Would we be justified in using electric shocks to reduce the occurrence of this behavior? In regard to Humphreys' resolution 1, we know that the means here is the electric shock, but what exactly are the ends? Until we know exactly what the ends might be, we have no way of deciding whether the means were justified or not. The implicit end of most behavior modification efforts is a well-func- tioning child, routinely emitting behaviors we consider normal or socially acceptable. I know of no very convincing evidence that such a state of affairs would be the realistic endpoint of any behavior shaping regimen. In fairness, it could be argued that Humphreys' first resolution involves no such unrealistic ends, but rather nothing more complicated than a reduction in the life- threatening head banging. If this tack is taken, the conflict here is not between means and ends, but rather between two ends, head banging vs. electric shocks. This conflict would still have to be resolved, but it should probably be resolved around the tight issue of which behavior is more deleterious at this point in time to the child's physical well-being. Thus, in regard to resolution 2, we have to make a choice between two short-range effects, the damage done by electric shocks vs. the damage done by head banging.

I am not sure how to apply to our example Humphreys' resolution 3 concerning the general good vs. the individual good. Who in our society is capable of defining what the general good might be? Furthermore, how exactly is the social good influenced by whether our hypothetical child bangs his head or is subjected to electric shock? We already know the primary criterion employed by society to determine whether individual or general social needs will be fulfilled, that is, the amount of common social resources (taxes) that must be expended. When informed that caring for an autistic child from infancy to maturity will cost several hundred thousand dollars, I am afraid the typical response of the government official who is the spokesman of the common good is that this is simply too great a cost for the society to bear, and it is therefore in the society's interest to find some less costly method of intervention. If this method involves the corporal punishment of the child, so be it. Whatever the needs of the child might be, the common social good and the husbanding of scarce tax dollars must take precedence over any individual life.

If this is what Professor Humphreys means by resolving every conflict between individual and social needs in favor of society, then I must reject his position. I find myself more concerned with the quality of life of that individual child than I am with some abstraction called "the general good." I prefer to think of society as being established to protect the rights and optimize the development of the individuals within the society. Thus when I see the rights of the individual in conflict with the values of society at large, I opt for defending the rights of the individual, since such rights have a certain primacy over the requirements of a smoothly functioning social body.

I have one final problem with Professor Humphreys' position which concerns his empirical and data orientation to the very serious conflicts that real people operating in the real world must resolve. Although he states sufficient data are available to support the use of aversive consequences, this is an empirical issue that is much further from resolution than he appears to believe. We still have no very satisfactory inventory of all of the positive and negative consequences of physically punishing children. Indeed, Professor Humphreys' support of the use of corporal punishment appears to exceed the support given by behavior modifiers themselves.

At some point in time, behavioral scientists will have to face squarely the problem of whether the use of corporal punishment with children is an empirical-scientific or a moral issue. Of course psychologists are trained to solve empirical questions and should rightly state that they have no special wisdom for resolving such a moral issue as whether one person should ever inflict physical harm upon another. Yet every person has a right to make moral judgments and I believe that psychologists should do more in exercising this right. We should speak out not only as empiricists but as human beings who genuinely care about those other human beings whom we study and quaintly call "subjects."

I would like to advance a moral position concerning corporal punishment. I believe that it is morally wrong for any human being to inflict punishment on any other human being. I am unconcerned here with those countless studies that have been done to document the long-range effects of physical punishment. Whatever these studies show, we would never again beat sailors with a cat-of-nine-tails. The best reason for not doing so is that we consider it to be wrong. I would like to see exactly the same argument made in regard to America's children. The thrust of history tells me that in some century hence, this point of view will be commonplace. The contemporary problem is how do we hurry along such a state of affairs. To begin with, I feel strongly that no parent should have the right to assign to some other party, for example, school personnel or therapists, the right to physically punish the parent's child. We must educate everyone in our society that physical punishment is a rare and unusual event to be engaged in after a close scrutiny of the case in question. To return to my example of a head-banging child, I would think that our court system would be the appropriate arena in which such individual cases could be decided. Let adults come before the court and make a case for the corporal punishment they are planning to inflict upon the child. If a convincing case can be made that the corporal punishment is necessary to maintain life, the court could use all the expertise available to it in deciding whether to allow such punishment or not.[113] What better way to give our society the message that we will not tolerate the indiscriminate physical abuse of children?

Conclusion

The total foregoing analysis leads me to conclude that we will make little progress over the next few years in reducing the incidence of child abuse. We simply do not have the knowledge and resources to deal very effectively with even the symptomatic treatment of child abuse in our society. I even find myself conflicted about the value of the Child Abuse Prevention and Treatment Act of 1974. Since I consider the architect of this bill, Senator Walter Mondale, to be one of our nation's most effective workers for the improvement of child-family life, I would like to make crystal clear my concerns over the Child Abuse Act. The bill simply provides too little in the way of resources and direction for us to make any significant impact on our child abuse incidence figures. A $20 million bill to fight child abuse in America amounts to little more than putting a band aid on a cancer.

We must be willing to entertain the possibility that history will show that this particular bill actually proved to be counterproductive. My view here is that we do not legislate away major social problems like child abuse with a single bill. Social change is produced not by the stroke of a pen, but by intensive and persistent efforts to change the human ecology within which the social target is embedded. Laws such as the Child Abuse Act do little more than give us the false sense of security that something meaningful has been done, thus interfering with our mounting truly effective measures.

Such tokenistic bills have other insidious effects, not the least of which is to call into question the credibility of the entire governmental apparatus. The Child Abuse Act simply promises more than it can possibly deliver. I agree with the Wirtz report which stated:

> The American people today are deeply skeptical about any grandiose representation. They have been oversold for too many years on too many grand initiatives . ,. the first demand on policy today is that it be totally credible. And the second demand is that it be fiscally responsible.[114]

I find the Child Abuse Act to be neither credible nor fiscally responsible, although I am not sure what a fiscally responsible child abuse act would look like. I suggest that members of both our legislative and executive branches of government begin the difficult task of costing out the tax payers' bill for significantly impacting child abuse in America. (I am reminded of an exchange that I had with another public figure whom I admire greatly, Elliot Richardson. This humane, wise, and dedicated public servant became interested in the cost of reducing lead paint poisoning among children. He asked the assistant secretary of HEW for Planning and Evaluation to do a cost analysis on this problem, and he discovered the cost to the nation would be many billions of dollars. He sadly had to conclude that such vast sums of money were simply not available to solve a problem whose technological aspects pose no difficulty.)

Examples for the cost of reducing the incidence of child abuse might come from the good work that is being done here and there around the country. I am favorably impressed with the social services and child advocacy approach currently being utilized at Boston's Children's Hospital, although I cannot find in the reports of this effort the dollar cost per child abuse case. Let us accept at face value that the incidence of child abuse is the million cases per year recently reported by HEW's Child Abuse Center. If the cost of effective intervention is no more than $5,000 per family (an extremely conservative estimate), the cost of successfully impacting child abuse in America would be something on the order of $5 billion per year. My best hunch is that the realistic cost would prove to be many times that amount annually. Given the current fiscal austerity on our nation, from where are these many billions to come? I am afraid for the time being that child abuse will have to take its place alongside prematurity and lead paint poisoning (which, by the way, is another socially tolerated form of child abuse) as another problem that our society has neither the commitment nor the resources to solve.

I must confess that I am surprised at the depth of my pessimism concerning our nation's ability to reduce the incidence of child abuse. This pessimism should not be misinterpreted as some sort of plea for adopting a stance of apathy or inaction. There is much that could and should be done in this area, including: (1) an invigorated research and data collection program, (2) increased efforts in the family planning area, (3) widespread implementation of programs dealing with education for parenthood, (4) a massive effort to do all we can to reduce the number of premature births in America, (5) an increase in the availability of homemaker services, and (6) an immediate increase in the availability of child care in America. Finally and perhaps most importantly, we will need a willingness to examine our society's value system, and a commitment to reduce the acceptability of man's violence to man, of which child abuse is but one manifestation.

References

1. M. Hurt, Jr., *Child Abuse and Neglect: A Report on the Status of the Research* (Washington, D.C.: U.S. Department of Health, Education and Welfare,

1975), p. 5; S.B. Kamerman, "Cross-National Perspectives on Child Abuse and Neglect," *Children Today* 4 (May/June 1975):34.

2. Hurt, *Child Abuse and Neglect*, p. 5; F.N. Silverman, "Radiologic Aspects of the Battered Child Syndrome," in *The Battered Child*, 2nd ed., ed. R.E. Helfer and C.H. Kempe (Chicago: University of Chicago Press, 1974).

3. D.G. Gil, "Physical Abuse of Children: Findings and Implications of a Nationwide Survey," *Pediatrics* 44 (May 1969):857.

4. D.G. Gil, *Violence Against Children: Physical Child Abuse in the United States* (Cambridge, Massachusetts: Harvard University Press, 1970).

5. Ibid., p. 59-60.

6. H. Kravitz, et al., "Accidental Falls from Elevated Surfaces in Infants from Birth to One Year of Age," *Pediatrics* 44 (May 1969):869.

7. E.H. Newberger et al., "Toward an Etiologic Classification of Pediatric Social Illness: A Descriptive Epidemiology of Child Abuse and Neglect, Failure to Thrive, Accidents and Poisonings in Children Under Four Years of Age." Paper presented at the biennial meeting of the Society for Research in Child Development, Denver, Colorado, April 11, 1975. Published in expanded form as "Pediatric Social Illness: Toward an Etiologic Classification," *Pediatrics* 52 (August 1977):178-185.

8. P.G. Zimbardo and F.L. Ruch, *Psychology and Life*, 9th ed. (Glenview, Illinois: Scott, Foresman, 1975).

9. Gil, *Violence Against Children*.

10. E.H. Newberger and J.N. Hyde, "Child Abuse: Principles and Implications of Current Pediatric Practice," *Pediatric Clinics of North America* 22 (August 1975):706.

11. P. Aries, *Centuries of Childhood*, (New York: Alfred Knopf, 1962); N.F. Chase, *A Child Is Being Beaten*, (New York: Holt, Rinehart and Winston, 1975); L. DeMause, ed., *The History of Childhood* (New York: Psychohistory Press, 1974); S.X. Radbill, "A History of Child Abuse and Infanticide," in *The Battered Child*, 2nd ed., ed. R.E. Helfer and C.H. Kempe (Chicago: University of Chicago Press, 1974); E. Shorter, *The Making of the Modern Family*, (New York: Basic Books, 1975).

12. Gil, "Physical Abuse of Children," p. 862; A. Maurer, "Corporal Punishment," *American Psychologist* 29 (September/October 1974):614-626.

13. Newberger and Hyde, "Child Abuse: Principles and Implications," p. 696.

14. Chase, *A Child Is Being Beaten*, 184.

15. K.T. Alvy, "Preventing Child Abuse," *American Psychologist* 30 (September 1975):921-928; Hurt, *Child Abuse and Neglect*, p. 6; Maurer, "Corporal Punishment," p. 615; Newberger and Hyde, "Child Abuse: Principles and Implications," p. 696.

16. I.E. Farber, "Sane and Insane: Constructions and Misconstructions," *Journal of Abnormal Psychology* 84 (September 1975):589-620; E. Zigler, "Metatheoretical Issues in Developmental Psychology," in *Psychological Theory*, 2nd ed., ed. M. Marx (New York: Macmillan, 1963), p. 350.

17. E.H. Newberger, "The Myth of the Battered Child Syndrome," *Current Medical Dialog* 40 (April 1973):327-334. Reprinted in *Annual Progress in Child Psychiatry and Child Development*, ed. S. Chess and A. Thomas (New York: Brunner/Mazel, 1975).

18. A. Haim, *Adolescent Suicide* (New York: International Universities Press, 1974), p. 24.

19. C.H. Kempe, et al., "The Battered Child Syndrome," *Journal of the American Medical Association* 181 (July 7, 1962):17-24.

20. V.J. Fontana, *The Maltreated Child: the Maltreatment Syndrome in Children*, 2nd ed. (Springfield, Ill.: C.C. Thomas, 1970).

21. Alvy, "Preventing Child Abuse."

22. E. Zigler. Testimony delivered before the Subcommittee on Children and Youth hearings: American families, trends and pressures. *Congressional Record-Senate*. September 26, 1973, S17792-S17795.

23. Alvy, "Preventing Child Abuse"; Hurt, Jr., *Child Abuse and Neglect*; Maurer, "Corporal Punishment."

24. Gil, *Violence Against Children*, pp. 134-135.

25. Alvy, "Preventing Child Abuse"; Maurer, "Corporal Punishment."

26. I.E. Farber, "Sane and Insane"; E. Zigler and L. Phillips, "Psychiatric Diagnosis: A Critique," *Journal of Abnormal and Social Psychology* 63 (January 1961):607-618.

27. Newberger et al., "Pediatric Social Illness."

28. J. Holt, *Escape from Childhood* (New York: E.P. Dutton, 1974).

29. H.S. Becker, *Outsiders* (New York: Free Press, 1963).

30. Alvy, "Preventing Child Abuse."

31. Ibid; R.J. Gelles, "Child Abuse as Psychopathology: A Sociological Critique and Reformulation," *American Journal of Orthopsychiatry* 41 (July 1973):611-621.

32. See previously cited works by K.T. Alvy, R.J. Gelles, M. Hurt, Jr., A. Maurer, and E.H. Newberger and J. Hyde.

33. Gelles, "Child Abuse as Psychopathology."

34. E. Zigler and I. Child, "Socialization" in *Handbook of Social Psychology*, 2nd ed., ed. G. Lindzey and E. Aronson (Reading, Massachusetts: Addison-Wesley, 1969).

35. R. Light, "Abused and Neglected Children in America: A Study of Alternative Policies," *Harvard Educational Review* 43 (November 1973):556-598.

36. Gelles, "Child Abuse as Psychopathology."

37. R.I. Evans, *Konrad Lorenz: the Man and His Ideas.* (New York: Harcourt, Brace, Jovanovitch, 1975).

38. J. Dollard et al., *Frustration and Aggression* (New Haven, Connecticut: Yale University Press, 1939).

39. A. Bandura and R.H. Walters, *Social Learning and Personality Development* (New York: Holt, Rinehart and Winston, 1963).

40. D. Morris, *The Naked Ape* (New York: McGraw-Hill, 1967), p. 137.

41. H.F. Harlow and M.K. Harlow, "Psychopathology in Monkeys," in *Experimental Psychopathology: Recent Research and Theory*, ed. H.D. Kimmel (New York: Academic Press, 1971).

42. R.L. Masland, S.B. Sarason, and T. Gladwin, *Mental Subnormality: Biological, Psychological and Cultural Factors* (New York: Basic Books, 1958).

43. Zimbardo and Ruch, *Psychology and Life.*

44. Farber, "Sane and Insane."

45. Alvy, "Preventing Child Abuse"; Gelles, "Child Abuse as Psychopathology"; Gil, "Physical Abuse of Children," pp. 857-864; Hurt, *Child Abuse and Neglect*; E.H. Newberger et al., "Pediatric Social Illness," Zimbardo and Ruch, *Psychology and Life.*

46. Gil, "Violence Against Children"; I.D. Milowe and R.S. Lourie, "The Child's Role in the Battered Child Syndrome," *Abstracts of the Society for Pediatric Research* (1964):1079.

47. Hurt, *Child Abuse and Neglect.*

48. G. Caplan, E.A. Mason, and D.M. Kaplan, "Four Studies of Crisis in Parents of Prematures," *Community Mental Health Journal* 1 (January 1965):149-161; Hurt, *Child Abuse and Neglect*; D.M. Kaplan et al., "Family Mediation of Stress," *Social Work* 43 (January 1973):60-69; Newberger and Hyde, "Child Abuse: Principles and Implications"; L. Stern, "Prematurity as a Factor in Child Abuse," *Hospital Practice* 8 (February 1973):117-123.

49. Caplan, Mason, and Kaplan, "Parents of Prematures"; Kaplan et al., "Family Mediation of Stress."

50. Gelles, "Child Abuse as Psychopathology."

51. Gil, *Violence Against Children.*

52. Alvy, "Preventing Child Abuse"; U. Bronfenbrenner, "The Origins of Alienation," *Scientific American* 231 (August 1974):53-57; J.H. Daniel and J.N. Hyde, "Working With High-Risk Families," *Children Today* 4 (November/December 1975):23-25; J. Garbarino, "A Preliminary Study of Some Ecological Correlates of Child Abuse: The Impact of Socioeconomic Stress on Mothers," *Child Development* 47 (March 1976):178-185; Hurt, *Child Abuse and Neglect*; Newberger and Hyde, "Child Abuse: Principles and Implications"; Newberger et al.

53. Hurt, *Child Abuse and Neglect.*

54. Daniel and Hyde, "High-Risk Families."

55. Newberger, "Myth of the Battered Child Syndrome"; Newberger and Hyde, "Child Abuse: Principles and Implications."
56. L.B. Silver, C.C. Dublin and R.S. Lourie, "Does Violence Breed Violence? Contributions from a Study of the Child Abuse Syndrome," *American Journal of Psychiatry* 126 (March 1969):152-155; Gelles, "Child Abuse as Psychopathology"; Gil, "Physical Abuse of Children," p. 860.
57. L. DeMause, "Our Forbears Made Childhood a Nightmare," *Psychology Today* 8 (April 1975):85-88.
58. Gil, "Physical Abuse of Children."
59. Newberger et al., "Pediatric Social Illness."
60. Gelles, "Child Abuse as Psychopathology"; Gil, "Violence Against Children."
61. Gil, "Physical Abuse of Children."
62. Gelles, "Child Abuse as Psychopathology."
63. Garbarino, "Ecological Correlates of Child Abuse."
64. Zigler and Child, "Socialization."
65. Ibid. for a more complete discussion of this point.
66. Gil, "Violence Against Children"; Newberger and Hyde, "Child Abuse: Principles and Implications."
67. Alvy, "Preventing Child Abuse"; Daniel and Hyde, "High-Risk Families"; E. Elmer, *Children in Jeopardy* (Pittsburgh, Pennsylvania: University of Pittsburgh Press, 1967); Gelles, "Child Abuse as Psychopathology"; Hurt, *Child Abuse and Neglect*; Newberger and Hyde, "Child Abuse: Principles and Implications."
68. D.M. Bullard et al., "Failure to Thrive in the 'Neglected' Child," *American Journal of Orthopsychiatry* 37 (May 1967):680-690; V. DeLissovoy, "Child Care by Adolescent Parents," *Children Today* 2 (July/August 1973):23-25; S.L. Evans et al., "Failure to Thrive: A Study of Forty-five Children and Their Families." Paper presented at the Twenty-Second Annual Meeting of the American Association of Psychiatric Services for Children, Philadelphia, Pennsylvania, November, 1970.
69. See E. Zigler, "On Growing Up, Learning, and Loving," *Human Behavior* (1973):65-67 for a more complete discussion of this point.
70. R. Roberts, "Strike Out Little League," *Newsweek* (July 21, 1975):11.
71. J. Stevens, "Who Speaks on Behalf of the Children?" *New York Times* (January 4, 1975):25.
72. Alvy, "Preventing Child Abuse"; T.J. Cottle, "Review of N.F. Chase, *A Child Is Being Beaten*" *New Republic* 173 (November 22, 1975):28; Daniel and Hyde, "High-Risk Families"; R. Galdston, "Observations of Children Who Have Been Physically Abused by Their Parents," *American Journal of Psychiatry* 122 (April, 1965):440-443; Garbarino, "Ecological Correlates of Child Abuse"; Gelles, "Child Abuse as Psychopathology"; Gil, "Violence Against Children"; Hurt, *Child Abuse and Neglect*; Kempe, et al., "Battered Child Syndrome";

Newberger and Hyde, "Child Abuse: Principles and Implications"; Newberger et al., "Pediatric Social Illness"; B. Steele and C. Pollick, "A Psychiatric Study of Parents Who Abuse Infants and Small Children," in *The Battered Child*, 2nd ed., ed. R.E. Helfer and C.H. Kempe (Chicago: University of Chicago Press, 1974).

73. D.J. Bem, "Constructing Cross-situational Consistencies in Behavior: Some Thoughts on Alker's Critique of Mischel," *Journal of Personality* 40 (January 1972):17-26; K. Bowers, "Situationism in Psychology: An Analysis and A Critique," *Psychological Review* 70 (May 1973):307-336; W. Mischel, "Continuity and Change in Personality," *American Psychologist* 24 (July 1969):252-283; W. Mischel, "Toward a Cognitive Social Learning Reconceptualization of Personality," *Psychological Review* 80 (April 1973):252-283.

74. Becker, *Outsiders*.

75. Gil, "Physical Abuse of Children," p. 861.

76. J. Richmond and H.L. Weinberger, "Program Implications of New Knowledge Regarding the Physical, Intellectual and Emotional Growth and Development and the Unmet Needs of Children and Youth," *American Journal of Public Health* 40 (April 1970, Supplement)23-67.

77. Newberger and Hyde, "Child Abuse: Principles and Implications," p. 703.

78. A. Murphy, "Child Abuse Increases During Yule Season," *Behavior Today* 7 (January 12, 1976):4.

79. Newberger and Hyde, "Child Abuse: Principles and Implications," p. 706.

80. J.P. Comer, "Spanking," *New York Times* (December 29, 1975):55; E. Zigler, "Child Care in the Seventies," *Inequality in Education* (Cambridge, Massachusetts: Harvard Center for Law and Education, December, 1972), pp. 17-28.

81. Comer, "Spanking."

82. V. Packard, *A Nation of Strangers* (New York: Simon and Schuster, 1974).

83. Gil, "Violence Against Children."

84. Daniel and Hyde, "High-Risk Families."

85. A.D. Murray, "Maternal Employment Reconsidered: Effects on Infants," *American Journal of Orthopsychiatry* 45 (October 1975):773-790.

86. A.J. Kahn and S.B. Kamerman, *Not for the Poor Alone* (Philadelphia, Pennsylvania: Temple University Press), 1976.

87. White House Conference on Children, 1970. *Report to the President.* (Washington, D.C.: Department of Health, Education and Welfare), 1971.

88. Garbarino, "Ecological Correlates of Child Abuse"; Gelles, "Child Abuse as Psychopathology."

89. D.T. Campbell, "On the Conflicts Between Biological and Social Evolution and Between Psychology and Moral Tradition," *American Psychologist* 30 (December 1975):1103-1126.

90. E. Maccoby and C. Jacklin, *The Psychology of Sex Differences* (Stanford, California: Stanford University Press), 1974.

91. Zigler and Phillips, "Psychiatric Diagnosis."

92. Cottle, "Review of *A Child Is Being Beaten*."

93. J. Mitchell, "Review of L. Tiger and J. Shepher, *Women in the Kibbutz*," *New York Times Book Review* (January 4, 1976):4.

94. Gil, "Physical Abuse of Children."

95. B. Blatt, *Exodus from Pandemonium: Human Abuse and a Reformation of Public Policy* (Boston, Massachusetts: Allyn and Bacon), 1970.

96. Quoted in Maurer, "Corporal Punishment," p. 617.

97. Ibid.

98. S.K. Escalona, "Children in a Warring World," *American Journal of Orthopsychiatry* 45 (October 1975):765-772.

99. *New York Times* (January 10, 1976).

100. *New Haven Journal-Courier* (January 1, 1976):40.

101. Gil, *Violence Against Children*.

102. J. McNamara, "There are No Kojaks in K.C.!" *Kansas City Town Squire* (November 1976):46.

103. S.B. Stolz, L.A. Wienckowski, and B.S. Brown, "Behavior Modification: A Perspective on Critical Issues," *American Psychologist* 30 (November 1975):1027-1048.

104. *New York Times Book Review* (October 26, 1975):43.

105. Ibid., p. 43.

106. *New York Times* (October 24, 1975).

107. *New Haven Register* (November 2, 1975):33A.

108. O.I. Lovaas and B.D. Bucher, *Perspectives in Behavior Modification with Deviant Children* (Englewood Cliffs, N.J.: Prentice-Hall, 1974).

109. Maurer, "Corporal Punishment."

110. L. Humphreys, "Corporal Punishment," *American Psychologist* 30 (September 1975):708-709.

111. Ibid., p. 709.

112. Ibid.

113. J. Goldstein, A. Freud and A.J. Solnit, *Beyond the Best Interests of the Child* (New York: Free Press, 1973).

114. Quoted in J. Reston, "On Learning and Earning," *New York Times* (December 7, 1975):15E.

Index

Index

Abused children: absence of literature on relations of, with siblings and peers, 180; characteristics of, 9-10, 182-185. *See also* Child abuse

Abusing parents: abuse of, as children, 8, 185-186; characteristics of, 185-186; consequences of treatment for, 149-150

Accidents, children's injuries viewed as, 21

Advertising and public relations campaigns, for prevention of child abuse, 10

Advocacy, 16, 37

Agency investigation, expanding scope of, 123-124

Age of child, violence toward children by, 62-63, 184

Agression: child abuse and other forms of, 179-180; leading to escalated level of violence, 200

Aid to Families with Dependent Children (AFDC), 71

Alcoholics Anonymous, 11

Alcoholism, child abuse and, 15, 28, 76, 83, 113, 147, 185

Alvy, K.T., 175, 177, 198

American Academy of Pediatrics, 162

American Bar Association, 89, 97, 140

American Civil Liberties Union, 199

American Humane Association, 162-163; Children's Division of, 54

American Journal of Public Health, 16

American Psychological Association, 195

Analytic concepts, for studying nature of child abuse, 70

Anger, importance of overcoming, for professionals in child abuse cases, 29

Attachment bond, parent-child, and child abuse, 184-185

Battered child syndrome, 143, 172; characteristics identified with, 147; Kempe and Helfer's definition of, 6, 20, 27, 81, 142; myth of, 15-18. *See also* Child abuse

Battered women. *See* Spouse abuse

Becker, H.S., 190

Behavior modification, 201-206

Bernstein, B., 47

Besharov, Douglas, 41, 200

Best interests of the child, 30-31, 89, 98, 107, 108, 110, 141

Beyond the Best Interests of the Child (J. Goldstein et al.), 30-31, 141

Bias, sampling, 22-23

Blatt, Burton, 198

Boston Juvenile Court, 144

Brademas, John, 165, 166

Brazelton, T. Berry, 184

Briar, S., 148

Bronfenbrenner, Urie, 179, 191, 200; on American service institutions, 32; on bond between parents and children, 185; on violence toward children by age of child, 62

Brown, Claude, *Manchild in the Promised Land,* 187

Bulcroft, R., 58

Burden of proof, 107, 108-109

Bureau of Labor Statistics, U.S., 71

Campbell, D.T., 195

Care and Protection cases, 144-145

Casework, 29-34, 83-86, 101-102, 104-106, 109

Causal dimensions of child abuse, 72-77

Causes of child abuse, 6; cultural, 6-7; economic, 7; familial, 7, 10; psychological, 7-10

Central registry, 35, 90, 117

Child, I., 178, 192

Child abuse: analytic concepts for studying nature of, 70; behavior

217

About the Contributors

Jessica H. Daniel is a staff psychologist at the Children's Hospital Medical Center and the Judge Baker Guidance Center, Boston, Massachusetts, and a lecturer on child psychiatry at Harvard Medical School, Boston, Massachusetts.

Elizabeth E. Elmer is Director of Research and Training at the Parental Stress Center, Pittsburgh, Pennsylvania, and an associate professor of child psychiatry (social work) in the Department of Psychiatry, University of Pittsburgh School of Medicine, Pittsburgh, Pennsylvania.

Ellen J. Flannery is editor-in-chief, Boston University Law Review.

Richard J. Gelles is an associate professor of sociology at the University of Rhode Island, Kingston, Rhode Island.

David G. Gil is a professor of social policy at the Florence Heller Graduate School for Advanced Studies in Social Welfare, Brandeis University, Waltham, Massachusetts.

Ellen Hoffman is Director of Governmental Affairs at the Children's Defense Fund of the Washington Research Project, Inc., Washington, D.C.

James N. Hyde, Jr. is Director, Preventive Medicine of the Commonwealth of Massachusetts Department of Public Health, Boston, Massachusetts.

Alvin A. Rosenfeld is an assistant professor of child psychiatry at Stanford University Medical School, Stanford, California.

Edward Zigler is Sterling Professor of Psychology and Director of the Psychology Unit at the Child Study Center, Yale University, New Haven, Connecticut.

About the Editors

Richard Bourne received the Ph.D in sociology from Harvard University (1973) and his J.D. degree from the Boston University School of Law (1974). A member of the Massachusetts and Connecticut bars, he is currently an associate of the Office of Legal Counsel, Children's Hospital Medical Center, Boston, and an assistant professor of sociology, Northeastern University, Boston. He is a consultant on child abuse law and management to the Judge Baker Guidance Center, the Massachusetts Mental Health Center, the Massachusetts Criminal Justice Counsel, the Massachusetts Committee on Children and Youth, among other groups. His sociological interests include social deviance, criminology, and the sociology of law.

Eli H. Newberger received the M.D. from Yale University and after an internship in internal medicine at Yale served for two years in the Peace Corps in Upper Volta, West Africa. He there became interested in pediatrics and public health.

During his pediatric residency at Boston Children's Hospital, he completed a master's degree in epidemiology at the Harvard School of Public Health and organized the Trauma X Group at Children's, one of the first interdisciplinary child abuse consultation units in the United States. As director of the Family Development Study since 1972, he has been concerned to develop a more adequate classification system and theory base for clinical practice and prevention of childhood illnesses of social and familial origin.

He was given the Annual Award for Improving the Welfare of Children by the Massachusetts Society for the Prevention of Cruelty to Children for 1976.

In 1977, he was elected president of the Massachusetts Committee on Children and Youth. He is assistant professor of pediatrics at the Harvard Medical School and lecturer on maternal and child health at the Harvard School of Public Health.